GREEK-ENGLISH LEXICON

OF THE

NEW TESTAMENT

BASED ON
SEMANTIC DOMAINS

Volume 2
Indices

Johannes P. Louw
Editor
Eugene A. Nida
Editor

Rondal B. Smith
Part-time editor
Karen A. Munson
Associate editor

United Bible Societies

GREEK-ENGLISH
LEXICON
of the
New Testament
based on
Semantic Domains

Volume 2

First edition 1988
© United Bible Societies 1988

Published by the United Bible Societies, 1865 Broadway,
New York, NY 10023, USA.

Library of Congress Cataloging-in-Publication Data

Greek-English lexicon of the New Testament: based on semantic domains /
Johannes P. Louw, editor, Eugene A. Nida, editor;
Rondal B. Smith, part-time editor; Karen A. Munson, associate editor.
p. cm.
Bibliography: v. 1, p.
Includes indices.
Contents: v. 1. Introduction & domains − v. 2. Indices.
ISBN 0-8267-0340-2 (set). ISBN 0-8267-0341-0 (v. 1). ISBN 0-8267-0342-9 (v. 2)
1. Greek language, Biblical − Glossaries, vocabularies, etc.
2. Greek language, Biblical − Dictionaries − English.
3. Greek language, Biblical − Semantics.
4. Bible. N.T. − Language, style.
I. Louw, Johannes Petrus, 1932−. II. Nida, Eugene Albert, 1914−.
PA881.G68 1988
487'.4 − dc 19
87-36866
CIP

© Maps − United Bible Societies, EPF,
used by kind permission.

ISBN 0 8267-0342-9 (Volume 2)
ISBN 0 8267-0340-2 (2 Volume Set)

Printed by NBP CT
Type 11/11 Plantin

ABS − 1988 − 3m − 56496

CONTENTS

PREFACE

This volume offers three indices: *Greek-English, English* and *Passages* quoted. The first contains a complete listing of all the Greek terms occurring in the text and apparatus of the 3rd edition of the Greek New Testament published by the United Bible Societies. It also includes a number of irregular forms of words that may help users to find the corresponding base forms.

To a certain extent the first index (Greek-English) resembles the listing in most dictionaries, namely, Greek terms in alphabetical order followed by a number of English glosses representing the various meanings which the editors have proposed. The Greek-English index is almost a concise dictionary in the regular sense of the word. Glosses were used in this index since complete definitions of meanings, such as those occurring in the domains of Volume 1, would be too extensive and cumbersome for ready reference. The glosses are, in fact, merely pointers and should not be used as lexical meanings without consulting the specific definitions of meaning offered in the entries belonging to the various domains. The Greek-English index is simply an alphabetical guide to the domains, thus enabling the reader to find the location where a particular meaning is discussed in Volume 1. At the same time, however, this index also summarizes the *range of meanings* for which a particular Greek term occurs in the Greek New Testament, and as such it offers in a nutshell the primary distinctions recognized by the editors. Users of this lexicon will get far more out of it if they can readily see the relationship between the material on specific meanings of words in the light of the broader pattern of the domain structure. For this reason the lexicon is in two volumes so that the indices may be used throughout in close conjunction with the data on the specific Greek meanings.

The second index (English) is in no way complete, since its purpose is merely to serve as a help to the reader in locating an *area of meaning* on the basis of English translational equivalents. Therefore, this index offers primarily those keywords that can direct the reader to a domain where fuller information is to be found. The English index should in no way be used as a guide to lexical meanings; in fact, it clearly shows the inadequacy of glosses as definitions of meanings. The English words only indicate that within or between the reference numbers quoted, the particular English word will be part of the glosses or titles or even in some instances of the proposed definitions. The reader, however, should not only look up the reference numbers cited, but should also compare the entries preceding and following the cited section or sections in order to grasp fully the total range of meaning. This is imperative since not all possible glosses are quoted with each item, and a particular gloss may occasionally be used to translate other items in the same subdomain.

The third index (Passages) lists the references from the New Testament quoted as illustrative examples to explain the meanings discussed in the domains. It can also serve as a means of finding what the lexicon has to say on problems involved in the understanding of various New Testament expressions.

α
first 60.46

Ἀαρών *m*
Aaron............. 93.1

Ἀβαδδών *m*
Abaddon 93.2

ἀβαρής, ές
not financially
burdensome........ 57.225

αββα *m*
Father (a title for
God) 12.12

Ἄβελ *m*
Abel 93.3

Ἀβιά *m*
Abijah 93.4

Ἀβιαθάρ *m*
Abiathar 93.5

Ἀβιληνή, ῆς *f*
Abilene 93.389

Ἀβιούδ *m*
Abiud............. 93.6

Ἀβραάμ *m*
Abraham 93.7
Ἀβραάμ : unit
χόλπος Ἀβραάμ
heaven 1.16

ἄβυσσος, ου *f*
very deep place 1.20

Ἄγαβος, ου *m*
Agabus............ 93.8

ἀγαγεῖν
see ἄγω

ἀγαθοεργέω
do good 88.3

ἀγαθοποιέω
do good 88.3

ἀγαθοποιΐα, ας *f*
good deeds 88.3

ἀγαθοποιός, οῦ *m*
one doing good deeds 88.8

ἀγαθός, ή, όν
a good (moral) 88.1
b good (value) 65.20
c generous 57.110
ἀγαθός : unit
τὰ ἀγαθά
possessions 57.33

ἀγαθουργέω
see ἀγαθοεργέω

ἀγαθωσύνη, ης *f*
a goodness 88.1
b generosity 57.109

ἀγαλλίασις, εως *f*
extreme joy 25.132

ἀγαλλιάω
be extremely joyful ... 25.133

ἄγαμος, ου *f* or *m*
unmarried 34.76

ἀγανακτέω
be indignant 88.187

ἀγανάκτησις, εως *f*
indignation 88.186

ἀγαπάω
a love 25.43
b show love 25.44
c take pleasure in 25.104

ἀγάπη, ης f
  a love . . 25.43
  b fellowship meal 23.28

ἀγαπητός, ή, όν
  a beloved 25.45
  b only dear 58.53

Ἀγάρ f
  Hagar 93.9

ἀγγαρεύω
  force to carry 37.34

ἀγγεῖον, ου n
  container 6.120

ἀγγελία, ας f
  message 33.193

ἀγγέλλω
  (aor ἤγγειλα)
  inform 33.189

ἄγγελος, ου m
  a messenger 33.195
  b angel 12.28

ἄγγος, ους n
  container 6.120

ἄγε
  look 91.13

ἀγέλη, ης f
  herd 4.8

ἀγενεαλόγητος, ον
  without record of
  ancestors 10.27

ἀγενής, ές
  inferior 87.59

ἄγια, ων n
  a sanctuary 7.18
  b the holy place 7.35

ἁγιάζω
  a dedicate 53.44
  b make holy 88.26
  c honor as holy 88.27

ἁγιασμός, οῦ m
  dedication 53.44

ἅγιον, ου n
  sanctuary 7.18

ἅγιος, α, ον
  a holy 88.24
  b dedicated 53.46
  ἅγιος : unit
  οἱ ἅγιοι
    God's people 11.27

ἁγιότης, ητος f
  holiness 88.25

ἁγιωσύνη, ης f
  a holiness 88.25
  b dedication 53.45

ἀγκάλη, ης f
  bent arm 8.28

ἄγκιστρον, ου n
  fish hook 6.10

ἄγκυρα, ας f
  anchor 6.48

ἄγναφος, ον
  unshrunken 48.8

ἁγνεία, ας f
  purity 88.29

ἁγνίζω
  a purify (ritual) 53.30
  b purify (moral) 88.30

ἁγνισμός, οῦ m
  purification (ritual) . . . 53.30

ἀγνοέω
  a not know 28.13
  b ignore 30.38
  c fail to understand . . 32.7

ἀγνόημα, τος *n*
sin through ignorance   *88.302*

ἄγνοια, ας *f*
ignorance *28.13*

ἀγνός, ή, όν
pure *88.28*

ἀγνότης, ητος *f*
purity *88.29*

ἀγνῶς
sincerely *88.45*

ἀγνωσία, ας *f*
a lack of knowledge . . *28.16*
b failure to under-
   stand *32.7*
c what is not under-
   stood *32.8*

ἄγνωστος, ον
unknown *28.27*

ἀγορά, ᾶς *f*
market *57.207*

ἀγοράζω
a buy *57.188*
b redeem *37.131*

ἀγοραῖος, ου *m*
a loafer *88.251*
b court of justice *56.1*

ἄγρα, ας *f*
catch *18.8*

ἀγράμματος, ον
uneducated *27.23*

ἀγραυλέω
remain outdoors *85.64*

ἀγρεύω
catch in mistake *27.30*

ἀγριέλαιος, ου *f*
wild olive tree *3.11*

ἄγριος, α, ον
violent *20.6*

Ἀγρίππας, α *m*
Agrippa *93.10*

ἀγρός, οῦ *m*
a field *1.95*
b countryside *1.87*
c farm settlement *1.93*

ἀγρυπνέω
a be alert *27.57*
b take care of *35.41*

ἀγρυπνία, ας *f*
sleeplessness *23.73*

ἄγω
(aor ἤγαγον, inf ἀγα-
γεῖν, aor pass ἤχθην,
fut pass ἀχθήσομαι)
a bring *15.165*
b carry *15.210*
c go away *15.34*
d guide *36.1*
c function *42.1*
f occur *67.64*
g spend time *67.79*

ἀγωγή, ῆς *f*
behavior *41.3*

ἀγών, ῶνος *m*
a fight *39.29*
b race *50.4*

ἀγωνία, ας *f*
intense sorrow *25.283*

ἀγωνίζομαι
a fight *39.29*
b compete *50.1*
c make effort *68.74*

Ἀδάμ *m*
Adam *93.11*

ἀδάπανος, ον
free of charge *57.164*

Ἀδδί, m
Addi 93.12

ἀδελφή, ῆς f
  a sister 10.50
  b fellow believer 11.24

ἀδελφός, οῦ m
  a brother 10.49
  b fellow believer 11.23
  c fellow Jew 11.25
  d fellow countryman . 11.57
  e neighbor 11.89

ἀδελφότης, ητος f
  brotherhood 11.22

ἄδηλος, ον
  not evident 24.95

ἀδηλότης, ητος f
  uncertainty 71.20

ἀδήλως
  aimlessly 30.65

ἀδημονέω
  be upset 25.247

ᾅδης, ου m
  a world of the dead . . . 1.19
  b death 23.108
  ᾅδης : unit
  πύλαι ᾅδου
   death (supernatural
   power) 12.50

ἀδιάκριτος, ον
  impartial 88.242

ἀδιάλειπτος, ον
  continuously 68.55

ἀδιαλείπτως
  continuously 68.55

ἀδικέω
  a hurt 20.25
  b act unjustly 88.22
  c mistreat 88.128

ἀδίκημα, τος n
  unrighteous act 88.23

ἀδικία, ας f
  unjust deed 88.21

ἄδικος, ον
  unjust 88.20

ἄδικος, ου m
  unbeliever 11.20

ἀδίκως
  unjustly 88.20

Ἀδμίν m
  Admin 93.13

ἀδόκιμος, ον
  a bad 88.111
  b worthless 65.13

ἄδολος, ον
  pure 79.98

Ἀδραμυττηνός, ή, όν
  Adramyttium 93.390

Ἀδρίας, ου m
  Adriatic Sea 93.391

ἀδρότης, ητος f
  abundance 59.60

ἀδυνατεῖ
  impossible 71.3

ἀδύνατος, ον
  a incapable 74.22
  b impossible 71.3

ᾄδω
  sing 33.109

ἀεί
  always 67.86

ἀετός, οῦ m
  eagle, vulture 4.42

ἄζυμος, ον
  without yeast 5.13

'Αζώρ m
  Azor 93.14

"Αζωτος, ου f
  Azotus 93.392

ἀήρ, έρος m
  a air (location) 1.6
  b air (substance) 2.2
  c sky 1.7
  ἀήρ : unit
  ἄρχων τῆς ἐξουσίας
  τοῦ ἀέρος
    supernatural power   12.44

αθα
  see θα

ἀθανασία, ας f
  immortality 23.126

ἀθέμιτος, ον
  a forbidden 13.144
  b disgusting 88.143

ἄθεος, ον
  without God 12.2

ἄθεσμος, ον
  lawless 88.141

ἀθετέω
  a reject 31.100
  b regard as invalid . . . 76.24

ἀθέτησις, εως f
  a annulment 76.24
  b removal 13.36

'Αθῆναι, ῶν f
  Athens 93.393

'Αθηναῖος, α, ον
  Athenian 93.394

'Αθηναῖος, ου m
  Athenian 93.395

ἀθλέω
  compete 50.2

ἄθλησις, εως f
  a struggle 50.3
  b challenge 74.13

ἀθροίζομαι
  come together 15.129

ἀθυμέω
  be disheartened 25.292

ἀθῷος, ον
  innocent 88.316

αἱ
  see ὁ

αἴγειος, α, ον
  of a goat 4.20

αἰγιαλός, οῦ m
  shore 1.63

Αἰγύπτιος, α, ον
  Egyptian 93.396

Αἰγύπτιος, ου m
  Egyptian 93.397

Αἴγυπτος, ου f
  Egypt 93.398

ἀΐδιος, ον
  eternal 67.96

αἰδώς, οῦς f
  modesty 88.49

Αἰθίοψ, οπος m
  Ethiopian 93.399

αἷμα, τος n
  a blood 8.64
  b death 23.107
  c killing 20.83
  αἷμα : units
  αἷμα ἐκχέω/ἐκχύννω
    kill 20.84

ἐκχύννεται τὸ αἷμα
  die as sacrifice 23.112
πηγὴ αἵματος
  menstrual flow 23.182
ῥύσις αἵματος
  menstrual flow 23.182
σὰρξ καὶ αἷμα
  human being 9.14
κοινωνέω αἵματος καὶ
σαρκός
  be a person 9.15

αἱματεκχυσία, ας f
  cause flow of blood . . . 23.183

αἱμορροέω
  bleed 23.181

Αἰνέας, ου m
  Aeneas 93.15

αἴνεσις, εως f
  praise 33.354

αἰνέω
  praise 33.354

αἴνιγμα, τος n
  a riddle 32.21
  b dim image 24.37

αἶνος, ου m
  praise 33.354

Αἰνών f
  Aenon 93.400

αἱρέομαι
  (aor εἱλάμην, ptc ἑλό-
  μενος)
  a select 30.86
  b choose 30.91

αἵρεσις, εως f
  a religious party 11.50
  b false teaching 33.241
  c division 63.27

αἱρετίζω
  choose 30.91

αἱρετικός, ή, όν
  divisive 39.17

αἴρω
  (fut 3 sg ἀρεῖ, aor
  ἦρα, inf ἆραι, pf
  ἦρκα, pf pass ἦρμαι,
  aor pass ἤρθην, fut
  pass ἀρθήσομαι)
  a carry 15.203
  b destroy 20.43
  c execute 20.65
  d withdraw 57.218
αἴρω : units
αἴρω ἀπό
  cause to no longer
  experience 90.96
αἴρω τὸν σταυρόν
  suffer unto death . . . 24.83
αἴρω τὴν ψυχήν τινος
  keep in suspense . . . 30.36

αἰσθάνομαι
  able to understand 32.28

αἴσθησις, εως f
  capacity to understand 32.28

αἰσθητήριον, ου n
  capacity to understand 32.28

αἰσχροκερδής, ές
  shamefully greedy 25.26

αἰσχροκερδῶς
  shamefully greedy 25.26

αἰσχρολογία, ας f
  dirty talk 33.33

αἰσχρός, ά, όν
  disgraceful 88.150

αἰσχρότης, ητος f
  indecent behavior 88.149

αἰσχύνη, ης f
  a shame 25.189
  b what causes shame . . 25.191
  c indecent behavior . . 88.149

αἰσχύνομαι
  be ashamed 25.190

αἰτέω
  ask for 33.163

αἴτημα, τος n
  request 33.164

αἰτία, ας f
  a reason 89.15
  b reason for accusation 56.4
  c accusation 56.5
  d guilt 88.315
  e relation 89.1

αἴτιον, ου n
  a reason 89.15
  b guilt 88.315

αἴτιος, ου m
  reason 89.15

αἰτίωμα, τος n
  accusation 56.5

αἰφνίδιος, ον
  immediately 67.113

αἰχμαλωσία, ας f
  captivity 55.23

αἰχμαλωτεύω
  take captive 55.24

αἰχμαλωτίζω
  a take captive 55.24
  b get control of 37.29

αἰχμάλωτος, ου m
  captive 55.25

αἰών, ῶνος m
  a era 67.143
  b universe 1.2
  c world system 41.38
  αἰών : units
  ἀπ' αἰῶνος
    long ago 67.25
  ἀπὸ τῶν αἰώνων
    since all time 67.133

ἐκ τοῦ αἰῶνος
    since all time 67.133
  πρὸ παντὸς τοῦ αἰῶνος
    since all time 67.133
  εἰς (τὸν) αἰῶνα (τοῦ
  αἰῶνος / τῶν αἰώνων)
    forever 67.95
  (εἰς) (παντὰς) τοὺς
  αἰῶνας (τῶν αἰώνων)
    forever 67.95
  αἰὼν τοῦ κόσμου τούτου
    supernatural
    power 12.44
  ὁ θεὸς τοῦ αἰῶνος τούτου
    the Devil 12.24
  υἱοὶ τοῦ αἰῶνος τούτου
    non-religious people 11.16
  ἐχθὲς καὶ σήμερον καὶ
  εἰς τοὺς αἰῶνας
    eternally 67.87
  εἰς ἡμέραν αἰῶνος
    forever 67.95

αἰώνιος, ον
  eternal 67.96
  αἰώνιος : units
  χρόνοις αἰωνίοις
    since all time 67.133
  πρὸ χρόνων αἰωνίων
    since all time 67.133

ἀκαθαρσία, ας f
  a immorality 88.261
  b filth 79.54

ἀκάθαρτος, ον
  defiled (religiously) . . . 53.39
  ἀκάθαρτος : unit
  πνεῦμα ἀκάθαρτον
    unclean spirit 12.39

ἀκαιρέομαι
  lack opportunity 67.7

ἀκαίρως
  unfavorable 67.8

ἄκακος, ον
  a without fault 88.2
  b unsuspecting 31.34

ἄκανθα, ης *f*
thorn plant 3.17

ἀκάνθινος, η, ον
thorny 3.18

ἄκαρπος, ον
a without fruit 23.202
b useless 65.34

ἀκατάγνωστος, ον
above criticism 33.415

ἀκατακάλυπτος, ον
uncovered 79.116

ἀκατάκριτος, ον
without trial 56.19

ἀκατάλυτος, ον
cannot be ended 13.47

ἀκατάπαυστος, ον
never ceasing 68.56

ἀκαταστασία, ας *f*
a rebellion 39.34
b riot 39.36

ἀκατάστατος, ον
not controlled by 37.32

Ἀκελδαμάχ
Akeldama 93.401

ἀκέραιος, ον
pure 88.32

ἀκήκοα
see ἀκούω

ἀκλινής, ές
firmly 31.80

ἀκμάζω
ripen 23.197

ἀκμήν
yet, still 67.128

ἀκοή, ῆς *f*
a hearing 24.52
b ability to hear 24.53
c what is heard 24.57
d news 33.213
e pay attention to 31.56
ἀκοή : units
ἀκοῇ ἀκούω
  listen carefully 24.63
κνήθομαι τὴν ἀκοήν
  desirous of hearing 25.11
ἀνοίγουσιν αἱ ἀκοαί
  become able to hear 24.69
εἰσφέρω εἰς τὰς ἀκοάς
  a cause to hear 24.55
  b speak about 33.92
νωθρὸς ταῖς ἀκοαῖς
  slow to understand . . 32.47

ἀκολουθέω
a go/come behind 15.144
b accompany as
  follower 15.156
c be a disciple 36.31

ἀκούω
(pf ἀκήκοα, aor pass
ptc ἀκουσθείς)
a hear 24.52
b be able to hear 24.58
c receive news 33.212
d pay attention to 31.56
e obey 36.14
f understand 32.1
g hear legal case 56.13
ἀκούω : units
ἀκοῇ ἀκούω
  listen carefully 24.63
ἀκούω εἰς τὸ οὖς
  hear in secret 24.67
τοῖς ὠσὶν βαρέως ἀκούω
  be mentally dull 32.46

ἀκρασία, ας *f*
lack of self-control 88.91

ἀκρατής, ές
lacking self-control . . . 88.92

ἄκρατος, ον
pure 79.99

ἀκρίβεια, ας *f*
accurateness *72.20*

ἀκριβής, ές
accurate *72.19*

ἀκριβόω
learn exactly *27.9*

ἀκριβῶς
accurately *72.19*

ἀκρίς, ίδος *f*
locust *4.47*

ἀκροατήριον, ου *n*
audience hall *7.13*

ἀκροατής, οῦ *m*
hearer *24.56*

ἀκροβυστία, ας *f*
a being uncircumcised *11.52*
b Gentiles *11.53*

ἀκρογωνιαῖος, ου *m*
cornerstone *7.44*

ἀκροθίνιον, ου *n*
finest booty *57.244*

ἄκρον, ου *n*
a extreme boundary .. *80.7*
b tip, top *79.104*

᾽Ακύλας *m*
Aquila *93.16*

ἀκυρόω
invalidate authority of *76.25*

ἀκωλύτως
freely *13.151*

ἄκων
not willing *25.67*

ἀλάβαστρον, ου *n*
alabaster jar *6.131*

ἀλαζονεία, ας *f*
false pride *88.219*

ἀλαζών, όνος *m*
arrogant person *88.220*

ἀλαλάζω
a clang *14.82*
b weep loudly *25.139*

ἀλάλητος, ον
cannot be expressed .. *33.96*

ἄλαλος, ον
mute *33.106*

ἄλας, ατος *n*
salt *5.25*

ἀλείφω
anoint *47.14*

ἀλεκτοροφωνία, ας *f*
before dawn *67.198*

ἀλέκτωρ, ορος *m*
rooster *4.45*

᾽Αλεξανδρεύς, έως *m*
an Alexandrian *93.402*

᾽Αλεξανδρῖνος, η, ον
Alexandrian *93.403*

᾽Αλέξανδρος, ου *m*
Alexander *93.17*

ἄλευρον, ου *n*
wheat flour *5.9*

ἀλήθεια, ας *f*
truth *72.2*
ἀλήθεια : units
ἐπ᾽ ἀληθείας
really *70.4*
ἐν ἀληθείᾳ
really *70.4*
κατ᾽ ἀλήθειαν
really *70.4*

ἀληθεύω
speak truth 33.251

ἀληθής, ές
a true 72.1
b real 70.3
c honest 88.39

ἀληθινός, ή, όν
a real 70.3
b true 72.1
c genuine 73.2

ἀλήθω
grind grain 46.16

ἀληθῶς
really 70.3

ἁλιεύς, έως m
fisherman 44.10

ἁλιεύω
catch fish 44.7

ἁλίζω
(fut pass ἁλισθήσομαι,
ἁλισγηθήσομαι)
salt 5.28

ἁλίσγημα, τος n
a thing defiled (ritually) 53.37

ἀλλά
a but 89.125
b and 89.96
c yet 91.2
d certainly 91.11
see also μέν . . . ἀλλά
ἀλλά : units
ἀλλὰ μᾶλλον
but 89.125
ἀλλ' ἤ
but 89.125

ἀλλάσσω
(fut pass ἀλλαγήσομαι)
a change 58.43
b exchange 57.142

ἀλλαχόθεν
from elsewhere 84.8

ἀλλαχοῦ
elsewhere 83.4

ἀλληγορέω
speak allegorically 33.18

ἀλληλουϊά
hallelujah 33.363

ἀλλήλων, οις, ους
each other 92.26

ἀλλογενής, οῦς m
foreigner 11.76

ἅλλομαι
(aor ἡλάμην)
a jump 15.238
b bubble up 14.30

ἄλλος, η, ο
a different 58.36
b another 58.37

ἀλλοτριεπίσκοπος, ου m
busybody 88.245

ἀλλότριος, α, ον
a belonging to another 92.20
b foreigner 11.74
c be enemy of 39.12

ἀλλόφυλος, ου m
heathen 11.43

ἄλλως
differently 58.36

'Αλμεί m
Almi 93.18

ἀλοάω
thresh 43.19

ἄλογος, ον
a not able to reason . . . 30.12
b without basis 89.19

ἀλόη, ης f
aloes 6.209

ἅλς, ἁλός m
salt 5.25

ἁλυκός, ή, όν
salty 5.26

ἀλυπότερος, α, ον
relieved of anxiety 25.278

ἅλυσις, εως f
a chain 6.16
b imprisonment 37.115

ἀλυσιτελής, ές
of no advantage 65.49

Ἄλφα n
first 61.7

Ἀλφαῖος, ου m
Alphaeus 93.19

ἅλων, ος f
a threshing floor 7.65
b threshed grain 3.43

ἀλώπηξ, εχος f
a fox 4.10
b wicked person 88.120

ἅλωσις, εως f
capture 44.11

ἅμα
a at the same time 67.34
b together with 89.114

ἀμαθής, ές
uneducated 27.24

ἀμαράντινος, η, ον
unfading 79.23

ἀμάραντος, ον
unfading 79.23

ἁμαρτάνω
(aor ἥμαρτον, often
ἁμαρτησ- in moods
other than the ind,
pf ἡμάρτηκα)
sin 88.289

ἁμάρτημα, τος n
sin 88.290

ἁμαρτία, ας f
a sin 88.289
b being evil 88.118
c guilt 88.310

ἀμάρτυρος, ον
without witness 33.267

ἁμαρτωλός, όν
sinful 88.294

ἁμαρτωλός, οῦ m
sinner 88.295

ἄμαχος, ον
peaceful 39.24

ἀμάω
mow 43.13

ἀμέθυστος, ου f
amethyst 2.42

ἀμελέω
disregard 30.50

ἄμεμπτος, ον
blameless 88.317

ἀμέμπτως
blameless 88.317

ἀμέριμνος, ον
without worry 25.226

ἀμετάθετος, ον
unchanging 13.61

ἀμετακίνητος, ον
firm 31.81

ἀμεταμέλητος, ον
   not regretful 25.271

ἀμετανόητος, ον
   unrepentant 41.54

ἄμετρος, ον
   ἄμετρος : unit
   εἰς τὰ ἄμετρα
      excessive 78.27

ἀμήν
   truly 72.6

ἀμήτωρ, ορος
   without mother 10.17

ἀμίαντος, ον
   undefiled 53.36

'Αμιναδάβ m
   Amminadab 93.20

ἄμμος, ου f
   a sand 2.28
   b beach 1.64

'Αμμών m
   Ammon 93.22

ἀμνός, οῦ m
   lamb 4.24

ἀμοιβή, ῆς f
   repayment 57.168

ἄμπελος, ου f
   grapevine 3.27

ἀμπελουργός, οῦ m
   vinedresser . . . . ! . 43.21

ἀμπελών, ῶνος m
   vineyard 3.28

'Αμπλιᾶτος, ου m
   Ampliatus 93.21

ἀμύνομαι
   help 35.3

ἀμφιάζω
   a clothe 49.3
   b adorn 49.5

ἀμφιβάλλω
   cast a fishnet 44.8

ἀμφίβληστρον, ου n
   casting-net 6.12

ἀμφιέννυμι
   (pf pass ἠμφίεσμαι)
   a clothe 49.3
   b adorn 49.5

'Αμφίπολις, εως f
   Amphipolis 93.404

ἄμφοδον, ου n
   city street 1.101

ἀμφότεροι, αι, α
   a both 59.25
   b all 59.26

ἀμώμητος, ον
   blameless 88.35

ἄμωμον, ου n
   spice 5.23

ἄμωμος, ον
   a without defect 79.61
   b blameless 88.34

'Αμών m
   Amon 93.22

'Αμώς m
   Amos 93.23

ἄν
   a would 71.14
   b ever 71.8
   ἄν : unit
   ἡνίκα ἄν
      whenever 67.36

ἀνά
each *89.91*
ἀνά : units
ἀνὰ μέσον
  a among *83.9*
  b in the middle *83.10*
  c between *89.143*
ἀνὰ μέρος
  in succession *61.4*

ἀναβαθμός, οῦ *m*
stairs *7.52*

ἀναβαίνω
(aor ἀνέβην, pf
ἀναβέβηκα)
  a go up *15.101*
  b go aboard *15.99*
  c sprout and grow ... *23.196*
  d grow up *23.189*
ἀναβαίνω : unit
ἀναβαίνω ἐπὶ καρδίαν
  begin to think *30.17*

ἀναβάλλω
adjourn a hearing *56.18*

ἀναβιβάζω
pull up *15.213*

ἀναβλέπω
  a look up *24.10*
  b gain sight *24.42*

ἀνάβλεψις, εως *f*
gaining sight *24.42*

ἀναβοάω
shout *33.81*

ἀναβολή, ῆς *f*
postponement *67.127*

ἀνάγαιον, ου *n*
upstairs room *7.27*

ἀναγγέλλω
(fut ἀναγγελῶ, aor
ἀνήγγειλα, inf ἀν-
αγγεῖλαι, aor pass
ἀνηγγέλην)
inform *33.197*

ἀναγεννάω
cause to be born again *13.55*

ἀναγινώσκω
(aor ἀνέγνων, inf
ἀναγνῶναι, ptc
ἀναγνούς, aor pass
inf ἀναγνωσθῆναι)
read *33.68*

ἀναγκάζω
compel *37.33*

ἀναγκαῖος, α, ον
  a necessary *71.39*
  b intimate *34.14*

ἀναγκαστῶς
out of obligation *71.31*

ἀνάγκη, ης *f*
  a trouble *22.1*
  b complete obligation *71.38*
  c inevitability *71.30*

ἀναγνωρίζομαι
make known again.... *27.62*

ἀνάγνωσις, εως *f*
reading *33.68*

ἀνάγομαι
set sail *54.4*

ἀνάγω
(aor ἀνήγαγον, aor pass
ἀνήχθην, inf ἀναχθῆναι)
  a lead up *15.176*
  b offer to *15.211*

ἀναδείκνυμι
(aor ἀνέδειξα)
  a make known *28.54*
  b give a task *37.96*

ἀνάδειξις, εως f
revelation 28.54

ἀναδέχομαι
a welcome 34.53
b experience 90.75

ἀναδίδωμι
(aor ptc ἀναδούς)
deliver 57.76

ἀναζάω
a live again 23.93
b begin to function . . . 42.6

ἀναζητέω
try to find out 27.42

ἀναζώννυμαι
(aor midd ptc ἀνα-
ζωσάμενος)
ἀναζώννυμαι : unit
ἀναζώννυμαι τὰς
ὀσφύας τῆς διανοίας
  be ready to learn . . . 27.55

ἀναζωπυρέω
reactivate 68.8

ἀναθάλλω
(aor ἀνέθαλον)
be again 13.23

ἀνάθεμα, τος n
a a curse 33.473
b cursed 33.474

ἀναθεματίζω
curse 33.472

ἀναθεωρέω
a observe 24.47
b reflect upon 30.28

ἀνάθημα, τος n
offering 53.18

ἀναίδεια, ας f
insolence 66.12

ἀναιρέομαι
adopt 35.53

ἀναίρεσις, εως f
killing 20.71

ἀναιρέω
(fut ἀνελῶ, 3 sg ἀνελεῖ,
aor ἀνεῖλα, subj ἀνέλω,
inf ἀνελεῖν, opt 3 sg ἀνέλοι, aor pass ἀνῃρέθην)
a kill 20.71
b do away with 76.22

ἀναίτιος, ον
innocent 88.316

ἀνακαθίζω
sit up 17.16

ἀνακαινίζω
restore 13.67

ἀνακαινόω
a make new 58.72
b restore 13.67

ἀνακαίνωσις, εως f
renewal 58.72

ἀνακαλύπτω
uncover 79.117

ἀνακάμπτω
a return 15.89
b change to former
  belief 31.64

ἀνάκειμαι
a recline to eat 17.23
b eat a meal 23.21
ἀνάκειμαι : unit
ἀνάκειμαι ἐν τῷ κόλπῳ
  dine in place of
  honor 17.25

ἀνακεφαλαιόω
bring together 63.8

ἀνακλίνομαι
recline to eat 17.23

ἀνακλίνω
a cause to lie down ... *17.28*
b cause to recline to eat *17.24*

ἀνακράζω
shout *33.83*

ἀνακρίνω
(aor pass ἀνεκρίθην)
a study thoroughly ... *27.44*
b investigate in court . *56.12*
c criticize *33.412*
d evaluate carefully ... *30.109*

ἀνάκρισις, εως *f*
investigation in court *56.12*

ἀνακύπτω
straighten up *17.33*

ἀναλαμβάνω
(aor ἀνέλαβον, aor
pass ἀνελήμφθην)
a lift up and carry *15.203*
b take/bring along ... *15.168*
c take aboard *15.100*

ἀνάλημψις, εως *f*
ascension *15.103*

ἀναλίσκω
(fut 3 sg ἀναλώσει, aor
ἀνήλωσα, opt 3 sg ἀνα-
λοῖ, aor pass ἀνηλώθην)
destroy *20.47*

ἀναλογία, ας *f*
in proportion to *89.10*

ἀναλογίζομαι
consider carefully *30.10*

ἀναλοῖ
see ἀναλίσκω

ἄναλος, ον
without salt *5.27*

ἀναλόω
see ἀναλίσκω

ἀνάλυσις, εως *f*
death *23.101*

ἀναλύω
a return *15.89*
b die *23.101*

ἀναλώσει
see ἀναλίσκω

ἀναμάρτητος, ον
guiltless *88.311*

ἀναμένω
wait for *85.60*

ἀναμιμνήσκομαι
remember *29.9*

ἀναμιμνήσκω
(fut ἀναμνήσω, aor
pass ἀνεμνήσθην)
cause to remember ... *29.10*

ἀνάμνησις, εως *f*
reminder *29.11*

ἀνανεόω
make new *58.72*

ἀνανήφω
return to one's right
senses *30.27*

Ἀνανίας, ου *m*
Ananias *93.24*

ἀναντίρρητος, ον
indisputable *33.458*

ἀναντιρρήτως
indisputable *33.458*

ἀνάξιος, ον
unworthy *65.19*

ἀναξίως
a unworthily *65.19*
b improperly *66.7*

ἀναστρέφω
(aor pass ἀνεστράφην)
return *15.89*

ἀναστροφή, ῆς *f*
behavior *41.3*

ἀναστῶ
see ἀνίσταμαι

ἀνατάσσομαι
compile *62.3*

ἀνατέλλω
(aor ἀνέτειλα, pf
ἀνατέταλκα)
a rise *15.104*
b dawn *14.41*
c be a descendant *10.35*

ἀνατίθεμαι
(aor ἀνεθέμην)
explain *33.151*

ἀνατολή, ῆς *f*
a rising *15.104*
b east *82.1*
ἀνατολή : unit
ἀνατολὴ ἐξ ὕφους
the dawn from on
high *14.42*

ἀνατρέπω
a turn over *16.18*
b upset faith *31.72*

ἀνατρέφω
rear *35.51*
ἀνατρέφω : unit
ἀνατρέφω παρὰ τοὺς
πόδας
be taught by *33.232*

ἀναφαίνομαι
(2nd aor part ἀναφάνας)
come into view *24.23*

ἀναφέρω
(aor ἀνήνεγκον, inf
ἀνενέγκαι, ἀνενεγκεῖν)
a lead up *15.176*
b carry up *15.206*
c offer up *53.17*

ἀναφωνέω
cry out *33.77*

ἀναχθῆναι
see ἀνάγω

ἀνάχυσις, εως *f*
excessive *78.26*

ἀναχωρέω
a go away *15.53*
b return *15.89*

ἀνάψυξις, εως *f*
a relief *22.35*
b encouragement *25.148*

ἀναψύχω
encourage *25.149*

ἀνδραποδιστής, οῦ *m*
slave dealer *57.187*

᾽Ανδρέας, ου *m*
Andrew *93.25*

ἀνδρίζομαι
be courageous *25.165*

᾽Ανδρόνικος, ου *m*
Andronicus *93.26*

ἀνδροφόνος, ου *m*
murderer *20.85*

ἀνεβαλόμην
see ἀναβάλλομαι

ἀνέβην
see ἀναβαίνω

ἀνέγκλητος, ον
without accusation . . . *33.433*

ἀνέγνων
  see ἀναγινώσκω

ἀνέδειξα
  see ἀναδείκνυμι

ἀνέθαλον
  see ἀναθάλλω

ἀνεθέμην
  see ἀνατίθεμαι

ἀνέθην
  see ἀνίημι

ἀνεῖλον
  see ἀναιρέω

ἀνείς
  see ἀνίημι

ἀνειχόμην
  see ἀνέχομαι

ἀνεκδιήγητος, ον
  indescribable 33.202

ἀνεκλάλητος, ον
  cannot be expressed. . . 33.96

ἀνέκλειπτος, ον
  unfailing 13.99

ἀνεκρίθην
  see ἀνακρίνω

ἀνεκτός, όν
  endurable 25.172

ἀνέλαβον
  see ἀναλαμβάνω

ἀνελεήμων, ον
  unmerciful 88.82

ἀνελεῖ
  see ἀναιρέω

ἀνελεῖν
  see ἀναιρέω

ἀνέλεος, ον
  unmerciful 88.82

ἀνελήμφθην
  see ἀναλαμβάνω

ἀνέλοι
  see ἀναιρέω

ἀνέλω
  see ἀναιρέω

ἀνελῶ
  see ἀναιρέω

ἀνεμίζομαι
  be driven on by wind   15.164

ἀνεμνήσθην
  see ἀναμιμνήσκω

ἄνεμος, ου m
  wind 14.4

ἀνένδεκτος, ον
  impossible 71.5

ἀνενέγκαι
  see ἀναφέρω

ἀνενεγκεῖν
  see ἀναφέρω

ἀνεξεραύνητος, ον
  impossible to under-
  stand 32.23

ἀνεξίκακος, ον
  tolerant 25.170

ἀνεξιχνίαστος, ον
  impossible to
  understand 32.23

ἀνεπαίσχυντος, ον
  unashamed 25.192

ἀνέπεσον
  see ἀναπίπτω

ἀνεπίλημπτος, ον
above criticism 33.415

ἀνέρχομαι
(aor ἀνῆλθον)
move up 15.101

ἄνεσις, εως f
a relief 22.36
b some freedom 37.137

ἀνέστην
see ἀνίσταμαι

ἀνέστησα
see ἀνίστημι

ἀνεστράφην
see ἀναστρέφω

ἀνεσχόμην
see ἀνέχομαι

ἀνετάζω
interrogate 56.16

ἀνέτειλα
see ἀνατέλλω

ἄνευ
without 89.120

ἀνεύθετος, ον
unusable 65.35

ἀνευρίσκω
(aor ἀνεῦρον)
find by searching 27.28

ἀνέχομαι
(impf ἀνειχόμην,
aor ἀνεσχόμην)
a be patient with 25.171
b accept 31.54
ἀνέχομαι : unit
κατὰ λόγον ἀνέχομαι
accept a complaint .. 56.10

ἀνεψιός, οῦ m
cousin 10.52

ἀνέῳγα
see ἀνοίγω

ἀνέῳγμαι
see ἀνοίγω

ἀνέῳξα
see ἀνοίγω

ἀνεῴχθην
see ἀνοίγω

ἀνήγαγον
see ἀνάγω

ἀνήγγειλα
see ἀναγγέλλω

ἀνηγγέλην
see ἀναγγέλλω

ἄνηθον, ου n
dill 3.24

ἀνήκει
be fitting 66.1

ἀνῆλθον
see ἀνέρχομαι

ἀνηλώθην
see ἀναλίσκω

ἀνήλωσα
see ἀναλίσκω

ἀνήμερος, ον
fierce 20.5

ἀνήνεγκον
see ἀναφέρω

ἀνήρ, ἀνδρός m
a man 9.24
b human being 9.1
c husband 10.53
ἀνήρ : units
γίνομαι ἀνδρί
marry 34.69
νόμος τοῦ ἀνδρός
marriage law 33.341

ἀνῃρέθην
see ἀναιρέω

ἀνήφθην
see ἀνάπτω

ἀνήχθην
see ἀνάγω

ἀνθέξομαι
see ἀντέχομαι

ἀνθίστημι
(aor ἀντέστην, pf
ἀνθέστηκα)
a be hostile toward ... *39.1*
b resist *39.18*

ἀνθομολογέομαι
give thanks *33.351*

ἄνθος, ους *n*
flower *3.56*

ἀνθρακιά, ᾶς *f*
charcoal fire........ *2.6*

ἄνθραξ, ακος *m*
charcoal *3.67*
ἄνθραξ : unit
σωρεύω ἄνθρακας
πυρὸς ἐπὶ τὴν κεφαλήν
   cause to be ashamed *25.199*

ἀνθρωπάρεσκος, ον
pleasing people *25.98*

ἀνθρώπινος, η, ον
human *9.6*
ἀνθρώπινος : unit
χεὶρ ἀνθρωπίνη
   person *9.5*

ἀνθρωποκτόνος, ου *m*
murderer *20.85*

ἄνθρωπος, ου *m*
a human being *9.1*
b man *9.24*
c husband *10.53*

ἄνθρωπος : units
υἱὸς τοῦ ἀνθρώπου
   Son of Man *9.3*
υἱοὶ τῶν ἀνθρώπων
   people........... *9.2*
παλαιὸς ἄνθρωπος
   former behavior *41.43*
ὁ ἔξω ἄνθρωπος
   body *8.3*
ὁ ἔσω (ἄνθρωπος)
   inner being *26.1*
ὁ ἐν τῷ κρυπτῷ
(ἄνθρωπος)
   inner being *26.1*

ἀνθύπατος, ου *m*
proconsul *37.82*

ἀνίημι
(pres ptc ἀνιείς, aor
subj ἀνῶ, ptc ἀνείς,
aor pass ἀνέθην)
a loosen........... *18.19*
b forsake *35.54*
c give up *68.43*

ἄνιπτος, ον
not washed *47.13*

ἀνίσταμαι
(2 aor ἀνέστην, subj
ἀναστῶ, impv ἀνάστα,
ἀνάστηθι, inf ἀναστῆναι,
ptc ἀναστάς)
a stand up *17.6*
b go away *15.36*
c appear *13.81*
d live again *23.93*
e rebel against...... *39.34*

ἀνίστημι
(fut ἀναστήσω, 1 aor
ἀνέστησα, ptc ἀνα-
στήσας)
a cause to stand up ... *17.7*
b raise to life *23.94*
ἀνίστημι : unit
ἀνίστημι σπέρμα
   beget............. *23.59*

"Αννα, ας *f*
Anna *93.27*

"Αννας, α *m*
Annas *93.28*

ἀνόητος, ον
without understanding *32.50*

ἄνοια, ας *f*
a lack of understanding *32.51*
b extreme fury *88.183*

ἀνοίγω
(aor ἀνέῳξα, ἠνέῳξα,
ἤνοιξα, pf ἀνέῳγα, pf
pass ἀνέῳγμαι, ἠν-
έῳγμαι, aor pass
ἀνεῴχθην, ἠνεῴχθην,
ἠνοίχθην, ἠνοίγην)
open *79.110*
ἀνοίγω : units
ἀνοίγω τὸ στόμα
   start speaking *33.29*
ἀνοίγω θύραν
   make possible *71.9*
τὸ στόμα ἀνοίγω πρός
   speak complete truth *33.252*
ἀνοίγω τοὺς ὀφθαλμούς
   cause to be able to see *24.43*
ἀνοίγουσιν αἱ ἀκοαί
   become able to hear *24.69*

ἀνοικοδομέω
rebuild *45.3*

ἄνοιξις, εως *f*
ἄνοιξις : unit
ἄνοιξις τοῦ στόματος
   starting to speak *33.29*

ἀνομία, ας *f*
lawlessness *88.139*

ἄνομος, ον
a lawless *88.140*
b without the Law . . . *33.57*

ἄνομος, ου *m*
heathen *11.42*

ἀνόμως
without the Law *33.57*

ἀνορθόω
a build up again *45.4*
b straighten up *17.33*
ἀνορθόω : unit
τὰ παραλελυμένα
γόνατα ἀνορθόω
   become encouraged *25.152*

ἀνόσιος, ον
impious *53.47*

ἀνοχή, ῆς *f*
patience *25.171*

ἀνταγωνίζομαι
struggle against *39.31*

ἀντάλλαγμα, τος *n*
something given in
exchange *57.143*

ἀνταναπληρόω
fill up *59.34*

ἀνταποδίδωμι
(fut ἀνταποδώσω, aor
inf ἀνταποδοῦναι, fut
pass ἀνταποδοθήσυμαι)
a pay back *57.154*
b repay *38.19*

ἀνταπόδομα, τος *n*
a repayment *57.155*
b recompense *38.20*

ἀνταπόδοσις, εως *f*
recompense *38.20*

ἀνταποκρίνομαι
a answer *33.186*
b criticize in return . . . *33.413*

ἀντεῖπον
see ἀντιλέγω

ἀντελαβόμην
see ἀντιλαμβάνομαι

ἀντέστην
see ἀνθίστημι

ἀντέχομαι
(fut ἀνθέξομαι)
a adhere to 34.24
b cling to a belief 31.49
c help 35.1

ἀντί
a instead 89.133
b on behalf of 90.37
c for this reason 89.24
d so then 89.45
e in place of 57.145

ἀντιβάλλω
discuss 33.160

ἀντιδιατίθεμαι
be hostile toward 39.1

ἀντίδικος, ου m
a accuser 56.11
b adversary 39.9

ἀντίθεσις, εως f
contradiction 33.457

ἀντικαθίστημι
(aor ἀντικατέστην)
resist 39.18

ἀντικαλέω
invite back 33.317

ἀντίκειμαι
be hostile toward 39.1

ἄντικρυς
opposite to 83.44

ἀντιλαμβάνομαι
(aor ἀντελαβόμην)
a help 35.1
b devote oneself to ... 25.79
c enjoy benefit 65.48

ἀντιλέγω
(aor ἀντεῖπον)
oppose 33.455

ἀντίλημψις, εως f
ability to help 35.9

ἀντιλογία, ας f
a dispute 33.445
b contradiction 33.456
c rebellion.......... 39.35

ἀντιλοιδορέω
insult in return 33.394

ἀντίλυτρον, ου n
ransom.............. 37.130

ἀντιμετρέω
repay 57.93

ἀντιμισθία, ας f
recompense 38.15

Ἀντιόχεια, ας f
Antioch 93.405

Ἀντιοχεύς, έως m
Antiochean 93.406

ἀντιπαρέρχομαι
(aor ἀντιπαρῆλθον)
pass by on opposite
side 15.30

Ἀντιπᾶς, ᾶ m
Antipas 93.29

Ἀντιπατρίς, ίδος f
Antipatris 93.407

ἀντιπέρα
across from 83.43

ἀντιπίπτω
resist 39.18

ἀντιστρατεύομαι
actively oppose 39.2

ἀντιτάσσομαι
be hostile toward 39.1

ἀντίτυπος, ον
representation 58.69

ἀντίχριστος, ου *m*
  antichrist 53.83

ἀντλέω
  (pf ptc ἠντληκώς)
  draw water 47.1

ἄντλημα, τος *n*
  bucket 6.123

ἀντοφθαλμέω
  face into 82.9

ἄνυδρος, ον
  waterless 2.8

ἀνυπόκριτος, ον
  genuine 73.8

ἀνυπότακτος, ον
  a not subject to 37.32
  b disobedient 36.26

ἀνῶ
  see ἀνίημι

ἄνω
  a above 83.48
  b upwards 84.25

ἄνωθεν
  a from above 84.13
  b again 67.55
  c for a long time 67.90
  ἄνωθεν : unit
  γεννάω ἄνωθεν
    be born again 41.53

ἀνωτερικός, ή, όν
  inland 1.65

ἀνώτερον
  a preceding 61.6
  b higher status 87.29

ἀνωφελής, ές
  not advantageous 65.50

ἀξίνη, ης *f*
  axe 6.217

ἄξιος, α, ον
  a worthy 65.17
  b proper 66.6

ἀξιόω
  a regard worthy 65.18
  b choose 30.95
  c desire 25.5

ἀξίως
  a worthy 65.17
  b properly 66.6

ἀόρατος, ον
  invisible 24.4

Ἀουλία
  see Ἰουλία 93.30

ἀπαγγέλλω
  (fut ἀπαγγελῶ, aor
  ἀπήγγειλα, opt 3 sg
  ἀπαγγειλοι, aor pass
  ἀπηγγέλην)
  a inform 33.198
  b command 33.327

ἀπάγχομαι
  (aor ἀπηγξάμην)
  hang oneself 20.81

ἀπάγω
  (aor ἀπήγαγον, aor
  pass inf ἀπαχθῆναι)
  a lead away 15.177
  b lead off to punish-
     ment 56.38
  c execute 20.65
  d deceive 88.152
  e extend to 84.33

ἀπαίδευτος, ον
  uneducated 27.25

ἀπαίρω
  (aor pass 3 sg ἀπήρθη,
  subj ἀπαρθῶ)
  lead away 15.177

ἀπαιτέω
  ask back 33.165

ἀπαλγέω
lose feeling of shame . . *25.197*

ἀπαλλάσσομαι
(pf pass inf ἀπηλλάχθαι)
a settle with *40.3*
b cease *13.40*

ἀπαλλάσσω
set free *37.127*

ἀπαλλοτριόομαι
be foreigner *11.75*

ἀπαλός, ή, όν
tender *79.101*

ἀπαντάω
meet up with *15.78*

ἀπάντησις, εως f
meeting up with *15.78*

ἅπαξ
a once *60.67*
b once for all *60.68*
ἅπαξ : unit
ἅπαξ καὶ δίς
   several times *60.70*

ἀπαράβατος, ον
unchanging *13.61*

ἀπαρασκεύαστος, ον
unprepared *77.9*

ἀπαρθῶ
see ἀπαίρω

ἀπαρνέομαι
a deny *33.277*
b disregard *30.52*
c reject *34.49*

ἀπαρτισμός, οῦ m
completion *68.28*

ἀπαρχή, ῆς f
a first portion *53.23*
b first *61.8*
c foretaste *57.171*

ἅπας, ασα, αν
all *59.23*

ἀπασπάζομαι
take leave of *33.21*

ἀπατάω
deceive *31.12*

ἀπάτη, ης f
deception *31.12*

ἀπάτωρ, ορος
without father *10.15*

ἀπαύγασμα, τος n
radiance *14.48*

ἀπαχθῆναι
see ἀπάγω

ἀπέβαλον
see ἀποβάλλω

ἀπέβην
see ἀποβαίνω

ἀπέδειξα
see ἀποδείκνυμι

ἀπεδίδουν
see ἀποδίδωμι

ἀπεδόμην
see ἀποδίδωμι

ἀπέθανον
see ἀποθνήσκω

ἀπεθέμην
see ἀποτίθεμαι

ἀπείθεια, ας f
a disobedience *36.23*
b rejection of believe . *31.107*

ἀπειθέω
a disobey *36.23*
b reject belief *31.107*

ἀπειθής, ές
disobedient *36.24*

ἀπειλέω
threaten *33.291*

ἀπειλή, ῆς *f*
threatening *33.291*
ἀπειλή : unit
ἐμπνέω ἀπειλῆς
   threaten strongly ... *33.293*

ἄπειμι
(from εἶμι, impf 3 pl
ἀπῇεσαν or from
εἰμί, ptc ἀπών)
a go, come *15.8*
b be absent *85.27*

ἀπειπάμην
see ἀπολέγομαι

ἀπείραστος, ον
cannot be tempted *88.309*

ἄπειρος, ον
inexperienced *28.15*

ἀπεκαλύφθην
see ἀποκαλύπτω

ἀπεκατεστάθην
see ἀποκαθίστημι

ἀπεκατέστην
see ἀποκαθίστημι

ἀπεκδέχομαι
a look forward eagerly *25.63*
b wait for *13.28*

ἀπεκδύομαι
undress *49.20*

ἀπέκδυσις, εως *f*
undressing *49.20*

ἀπεκριθείς
see ἀποκρίνομαι

ἀπεκρίθην
see ἀποκρίνομαι

ἀπεκτάνθην
see ἀποκτείνω

ἀπέκτεινα
see ἀποκτείνω

ἀπέλαβον
see ἀπολαμβάνω

ἀπελαύνω
(aor ἀπήλασα)
drive away *15.56*

ἀπελεγμός, οῦ *m*
serious criticism *33.416*

ἀπελεύθερος, ου *m*
free person *87.85*

ἀπελεύσομαι
see ἀπέρχομαι

ἀπελήλυθα
see ἀπέρχομαι

ἀπέλιπον
see ἀπολείπω

'Απελλῆς, οῦ *m*
Apelles *93.31*

ἀπελπίζω
expect *30.54*

ἀπέναντι
a opposite *83.42*
b against *90.35*

ἀπενεγκεῖν
see ἀποφέρω

ἀπενεχθῆναι
see ἀποφέρω

ἀπέπεσα
see ἀποπίπτω

ἀπέπλευσα
see ἀποπλέω

ἀπεπνίγην
see ἀποπνίγω

ἀπέραντος, ον
endless 61.19

ἀπερισπάστως
not distracting 30.33

ἀπερίτμητος, ον
ἀπερίτμητος : unit
ἀπερίτμητος καρδία
καὶ τοῖς ὠσίν
   obstinate 88.224

ἀπέρχομαι
(fut ἀπελεύσομαι, aor
ἀπῆλθον, pf ἀπελήλυθα)
a go away 15.37
b pass away 13.93
ἀπέρχομαι : units
ἀπέρχομαι εἰς τὰ ὀπίσω
   no longer follow 36.36
ἀπέρχομαι πρὸς ἑαυτόν
   go back to one's
   place 15.92
ἀπέρχομαι ὀπίσω σαρκὸς
ἑτέρας
   have homosexual
   intercourse 88.279

ἀπεστάλην
see ἀποστέλλω

ἀπέσταλκα
see ἀποστέλλω

ἀπέστειλα
see ἀποστέλλω

ἀπέστην
see ἀφίσταμαι

ἀπέστησα
see ἀφίστημι

ἀπεστράφην
see ἀποστρέφομαι

ἀπέχομαι
avoid 13.158

ἀπέχω
a receive in full 57.137
b be away from 85.16
c be enough 59.47
d experience 90.67

ἀπήγαγον
see ἀπάγω

ἀπηγξάμην
see ἀπάγχομαι

ἀπῄεσαν
see ἄπειμι

ἀπήλασα
see ἀπελαύνω

ἀπῆλθον
see ἀπέρχομαι

ἀπηλλάχθαι
see ἀπαλλάσσω

ἀπήνεγκα
see ἀποφέρω

ἀπήρθη
see ἀπαίρω

ἀπιστέω
a not think true 31.39
b not trust 31.97
c not believe 31.105

ἀπιστία, ας f
a not trustworthy 31.89
b not trusting 31.97
c not believing 31.105

ἄπιστος, ον
a unbelievable 31.40
b lack in trust 31.98

ἄπιστος, ου m
a unbeliever 31.106
b non-Christian 11.19

ἁπλότης, ητος f
a sincerity 88.44
b generosity 57.106

ἁπλοῦς, ῆ, οῦν
a healthy 23.132
b generous 57.107

ἁπλῶς
generously 57.107

ἀπό
a from (dissociation) . . 89.122
b from (source) 90.15
c from (extension) . . . 84.3
d of (part-whole) 63.20
e of (substance) 89.142
f by (agent) 90.7
g by (instrument) 90.11
h since (time) 67.131
i because of (reason) . . 89.25
j upon (responsibility) 90.19
ἀπό : units
ἀπ' αἰῶνος
long ago 67.25
ἀπὸ τῶν αἰώνων
since all time 67.133
ἀφ' ἡμερῶν ἀρχαίων
long ago 67.26
ἀπὸ μέρους
a in part 63.15
b temporary 67.109
ἀπὸ μιᾶς
one by one 61.2
αἴρω ἀπό
cause to no longer
experience 90.96
στέλλομαι ἀπό
avoid association . . . 34.41
μετατίθεμαι ἀπό
abandon loyalty to . . 34.27
παραφέρω τὸ ποτήριον
ἀπό
cause not to expe-
rience 90.97
ἀπό . . . εἰς
from . . . to 13.62
καταφέρομαι ἀπὸ τοῦ
ὕπνου
be sound asleep 23.71

ἀποβαίνω
(fut ἀποβήσομαι, aor
ἀπέβην)
disembark 15.39
ἀποβαίνω : unit
ἀποβαίνω εἰς
result in 89.41

ἀποβάλλω
(aor ἀπέβαλον)
a throw off 49.19
b do away with 13.45

ἀποβλέπω
fix attention on 30.31

ἀπόβλητος, ον
be rejected 57.141

ἀποβολή, ῆς f
a rejection 34.38
b destruction 13.103

ἀπογίνομαι
a cease 68.40
b not respond to 74.27

ἀπογραφή, ῆς f
census 33.43

ἀπογράφω
register 33.42

ἀποδείκνυμι
(aor ἀπέδειξα, pf
midd ἀποδέδειγμαι)
a demonstrate 28.50
b show publicly 28.65
c show to be true 72.5

ἀπόδειξις, εως f
proof 28.52

ἀποδεκατόω
a give a tenth 57.114
b collect tithes 57.115

ἀπόδεκτος, ον
pleasing 25.85

27

ἀποδέχομαι
a welcome 34.53
b accept 31.52
c acknowledge 31.26

ἀποδημέω
leave home on a
journey 15.47

ἀπόδημος, ον
away on a journey 85.22

ἀποδίδομαι
sell 57.186

ἀποδίδωμι
(ptc ἀποδιδούς, ptc
neut ἀποδιδοῦν, impf
ἀπεδίδουν, aor subj
2 sg ἀποδῷς, 3 sg
ἀποδῷ, ἀποδοῖ, impv
ἀπόδος, inf ἀποδοῦ-
ναι, ptc ἀποδούς, aor
midd ἀπεδόμην, aor
pass inf ἀποδοθῆναι)
a pay 57.153
b reward 38.16
c cause to happen 13.136
d do 90.46
ἀποδίδωμι : unit
καρπὸν ἀποδίδωμι
bear fruit 23.199

ἀποδιορίζω
a cause divisions 39.16
b make a distinction . . 30.116

ἀποδοκιμάζω
regard unworthy 30.117

ἀποδοχή, ῆς f
acceptance 31.52

ἀποθανοῦμαι
see ἀποθνήσκω

ἀποθέμενος
see ἀποτίθεμαι

ἀποθέσθαι
see ἀποτίθεμαι

ἀπόθεσθε
see ἀποτίθεμαι

ἀπόθεσις, εως f
ἀπόθεσις : unit
ἀπόθεσις τοῦ
σκηνώματος
die 23.111

ἀποθήκη, ης f
storehouse 7.25

ἀποθησαυρίζω
treasure up 65.11

ἀποθλίβω
crowd against 19.44

ἀποθνήσκω
(fut ἀποθανοῦμαι, aor
ἀπέθανον)
a die 23.99
b likely to die 23.117
c not respond to 74.27
ἀποθνήσκω : unit
δὶς ἀποθάνων
completely dead 23.123

ἀποθῶμαι
see ἀποτίθεμαι

ἀποίσω
see ἀποφέρω

ἀποκαθιστάνω
see ἀποκαθίστημι

ἀποκαθίστημι
(fut ἀποκαταστήσω,
aor ἀπεχατέστην, aor
pass ἀπεχατεστάθην)
a restore 13.65
b send back 15.74

ἀποκαλύπτω
(aor pass ἀπεχαλύφθην)
reveal 28.38

ἀποκάλυψις, εως f
revelation 28.38

ἀποκαραδοκία, ας *f*
eager desire *25.64*

ἀποκαταλλάσσω
(aor pass ἀποκατηλλά-
γην)
reconcile *40.1*

ἀποκατάστασις, εως *f*
restoration *13.65*

ἀποκαταστήσω
see ἀποκαθίστημι

ἀπόκειμαι
a put away *85.53*
b exist *13.73*
c be necessary *71.37*

ἀποκεφαλίζω
cut head off *20.80*

ἀποκλείω
close *79.113*

ἀποκόπτω
cut down/off *19.18*

ἀποκριθείς
see ἀποκρίνομαι

ἀπόκριμα, τος *n*
verdict *56.26*

ἀποκρίνομαι
(aor pass ἀπεκρίθην,
ptc ἀποκριθείς)
a answer *33.184*
b speak *33.28*

ἀπόκρισις, εως *f*
answer *33.185*

ἀποκρύπτω
keep secret *28.80*

ἀπόκρυφος, ον
secret *28.70*

ἀποκτείνω
(fut ἀποκτενῶ, aor
ἀπέκτεινα, aor pass
ἀπεκτάνθην)
a kill *20.61*
b do away with *13.44*

ἀποκτέννω
see ἀποκτείνω

ἀποκυέω
a cause a state *13.12*
b cause to exist *13.87*

ἀποκυλίω
roll away *15.248*

ἀπολαμβάνω
(fut ἀπολήμφομαι,
aor ἀπέλαβον)
a obtain from *57.128*
b receive back *57.136*
c lead away *15.177*
d welcome *34.53*
e undergo *90.63*

ἀπόλαυσις, εως *f*
enjoyment *25.115*

ἀπολέγομαι
(aor ἀπειπάμην)
a put aside *13.156*
b denounce *33.220*

ἀπολείπομαι
exist *13.74*

ἀπολείπω
(aor ἀπέλιπον, ptc
ἀπολιπών)
a leave behind *85.65*
b abandon *15.59*
c allow *13.140*

ἀπολέσαι
see ἀπόλλυμι

ἀπολέσῃ
see ἀπόλλυμι

ἀπολέσω
    see ἀπόλλυμι

ἀπόλλυμαι
    (fut ἀπολοῦμαι, aor
    ἀπωλόμην)
    a die 23.106
    b disappear 13.96
    c be lost 21.32

ἀπόλλυμι
    (fut ἀπολέσω, ἀπολῶ,
    aor ἀπώλεσα, subj 3 sg
    ἀπολέσῃ, inf ἀπολέσαι,
    pf ptc ἀπολωλώς)
    a destroy 20.31
    b fail to get 57.67
    c lose 57.68
    d unaware of location 27.29
    ἀπόλλυμι : unit
    ἀπόλλυμι τὴν ψυχήν
      die 23.114

'Απολλύων, ονος m
    Apollyon 93.32

'Απολλωνία, ας f
    Apollonia 93.408

'Απολλῶς, ῶ m
    Apollos 93.33

ἀπολογέομαι
    defend oneself 33.435

ἀπολοῦμαι
    see ἀπόλλυμαι

ἀπολογία, ας f
    a defend oneself 33.435
    b defense 33.436

ἀπολούω
    make pure 88.30

ἀπολύομαι
    go away 15.38

ἀπολύτρωσις, εως f
    deliverance 37.128

ἀπολύω
    a dismiss 15.43
    b send 15.66
    c set free 37.127
    d divorce 34.78
    e forgive 40.8

ἀπολωλώς
    see ἀπόλλυμι

ἀπομάσσομαι
    wipe off 16.9

ἀπονέμω
    cause 90.54

ἀπονίπτω
    wash off 47.10

ἀποπίπτω
    (aor ἀπέπεσα)
    fall from 15.120

ἀποπλανάομαι
    stray from truth 31.67

ἀποπλανάω
    cause wrong views 31.11

ἀποπλέω
    (aor ἀπέπλευσα)
    sail from 54.7

ἀποπληρόω
    obey 36.17

ἀποπνίγομαι
    (aor ἀπεπνίγην)
    drown 23.119

ἀποπνίγω
    cause plants to die 23.120

ἀπορέω
    be at a loss 32.9

ἀπορία, ας f
    consternation 32.9

ἀπορίπτω
    jump off 15.242

ἀπορφανίζω
separate 85.17

ἀποσκίασμα, τος *n*
shadow 14.61

ἀποσπάομαι
go off 15.54

ἀποσπάω
a pull out 15.214
b lure away 31.74

ἀποστάς
see ἀφίσταμαι

ἀποστασία, ας *f*
rebellion 39.34

ἀποστάσιον, ου *n*
notice of divorce 33.41

ἀποστεγάζω
remove a roof 45.11

ἀποστέλλω
(fut ἀποστελῶ, aor
ἀπέστειλα, subj
ἀποστείλω, pf
ἀπέσταλκα, aor
pass ἀπεστάλην)
a send someone 15.66
b send a message 15.67
ἀποστέλλω : unit
ἀποστέλλω τὸ
δρέπανον
  begin to harvest 43.17

ἀποστερέω
a defraud 57.248
b deprive of 57.47

ἀποστῆναι
see ἀφίσταμαι

ἀποστήσομαι
see ἀφίσταμαι

ἀπόστητε
see ἀφίσταμαι

ἀποστολή, ῆς *f*
apostleship 53.73

ἀπόστολος, ου *m*
a apostle 53.74
b messenger 33.194

ἀποστοματίζω
ask hostile questions . . 33.183

ἀποστρέφομαι
(aor ἀπεστράφην)
a reject belief 31.62
b forsake 34.26
c refuse to help 35.18

ἀποστρέφω
a cause to change
  belief 31.70
b lead astray 88.264
c put back 85.52
d change 13.63
e stop 68.44

ἀποστυγέω
hate 88.203

ἀποσυνάγωγος, ον
expelled from
synagogue 11.46

ἀποτάσσομαι
a say goodbye 33.23
b take leave of 15.55
c part with possessions 57.70

ἀποτελέω
complete 68.22

ἀποτίθεμαι
(aor ἀπεθέμην, subj
ἀποθῶμαι, impv 2 pl
ἀπόθεσθε, inf ἀποθέσ-
θαι, ptc ἀποθέμενος)
a put away 85.44
b stop 68.37

ἀποτινάσσω
shake off 16.8

31

ἀποτίνω
(fut ἀποτίσω)
pay back 57.156

ἀποτολμάω
be very bold 25.163

ἀποτομία, ας f
harshness 88.73

ἀποτόμως
harshly 88.74

ἀποτρέπομαι
avoid 34.41

ἀπουσία, ας f
absence 85.28

ἀποφέρω
(fut ἀποίσω, aor ἀπή-
νεγκα, inf ἀπενεγκεῖν,
inf pass ἀπενεχθῆναι)
a carry away 15.202
b lead off 15.177

ἀποφεύγω
escape 21.14

ἀποφθέγγομαι
speak 33.76

ἀποφορτίζομαι
unload a cargo 15.209

ἀπόχρησις, εως f
consumption 42.24

ἀποχωρέω
go away 15.51

ἀποχωρίζομαι
a move away 15.14
b separate definitely . . 63.30

ἀποψύχω
a faint 23.184
b be discouraged 25.293

Ἀππίου Φόρον
Forum of Appius 93.409

ἀπρόσιτος, ον
unapproachable 15.80

ἀπρόσκοπος, ον
a blameless 88.318
b not causing offense 25.184

ἀπροσωπολήμπτως
impartially 88.240

ἄπταιστος, ον
free from sinning 88.292

ἅπτομαι
(aor ἡψάμην)
a hold on to 18.6
b touch 24.73
c harm 20.16
ἅπτομαι : unit
γυναικὸς ἅπτομαι
marry 34.70

ἅπτω
(aor ptc ἅψας)
start a fire 14.65

Ἀπφία, ας f
Apphia 93.34

ἀπωθέομαι
(aor ἀπωσάμην)
a push away 15.46
b reject 31.63

ἀπώλεια, ας f
a destruction 20.31
b waste 65.14

ἀπώλεσα
see ἀπόλλυμι

ἀπωλόμην
see ἀπόλλυμαι

ἀπών
see ἄπειμι

ἀπωσάμην
see ἀπωθέομαι

ἀρά, ᾶς f
curse 33.473

ἄρα
a as a result 89.46
b possible 71.7
c perhaps 71.19

ἆρα
indeed 69.14

Ἀραβία, ας f
Arabia 93.410

ἄραι
see αἴρω

Ἀράμ m
Aram 93.35

ἄραφος, ον
seamless 48.6

Ἄραψ, βος m
an Arab 93.411

ἀργέω
be idle 42.2

ἀργός, ή, όν
a idle 42.46
b lazy 88.248
c without thought . . . 30.44
d useless 65.36
e indifferent 72.21

ἀργύριον, ου n
a silver 2.51
b silver money 6.73
ἀργύριον : unit
ἀργύριον καὶ χρυσίον
    money 6.69

ἀργυροκόπος, ου m
silversmith 2.52

ἄργυρος, ου m
a silver 2.51
b silver money 6.73

ἀργυροῦς, ᾶ, οῦν
made of silver 2.53

ἀρεῖ
see αἴρω

Ἄρειος Πάγος m
a Areopagus 93.412
b council of
    Areopagus 11.81

Ἀρεοπαγίτης, ου m
member of council of
Areopagus 11.82

ἀρεσκεία, ας f
means of favor 25.91

ἀρέσκω
(aor ἤρεσα, inf ἀρέσαι)
please 25.90

ἀρεστός, ή, όν
a pleasing 25.92
b proper 66.8

Ἀρέτας, α m
Aretas 93.36

ἀρετή, ῆς f
a virtue 88.11
b wonderful act 76.14

Ἀρηί
see Ἀρνί 93.37

ἀρήν, ἀρνός m
lamb 4.24

ἀρθήσομαι
see αἴρω

ἀριθμέω
count 60.3

ἀριθμός, οῦ m
a number 60.1
b total 60.2

Ἀριμαθαία, ας f
Arimathea 93.413

33

Ἀρίσταρχος, ου *m*
Aristarchus 93.38

ἀριστάω
a eat a meal 23.20
b have breakfast 23.24

ἀριστερά, ᾶς *f*
left hand 8.33
ἀριστερά : units
μὴ γνώτω ἡ ἀριστερά
σου τί ποιεῖ ἡ δεξιά σου
  do secretly 28.74
ἐξ ἀριστερῶν καθίζω
  be in less high
  position 87.35

ἀριστερός, ά, όν
left 82.7

Ἀριστόβουλος, ου *m*
Aristobulus 93.39

ἄριστον, ου *n*
a meal 23.22
b noon meal 23.23

ἀρκετός, ή, όν
sufficient 59.45

ἀρκέομαι
be satisfied 25.81

ἀρκέω
be sufficient 59.46

ἄρκος, ου *m, f*
bear 4.12

ἅρμα, τος *n*
chariot 6.52

Ἀρμαγεδών
Armageddon 93.414

Ἀρμίν
see Ἀδμίν 93.40

ἁρμόζομαι
promise in marriage . . 34.74

ἁρμός, οῦ *m*
body joint 8.59

ἄρνας
see ἀρήν

ἀρνέομαι
a deny (verbal) 33.277
b deny (non-verbal) . . . 34.48
c refuse to agree 31.25
d disregard 30.52
e refuse to follow 36.43
f be false to oneself . . . 88.231

Ἀρνί *m*
Arni 93.41

ἀρνίον, ου *n*
a sheep 4.25
b follower of Christ . . 11.29
c Lamb (a title for
  Christ) 4.26

ἀροτριάω
plow 43.4

ἄροτρον, ου *n*
plow 6.4
ἄροτρον : unit
ἐπιβάλλω τὴν χεῖρα
ἐπ' ἄροτρον καὶ βλέπω
εἰς τὰ ὀπίσω
  start to do and then
  hesitate 68.6

ἁρπαγείς
see ἁρπάζω

ἁρπαγή, ῆς *f*
a plunder 57.235
b booty 57.237
c violent greed 25.24

ἁρπαγμός, οῦ *m*
a plunder 57.235
b something to hold by
  force 57.236

ἁρπάζω
(aor pass ἡρπάγην,
ptc ἁρπαγείς)
a snatch 18.4
b attack 39.49
c plunder 57.235
d gain control over . . . 37.28

ἅρπαξ, αγος m
robber 57.239

ἅρπαξ, αγος (adj)
a vicious 20.4
b violently greedy 25.25

ἀρραβών, ῶνος m
first installment 57.170

ἄρρητος, ον
what cannot be spoken 33.95

ἄρρωστος, ον
ill 23.147

ἀρσενοκοίτης, ου m
homosexual 88.280

ἄρσην, εν
male 79.102
ἄρσην : unit
ἄρσην διανοίγων μήτραν
firstborn son 10.45

Ἀρτεμᾶς, ᾶ m
Artemas 93.42

Ἄρτεμις, ιδος f
Artemis 93.43

ἀρτέμων, ωνος m
sail 6.49

ἄρτι
a now 67.38
b just now 67.39
c immediately 67.113
ἄρτι : unit
ἡ ἄρτι ὥρα
at this very moment 67.42

ἀρτιγέννητος, ον
newly born 23.48

ἄρτιος, α, ον
qualified 75.4

ἄρτος, ου m
a loaf of bread 5.8
b food 5.1
ἄρτος : units
τὸν ἑαυτοῦ ἄρτον
ἐσθίω
earn a living 57.190
ἄρτοι τῆς προθέσεως
consecrated bread . . 53.26
ἄρτον κλάω
have a meal 23.20

ἀρτύω
season 46.14

Ἀρφαξάδ m
Arphaxad 93.44

ἀρχάγγελος, ου m
archangel 12.31

ἀρχαῖος, α, ον
ancient 67.98
ἀρχαῖος : unit
ἀφ' ἡμερῶν ἀρχαίων
long ago 67.26

Ἀρχέλαος, ου m
Archelaus 93.45

ἀρχή, ῆς f
a beginning (aspect) . . 68.1
b beginning (time) . . . 67.65
c first cause 89.16
d sphere of authority 37.55
e ruler 37.56
f supernatural power 12.44
g elementary aspect . . 58.20
h corner 79.106

ἀρχηγός, οῦ m
a initiator 68.2
b pioneer leader 36.6

ἀρχιερατικός, όν
highpriestly 53.90

ἀρχιερεύς, έως m
a chief priest 53.88
b high priest 53.89

ἀρχιποίμην, ενος m
chief shepherd 44.5

Ἄρχιππος, ου m
Archippus 93.46

ἀρχισυνάγωγος, ου m
leader of a synagogue 53.93

ἀρχιτέκτων, ονος m
master builder 45.10

ἀρχιτελώνης, ου m
chief tax collector 57.185

ἀρχιτρίκλινος, ου m
head steward 46.7

ἄρχομαι
a begin (aspect) 68.1
b begin (time) 67.65

ἄρχω
rule 37.54

ἄρχων, οντος m
a ruler 37.56
b judge 56.29
ἄρχων : units
ἄρχων τῶν Ἰουδαίων
   member of Council 37.95
ἄρχων τῆς ἐξουσίας
τοῦ ἀέρος
   supernatural power 12.44

ἄρωμα, τος n
perfumed ointment . . . 6.207

Ἀσά
see Ἀσάφ 93.47

ἀσάλευτος, ον
a immovable 15.4
b unchangeable 13.31

Ἀσάφ m
Asaph 93.48

ἄσβεστος, ον
unquenchable 14.71

ἀσέβεια, ας f
godlessness 53.10

ἀσεβέω
live ungodly 53.10

ἀσεβής, ές
ungodly 53.11

ἀσέλγεια, ας f
licentiousness 88.272

ἄσημος, ον
inferior 87.59

Ἀσήρ m
Asher 93.49

ἀσθένεια, ας f
a incapacity 74.23
b illness 23.143
c timidity 25.269

ἀσθενέω
a be weak 74.26
b be ill 23.144

ἀσθένημα, τος n
weakness 74.24

ἀσθενής, ές
a unable 74.25
b morally weak 88.117
c illness 23.145
d helpless condition . . 22.3
e weak 79.69

Ἀσία, ας f
Asia 93.415

Ἀσιανός, οῦ m
an Asian 93.416

Ἀσιάρχης, ου m
provincial authority . . 37.81

ἀσιτία, ας f
without food 23.32

ἄσιτος, ον
without food 23.32

ἀσκέω
do one's best 68.72

ἀσκός, οῦ m
wineskin 6.132

ἀσμένως
gladly 25.128

ἄσοφος, ον
foolish 32.54

ἀσπάζομαι
a greet 33.20
b be happy about 25.130
c welcome 34.55

ἀσπασμός, οῦ m
greeting 33.20

ἄσπιλος, ον
a spotless 79.59
b pure 88.33

ἀσπίς, ίδος f
snake 4.53

ἄσπονδος, ον
irreconcilable........ 40.7

Ἀσσά
see Ἀσάφ 93.50

ἀσσάριον, ου n
penny............. 6.77

ἆσσον
very near 83.28

Ἄσσος, ου f
Assos 93.417

ἀστατέω
a wander 15.25
b be homeless 85.80

ἀστεῖος, α, ον
beautiful 79.11

ἀστήρ, έρος m
star, planet......... 1.30
ἀστήρ : unit
ἀστὴρ πρωϊνός
morning star 1.33

ἀστήρικτος, ον
unstable 31.79

ἄστοργος, ον
without love 25.42

ἀστοχέω
abandon truth 31.68

ἀστραπή, ῆς f
a lightning 14.16
b bright beam 14.46

ἀστράπτω
glisten 14.47

ἄστρον, ου n
a star, planet....... 1.30
b constellation 1.31

Ἀσύγκριτος, ου m
Asyncritus 93.51

ἀσύμφωνος, ον
be in disagreement ... 31.24

ἀσύνετος, ον
without understanding 32.49

ἀσύνθετος, ον
not keeping agreement 34.45

ἀσφάλεια, ας f
a safety 21.9
b certainty......... 31.41

ἀσφαλής, ές
a safe 21.10
b certain 31.42

ἀσφαλίζω
a make safe 21.11
b fasten 18.12

ἀσφαλῶς
a safely 21.10
b certainly 31.42

ἀσχημονέω
behave indecently 88.149

ἀσχημοσύνη, ης f
a indecent behavior . . 88.149
b shameful state 25.202

ἀσχήμων, ον
ugly 79.16

ἀσωτία, ας f
recklessness 88.96

ἀσώτως
recklessly 88.97

ἀτακτέω
be lazy 88.246

ἄτακτος, ον
lazy 88.247

ἀτάκτως
lazily 88.247

ἄτεκνος, ον
childless 10.41

ἀτενίζω
stare at 24.49

ἄτερ
without 89.120

ἀτιμάζω
a treat shamefully 88.127
b cause to be
   dishonored 87.74

ἀτιμία, ας f
dishonor 87.71

ἄτιμος, ον
lacking in honor 87.72

ἀτμίς, ίδος f
steam 1.36

ἄτομος, ον
moment 67.149

ἄτοπος, ον
a bad 88.111
b unusual 58.54

'Ατταλεια, ας f
Attalia 93.418

αὐγάζω
cause to be seen 28.37

αὐγή, ῆς f
dawn 67.73

Αὐγοῦστος, ου m
Augustus 93.52

αὐθάδης, ες
arrogant 88.206

αὐθαίρετος, ον
willing 25.66

αὐθεντέω
control 37.21

αὐλέω
play the flute 6.87

αὐλή, ῆς f
a courtyard 7.56
b dwelling 7.6

αὐλητής, οῦ m
flutist 6.88

αὐλίζομαι
spend the night 67.194

αὐλός, οῦ m
flute 6.86

αὐξάνομαι
increase (degree) *78.5*

αὐξάνω
(fut αὐξήσω, aor ηὔξησα,
aor pass ηὐξήθην)
a increase *59.62*
b cause to increase ... *59.63*
c grow *23.188*
d enjoy greater respect *87.37*

αὔξησις, εως *f*
growth *23.188*

αὔξω
see αὐξάνω

αὔριον
a tomorrow *67.207*
b soon *67.58*

αὐστηρός, ά, όν
exacting *88.138*

αὐτάρκεια, ας *f*
a contentment *25.83*
b adequacy *75.6*

αὐτάρκης, ες
content *25.84*

αὕτη
see οὗτος

αὐτοκατάκριτος, ον
condemned by own
actions *30.119*

αὐτόματος, η, ον
without any cause *89.21*

αὐτόπτης, ου *m*
eyewitness *24.46*

αὐτός, ή, ό
a same *58.31*
b he, she, it *92.11*
c self *92.37*
αὐτός : unit
οἱ παρ᾽ αὐτοῦ
his family *10.9*

αὐτοῦ
here, there *83.3*

αὐτόφωρος, ον
in the act *42.14*

αὐτόχειρ, ος
one's own hands *8.31*

αὐχέω
boast *33.368*

αὐχμηρός, ά, όν
dark and miserable ... *14.58*

ἀφ᾽
see ἀπό

ἀφαιρέω
(fut ἀφελῶ, aor ἀφεῖ-
λον, inf ἀφελεῖν, aor
subj ἀφέλω, ἀφέλωμαι)
a put away *85.44*
b take away from *68.47*
c do away with *13.38*

ἀφανής, ές
hidden *28.68*

ἀφανίζομαι
a become invisible ... *24.27*
b disappear *13.98*

ἀφανίζω
a destroy *20.46*
b make ugly *79.17*

ἀφανισμός, οῦ *m*
disappearance *13.98*

ἄφαντος, ον
invisible *24.28*

ἀφεδρών, ῶνος *m*
toilet *7.72*

ἀφέθην
see ἀφίημι

ἀφεθήσομαι
see ἀφίημι

39

ἀφειδία, ας *f*
severe self-control *88.90*

ἀφεῖλον
see ἀφαιρέω

ἀφείς
see ἀφίημι

ἀφεῖς
see ἀφίημι

ἀφελεῖν
see ἀφαιρέω

ἀφελότης, ητος *f*
humbleness *88.55*

ἀφελῶ
see ἀφαιρέω

ἀφέλω
see ἀφαιρέω

ἀφέλωμαι
see ἀφαιρέω

ἄφες
see ἀφίημι

ἄφεσις, εως *f*
a pardon *40.8*
b liberty *37.132*

ἄφετε
see ἀφίημι

ἀφέωνται
see ἀφίημι

ἀφή, ῆς *f*
ligament *8.60*

ἀφῆκα
see ἀφίημι

ἀφήσω
see ἀφίημι

ἀφθαρσία, ας *f*
a immortality *23.127*
b unceasing *68.57*

ἄφθαρτος, ον
immortal *23.128*

ἀφθορία, ας *f*
integrity *88.43*

ἀφίδω
see ἀφοράω

ἀφίημι
(pres 2 sg ἀφεῖς, 1 pl
ἀφίομεν, 3 pl ἀφίουσιν,
inf ἀφιέναι, impf 3 sg
ἤφιεν, fut ἀφήσω, aor
ἀφῆκα, impv ἄφες, 2 pl
ἄφετε, subj ἀφῶ, ptc
ἀφείς, aor pass ἀφέθην,
fut pass ἀφεθήσομαι, pf
pass 3 pl ἀφέωνται)
a dismiss *15.43*
b depart from *15.48*
c leave behind *85.45*
d leave in a place *85.62*
e divorce *34.78*
f forgive *40.8*
g cancel a debt *57.223*
h reject *31.63*
i stop (activity) *68.43*
j stop (state) *13.37*
k allow *13.140*
l produce *90.50*
ἀφίημι : units
ἀφίημι τὸ πνεῦμα
die *23.109*
ἄφες τοὺς νεκροὺς θάψαι
τοὺς ἑαυτῶν νεκρούς
that is not the issue *33.137*

ἀφικνέομαι
(aor ἀφικόμην)
become known *28.23*

ἀφιλάγαθος, ον
be against what is good *25.106*

ἀφιλάργυρος, ον
not loving money *25.109*

ἄφιξις, εως f
departure 15.37

ἀφίομεν
see ἀφίημι

ἀφίουσιν
see ἀφίημι

ἀφίσταμαι (+ 2 aor)
(aor ἀπέστην, subj
ἀποστῶ, impv 2 pl
ἀπόστητε, inf ἀπο-
στῆναι, ptc ἀποστάς,
fut ἀποστήσομαι,
impf 3 sg ἀφίστατο)
a depart 15.51
b forsake 34.26
c keep away from 34.41

ἀφίστημι
(aor ἀπέστησα)
cause to rebel 39.41

ἄφνω
immediately 67.113

ἀφόβως
a without fear 25.253
b disgracefully 88.151
c without reverence to
God 53.60

ἀφομοιόω
be similar to 64.4

ἀφοράω
(aor subj ἀφίδω)
a fix attention on 30.31
b learn about 27.6

ἀφορίζω
(fut ἀφοριῶ, ἀφορίσω)
a exclude 34.36
b appoint 37.97
c separate 63.28

ἀφορμή, ῆς f
a favorable circum-
stances 22.46
b excuse 89.22

ἀφρίζω
foam up 14.28

ἀφρός, οῦ m
foam 14.27

ἀφροσύνη, ης f
foolishness 32.53

ἄφρων, ον
foolish 32.52

ἀφυπνόω
fall asleep 23.70

ἀφυστερέω
withhold payment 57.159

ἀφῶ
see ἀφίημι

ἄφωνος, ον
a mute 33.106
b without meaning . . . 33.135

Ἀχάζ m
Ahaz 93.53

Ἀχαΐα, ας f
Achaia 93.419

Ἀχαϊκός, οῦ m
Achaicus 93.54

ἀχάριστος, ον
a unthankful 25.101
b ungrateful 33.353

ἀχειροποίητος, ον
not man-made 42.33

ἀχθήσομαι
see ἄγω

Ἀχίμ m
Achim 93.55

ἀχλύς, ύος f
ἀχλύς : unit
ἀχλὺς καὶ σκότος πίπτει
become blind 24.40

ἀχρειόομαι
become perverse *88.263*

ἀχρεῖος, ον
a useless *65.33*
b not worthy of praise *33.361*

ἄχρηστος, ον
useless *65.33*

ἄχρι
a until *67.119*
b later *67.49*
c as far as *84.19*
ἄχρι : units
ἄχρι οὗ
    a before *67.17*
    b until *67.119*
κολλάομαι ἄχρι τοῦ
οὐρανοῦ
    increase greatly *59.66*

ἄχρις
    ἄχρις : unit
    ἄχρις οὗ
      a until *67.119*
      b as long as *67.139*

ἄχυρον, ου n
chaff.............. *3.57*

ἄψας
see ἅπτω

ἀψευδής, ές
truthful *88.40*

ἄψινθος, ου m
a wormwood........ *3.21*
b bitter *79.43*

ἄψυχος, ον
lifeless *23.98*

β
second *60.49*

Βάαλ m
Baal *93.56*

Βαβυλών, ῶνος f
Babylon *93.420*

τὰ βαθέα
deep secrets *28.76*

τὰ βάθη
deep secrets *28.76*

βαθμός, οῦ m
status *87.3*

βάθος, ους n
a depth *81.8*
b deep place *81.9*
c extremely........ *78.22*
d the world below *1.18*
e powers of world
    below *12.47*
βάθος : unit
κατὰ βάθους
    extremely *78.22*

βαθύνω
make deep *81.11*

βαθύς, εῖα, ύ
a deep *81.10*
b extremely........ *78.22*

βάϊον, ου n
palm branch *3.53*

Βαλαάμ m
Balaam............ *93.57*

Βαλάκ m
Balak *93.58*

βαλλάντιον, ου n
money bag *6.144*

βάλλω
(fut βαλῶ, aor ἔβαλον,
pf βέβληκα, aor pass
ἐβλήθην, fut βληθήσο-
μαι, pf βέβλημαι, plpf
ἐβεβλήμην)
a throw *15.215*
b let fall........... *15.122*
c sweep down *15.112*

d pour 47.2
e put 85.34
f bring about 13.14
g do away with 13.45
h deposit 57.217
βάλλω : units
βάλλω τὸ δρέπανον
   begin to harvest 43.17
βάλλω εἰς κλίνην
   make sick 23.152
πῦρ βάλλω
   cause discord 39.15
βάλλω εἰς τὴν καρδίαν
   cause to think 30.29

βαπτίζομαι
   βαπτίζομαι : unit
   βάπτισμα βαπτίζομαι
     suffer severely 24.82

βαπτίζω
   a wash 53.31
   b baptize 53.41
   c cause religious
     experience 53.49

βάπτισμα, τος n
   baptism 53.41
   βάπτισμα : unit
   βάπτισμα βαπτίζομαι
     suffer severely 24.82

βαπτισμός, οῦ m
   a washing 53.31
   b baptism 53.41

βαπτιστής, οῦ m
   baptizer 53.42

βάπτω
   (pf pass βέβαμμαι)
   dip in 47.11

Βαραββᾶς, ᾶ m
   Barabbas 93.59

Βαράκ m
   Barak 93.60

Βαραχίας, ου m
   Barachiah 93.61

βάρβαρος, ον
   a non-Greek 11.95
   b native people 11.94
   c uncivilized 41.31

βαρέομαι
   be troubled 22.18
   βαρέομαι : units
   βαρέομαι ὕπνῳ
     be sound asleep 23.71
   ἦσαν οἱ ὀφθαλμοὶ
   βεβαρημένοι
     be very sleepy 23.69

βαρέως
   βαρέως : unit
   τοῖς ὠσὶν βαρέως ἀκούω
     be mentally dull 32.46

Βαρθολομαῖος, ου m
   Bartholomew 93.62

Βαριησοῦς, οῦ m
   Bar-Jesus 93.63

Βαριωνᾶ(ς), ᾶ m
   Bar-Jonas 93.64

Βαρναβᾶς, ᾶ m
   Barnabas 93.65

βάρος, ους n
   a hardship 22.4
   b tremendous 78.23
   βάρος : unit
   ἐν βάρει εἰμί
     claim importance . . . 65.56

Βαρσαββᾶς, ᾶ m
   Barsabbas 93.66

Βαρτιμαῖος, ου m
   Bartimaeus 93.67

βαρύς, εῖα, ύ
   a heavy 86.1
   b burdensome 22.30
   c important 65.55
   d fierce 20.7

βαρύτιμος, ον
   valuable 65.3

βασανίζω
   torture 38.13
   βασανίζω : unit
   ψυχὴν βασανίζω
     experience anguish   25.280

βασανισμός, οῦ m
   torment 24.90

βασανιστής, οῦ m
   prison guard 37.126

βάσανος, ου f
   torment 24.90

βασιλεία, ας f
   a reign 37.64
   b kingdom 1.82
   βασιλεία : units
   λαμβάνω βασιλείαν
     become a king 37.65
   διατίθεμαι βασιλείαν
     give right to rule . . . 37.105
   υἱοὶ τῆς βασιλείας
     people of God 11.13

βασίλειον, ου n
   palace 7.5

βασίλειος, ον
   royal 37.69

βασιλεύς, έως m
   king 37.67

βασιλεύω
   a be a king 37.64
   b control completely   37.22

βασιλικός, ή, όν
   royal 37.69

βασιλικός, οῦ m
   official of a king 37.84

βασίλισσα, ης f
   queen 37.68

βάσις, εως f
   foot 8.49

βασκαίνω
   a bewitch 53.98
   b deceive 88.159

βαστάζω
   a carry 15.188
   b remove 15.201
   c endure 25.177
   d provide for 35.32
   e undergo 90.80
   f accept 31.55
   βαστάζω : units
   ἡ κοιλία βαστάζει
     be pregnant with . . . 23.51
   βαστάζω ὄνομα
     inform 33.210
   βαστάζω τὸν σταυρόν
     suffer unto death . . . 24.83
   βαστάζω στίγματα
     experience being
     slave of 90.84

βάτος, ου m, f
   a thorn bush 3.16
   b bath (measure) 81.20

βάτραχος, ου m
   frog 4.55

βατταλογέω
   a use many words 33.88
   b babble 33.89

βδέλυγμα, τος n
   what is detestable 25.187
   βδέλυγμα : unit
   τὸ βδέλυγμα τῆς
   ἐρημώσεως
     horrible thing
     which defiles 53.38

βδελυκτός, ή, όν
   detested 25.188

βδελύσσομαι
   detest 25.186

βεβαιόομαι
increase in inner
strength *74.17*

βέβαιος, α, ον
a certain *71.15*
b trustworthy *31.90*
c verified *28.43*

βεβαιόω
a cause to believe *31.91*
b verify *28.44*

βεβαίωσις, εως *f*
verification *28.44*

βέβαμμαι
see βάπτω

βέβηλος, ον
worldly *88.115*

βεβηλόω
defile ritually *53.33*

βέβληκα
see βάλλω

βέβλημαι
see βάλλω

βεβρωκώς
see βιβρώσκω

Βεελζεβούλ *m*
Beelzebul *93.68*

Βελζεθά
Belzetha *93.421*

Βελιάρ *m*
Belial *93.69*

βελόνη, ης *f*
needle *6.215*

βέλος, ους *n*
arrow, dart *6.36*

βέλτιον
well *65.23*

Βενιαμ(ε)ίν *m*
Benjamin *93.70*

Βερνίκη, ης *f*
Bernice *93.71*

Βέροια, ας *f*
Beroea *93.422*

Βεροιαῖος, ου *m*
a Beroean *93.423*

Βέρος, ου *m*
Berus *93.72*

Βεωρσόρ
see Βεώρ *93.73*

Βεώρ *m*
Beor *93.74*

Βηδσαϊδά(ν) *f*
Bedsaida(n) *93.424*

Βηζαθά
Bezatha *93.425*

Βηθαβαρά *f*
Bethabara *93.426*

Βηθανία, ας *f*
Bethany *93.427*

Βηθαραβά *f*
Betharaba *93.428*

Βηθεσδά *f*
Bethesda *93.429*

Βηθζαθά *f*
Bethzatha *93.430*

Βηθλέεμ *f*
Bethlehem *93.431*

Βηθσαϊδά *f*
Bethsaida *93.432*

Βηθφαγή *f*
Bethphage *93.433*

βῆμα, τος *n*
  judgment seat *7.63*
  βῆμα : unit
  βῆμα ποδός
    square yard/meter . . *80.3*

Βηρεύς, έως *m*
  Bereus *93.75*

βήρυλλος, ου *m, f*
  beryl *2.38*

Βησσαϊδά *f*
  Bessaida *93.434*

βία, ας *f*
  violence *20.1*

βιάζομαι
  a suffer violence *20.9*
  b use violence *20.10*

βίαιος, α, ον
  violent *20.8*

βιαστής, οῦ *m*
  violent person *20.11*

βιβλαρίδιον, ου *n*
  little scroll *6.65*

βιβλίον, ου *n*
  a document *6.64*
  b book *33.52*
  c record *33.38*

βίβλος, ου *f*
  a book (object) *6.64*
  b book (content) *33.52*
  c record *33.38*

βιβρώσκω
  (pf ptc βεβρωκώς)
  eat *23.3*

Βιθαρά *f*
  Bithara *93.435*

Βιθυνία, ας *f*
  Bithynia *93.436*

βίος, ου *m*
  a daily life *41.18*
  b possessions *57.18*

βιόω
  conduct daily life *41.18*

βίωσις, εως *f*
  daily life *41.18*

βιωτικός, ή, όν
  of daily life *41.19*

βλαβερός, ά, όν
  harmful *20.13*

βλάπτω
  injure *20.12*

βλαστάνω
  (aor ἐβλάστησα)
  sprout leaves *23.195*
  βλαστάνω : unit
  χαρπὸν βλαστάνω
    bear fruit *23.199*

βλαστάω
  see βλαστάνω

Βλάστος, ου *m*
  Blastus *93.76*

βλασφημέω
  blaspheme *33.400*

βλασφημία, ας *f*
  a reviling *33.400*
  b blasphemy *33.401*

βλάσφημος, ον
  blasphemous *33.402*

βλάσφημος, ου *m*
  blasphemer *33.403*

βλέμμα, τος *n*
  what is seen *24.8*

βλέπω
  a see *24.7*
  b be able to see *24.41*

c watch out for 27.58
d think about 30.1
e understand........ 32.11
f cause to happen 13.134
g facing 82.10
βλέπω : units
βλέπω εἰς πρόσωπον
  judge on external
  appearance 30.120
ἐπιβάλλω τὴν χεῖρα
ἐπ᾽ ἄροτρον καὶ
βλέπω εἰς τὰ ὀπίσω
  start to do and then
  hesitate 68.6

βληθήσομαι
  see βάλλω

βλητέος, α, ον
  must be put 85.36

Βοανηργές
  Boanerges 93.77

βοάω
  shout 33.81

Βόες, m
  Boaz.............. 93.78

βοή, ῆς f
  shout 33.82

βοήθεια, ας f
  a help 35.1
  b support 35.10

βοηθέω
  help 35.1

βοηθός, οῦ m
  helper 35.11

βόθυνος, ου m
  pit, ditch 1.55

βολή, ῆς f
  throw 15.216

βολίζω
  drop a plummet 54.23

Βόος m
  Boaz............ 93.79

βόρβορος, ου m
  mud 2.17

βορρᾶς, ᾶ m
  north 82.3

βόσκομαι
  graze 23.9

βόσκω
  a feed animals 23.10
  b herd animals 44.1

Βοσόρ m
  Bosor 93.80

Βοσύρ
  see Βοσόρ 93.80

βοτάνη, ης f
  plant 3.14

βότρυς, υος m
  grapes 3.38

βουλεύομαι
  a intend.......... 30.56
  b think about carefully 30.8

βουλευτής, οῦ m
  member of council
  of Jews 11.85

βουλή, ῆς f
  intention 30.57
  βουλή : unit
  τίθημι βουλήν
    advise 33.296

βούλημα, τος n
  a desire 25.4
  b intention 30.57

βούλομαι
  (aor ἐβουλήθην)
  a desire 25.3
  b intend.......... 30.56

βουνός, οῦ *m*
hill *1.48*

βοῦς, βοός *m, f*
cattle *4.15*

βραβεῖον, ου *n*
prize. *57.120*

βραβεύω
control *37.20*

βραδύνω
be slow in *67.124*

βραδυπλοέω
sail slowly *54.2*

βραδύς, εῖα, ύ
slow *67.123*

βραδύτης, ητος *f*
slowness *67.124*

βραχίων, ονος *m*
power. *76.3*
βραχίων : unit
βραχίων ὑψηλός
great power *76.5*

βραχύς, εῖα, ύ
a few *59.4*
b little *59.14*
βραχύς : units
βραχύ τι
somewhat *78.43*
διὰ βραχέων
briefly *67.106*

βρέφος, ους *n*
a infant *9.45*
b childhood *67.152*

βρέχω
a rain. *14.10*
b send rain. *14.11*
c make wet *79.79*

βροντή, ῆς *f*
thunder *14.15*

βροχή, ῆς *f*
rain *14.10*

βρόχος, ου *m*
βρόχος : unit
βρόχον ἐπιβάλλω
impose restrictions *37.2*

βρυγμός, οῦ *m*
βρυγμός : unit
βρυγμὸς τῶν ὀδόντων
gnashing of teeth . . . *23.41*

βρύχω
βρύχω : unit
βρύχω τοὺς ὀδόντας
a gnash the teeth . . *23.41*
b be furious *88.184*

βρύω
cause to pour out *14.31*

βρῶμα, τος *n*
a food *5.1*
b meat *5.7*

βρώσιμος, ον
eatable *23.4*

βρῶσις, εως *f*
a eating *23.3*
b meal *23.22*
c food *5.1*
d meat *5.7*
e rusting *2.62*

βυθίζω
a sink *15.115*
b cause *90.95*

βυθός, οῦ *m*
open sea *1.73*

βυρσεύς, έως *m*
tanner *6.186*

βύσσινον, ου *n*
cloth of fine linen *6.167*

βύσσος, ου *f*
fine linen *6.166*

βωμός, οῦ *m*
  altar 6.115

γ
  third 60.50

Γαββαθα
  Gabbatha 93.437

Γαβριήλ *m*
  Gabriel 93.81

γάγγραινα, ης *f*
  gangrene 23.165

Γάδ *m*
  Gad 93.82

Γαδαρηνός, οῦ *m*
  Gadarene 93.438

Γάζα, ης *f*
  Gaza 93.139

γάζα, ης *f*
  treasury 57.36

Γαζαρηνός
  see Γαδαρηνός 93.440

γαζοφυλάκιον, ου *n*
  a treasury 7.33
  b offering box 6.141

Γάϊος, ου *m*
  Gaius 93.83

γάλα, γάλακτος *n*
  milk 5.19

Γαλάτης, ου *m*
  Galatian 93.441

Γαλατία, ας *f*
  Galatia 93.442

Γαλατικός, ή, όν
  Galatian 93.443

γαλήνη, ης *f*
  calm 14.23

Γαλιλαία, ας *f*
  Galilee 93.444

Γαλιλαῖος, ου *m*
  Galilean 93.445

Γαλλία, ας *f*
  Gaul 93.446

Γαλλίων, ωνος *m*
  Gallio 93.84

Γαμαλιήλ *m*
  Gamaliel 93.85

γαμέω
  (aor ἐγάμησα and ἔγημα,
  subj γήμω, ptc γήμας)
  marry 34.66

γαμίζω
  a marry 34.66
  b give in marriage 34.72

γαμίσκω
  give in marriage 34.72

γάμος, ου *m*
  a marriage 34.67
  b wedding 34.68
  c wedding hall 7.34

γάρ
  a because 89.23
  b then 91.1

γαστήρ, τρός *f*
  a belly 8.68
  b glutton 23.19
  γαστήρ : unit
  ἐν γαστρὶ ἔχω
    be pregnant 23.50

Γαύδη
  see Καῦδα 93.447

γέ
  indeed 91.6

γεγένημαι
see γίνομαι

γέγονα
see γίνομαι

γέγονει
see γίνομαι

γέγραπται
see γράφω

γέγραφα
see γράφω

Γεδεών m
Gideon 93.86

γέεννα, ης f
hell 1.21

Γεθσημανί
Gethsemane 93.448

γείτων, ονος m, f
neighbor 11.89

γελάω
laugh 25.135

γέλως, ωτος m
laughter 25.135

γεμίζω
fill 59.42

γέμω
be full 59.41

γενεά, ᾶς f
a same generation 11.4
b people of same kind 10.4
c descendants 10.28
d age 67.144

γενεαλογέομαι
be descended from . . . 10.25

γενεαλογία, ας f
genealogy 10.26

γενέσθαι
see γίνομαι

γενέσια, ων n
birthday celebration . . 51.12

γένεσις, εως f
a birth 23.46
b lineage 10.24
c history 33.19
d existence 13.71

γενετή, ῆς f
birth 23.46

γενηθήτω
see γίνομαι

γένημα, τος n
product 13.49

γενήσομαι
see γίνομαι

γεννάω
a beget 23.58
b give birth 23.52
c be born of 13.56
d cause to happen 13.129
γεννάω : unit
γεννάω ἄνωθεν
be born again 41.53

γέννημα, τος n
a offspring 23.53
b kind 58.26

Γεννησαρέτ f
Gennesaret 93.449

γέννησις, εως f
see γένεσις

γεννητός, ή, όν
born 23.47

γένοιτο
see γίνομαι

γενόμενος
see γίνομαι

γένος, ους *n*
  a descendant *10.32*
  b nation *10.1*
  c kind *58.23*

Γερασηνός, οῦ *m*
  Gerasene *93.450*

Γεργεσηνός, οῦ *m*
  Gergesene *93.451*

γερουσία, ας *f*
  high council of the
  Jews *11.83*

Γερσινός
  see Γεργεσηνός *93.452*

γέρων, οντος *m*
  old man *9.30*

γεύομαι
  a taste *24.72*
  b eat *23.3*
  c experience *90.78*

γεωργέω
  cultivate land *43.1*

γεώργιον, ου *n*
  field *1.96*

γεωργός, οῦ *m*
  farmer *43.2*

γῆ, γῆς *f*
  a earth *1.39*
  b land *1.60*
  c soil *2.14*
  d region *1.79*
  e people *9.22*
  γῆ : units
  ὁ οὐρανὸς καὶ ἡ γῆ
    universe *1.3*
  κλίνω τὸ πρόσωπον
  εἰς τὴν γήν
    prostrate oneself . . . *17.21*

γήμας
  see γαμέω

γήμω
  see γαμέω

γῆρας, ως/ους, dat γήρει *n*
  old age *67.157*

γηράσκω
  grow old *67.105*

γίνομαι
  (fut γενήσομαι, aor ἐγενόμην, opt 3 sg γένοιτο,
  inf γενέσθαι, ptc
  γενόμενος, pf γέγονα
  and γεγένημαι, aor pass
  ἐγενήθην, impv 3 sg
  γενηθήτω, plpf 3 sg
  ἐγεγόνει and γεγόνει)
  a come to exist *13.80*
  b be *13.3*
  c become *13.48*
  d happen *13.107*
  e move *15.1*
  f belong to *57.2*
  g behave *41.1*
  h be in a place *85.6*
  i come to be in a place *85.7*
  j there was *91.5*
  γίνομαι : units
  γίνομαι ἀνδρί
    marry *34.69*
  γίνομαι γνώμης
    make up mind *30.77*
  ὁρμὴ γίνομαι
    make up mind *30.78*

γινώσκω
  (fut γνώσομαι, aor
  ἔγνων, impv γνῶθι,
  γνώτω, subj 3 sg γνῶ
  and γνοῖ, inf γνῶναι,
  ptc γνούς, pf ἔγνωκα,
  plpf ἐγνώκειν, aor pass
  ἐγνώσθην, fut pass
  γνωσθήσομαι)
  a know *28.1*
  b learn *27.2*
  c be familiar with *27.18*
  d understand *32.16*
  e acknowledge *31.27*

f have sexual
   intercourse........ *23.61*
γινώσκω : unit
μὴ γνώτω ἡ ἀριστερά
σου τί ποιεῖ ἡ δεξιά σου
   do secretly *28.74*

γλεῦκος, ους *n*
   sweet wine.......... *6.199*

γλυκύς, εῖα, ύ
   sweet *79.39*

γλῶσσα, ης *f*
   a tongue *8.21*
   b language.......... *33.2*
   c ecstatic language ... *33.3*
   d speech (activity).... *33.74*
   e speech (faculty) *33.75*
   f utterance *33.101*
   g person *9.18*

γλωσσόκομον, ου *n*
   money box.......... *6.143*

γναφεύς, έως *m*
   bleacher *48.7*

γνήσιος, α, ον
   genuine *73.1*

γνησίως
   genuine *73.1*

γνοῖ
   see γινώσκω

γνούς, γνόντος
   see γινώσκω

γνόφος, ου *m*
   darkness............ *14.53*

γνῷ
   see γινώσκω

γνῶθι
   see γινώσκω

γνώμη, ης *f*
   a intention *30.67*

b opinion *31.3*
c agreement *31.14*
γνώμη : unit
γίνομαι γνώμης
   make up mind *30.77*

γνῶναι
   see γινώσκω

γνωρίζω
   a know *28.1*
   b make known *28.26*

γνωσθήσομαι
   see γινώσκω

γνῶσις, εως *f*
   a acquaintance *28.1*
   b knowledge *28.17*
   c esoteric knowledge *28.19*
   d understanding *32.16*

γνώσομαι
   see γινώσκω

γνώστης, ου *m*
   one who knows *28.11*

γνωστός, ή, όν
   a what is known *28.21*
   b well known *28.30*
   c remarkable........ *28.32*
   d what can be known *28.57*
   e friend............ *34.17*
   f extraordinary..... *58.55*

γνώτω
   see γινώσκω

γογγύζω
   complain *33.382*

γογγυσμός, οῦ *m*
   complaint *33.382*

γογγυστής, οῦ *m*
   grumbler *33.386*

γόης, ητος *m*
   impostor *88.232*

52

Γολγοθᾶ, acc ᾶν f
Golgotha 93.453

Γόμορρα, ας f
Gomorrah 93.454

γόμος, ου m
load 15.208

γονεύς, έως m
parents 10.18

γόνυ, γόνατος n
a knee 8.47
b person 9.16
γόνυ : units
τίθημι τὰ γόνατα
kneel (down) 17.19
κάμπτω τὸ γόνυ
worship 53.61
τὰ παραλελυμένα
γόνατα ἀνορθόω
become encouraged 25.152

γονυπετέω
kneel down 17.19

γράμμα, τος n
a letter of alphabet . . . 33.35
b a writing 33.50
c epistle 6.63
d record of debts 33.39

γράμματα, τῶν n
education 27.21

γραμματεύς, έως, m
a expert in the Law . . 53.94
b scholar 27.22
c town clerk 37.94

γραπτός, ή, όν
written 33.64

γραφαί, ῶν f
the Scriptures 33.54

γραφή, ῆς f
a passage 33.10
b Scripture 33.53

γράφω
(aor pass ἐγράφην, pf
γέγραφα, pf pass 3 sg
γέγραπται)
write 33.61
γράφω : unit
μὴ ὑπὲρ ἃ γέγραπται
observe rules 88.95

γραώδης, ες
of old women 9.38

γρηγορέω
a stay awake 23.72
b be alert 27.56
c be alive 23.97

Γύλλιον
Gyllium 93.455

γυμνάζω
a discipline oneself . . . 88.88
b train 36.11

γυμνασία, ας f
physical exercise 50.7

γυμνιτεύω
wear rags 49.24

γυμνός, ή, όν
a naked 49.22
b easily known 28.62

γυμνότης, ητος f
nakedness 49.23

γυναικάριον, ου n
foolish woman 9.35

γυναικεῖος, α, ον
female 9.36

γυνή, αικός f
a woman 9.34
b wife 10.54
γυνή : unit
γυναικὸς ἅπτομαι
marry 34.70

Γώγ m
Gog 93.87

γωνία, ας f
corner 79.107
γωνία : unit
χεφαλή γωνίας
cornerstone 7.44

Δαδδαῖος
see Θαδδαῖος 93.88

δαιμονίζομαι
be demon possessed . . 12.41

δαιμόνιον, ου n
a demon 12.37
b god 12.26

δαιμονιώδης, ες
demonic 12.40

δαίμων, ονος m
demon 12.37

δάκνω
harm 20.26

δάκρυον, ου n
tear 8.73

δακρύω
weep 25.137

δακτύλιος, ου m
ring 6.190

δάκτυλος, ου m
a finger 8.34
b power 76.3

Δαλμανουθά f
Dalmanutha 93.456

Δαλματία, ας f
Dalmatia 93.457

δαμάζω
bring under control . . . 37.1

δάμαλις, εως f
heifer 4.18

Δάμαρις, ιδος f
Damaris 93.89

Δαμασκηνός, οῦ m
Damascene 93.458

Δαμασκός, οῦ f
Damascus 93.459

δανείζομαι
borrow money 57.213

δανείζω
(aor subj δανίσω)
give a loan 57.209

δάνειον, ου n
debt 57.210

Δανιήλ m
Daniel 93.90

δανιστής, οῦ m
moneylender 57.211

δαπανάω
a spend 57.146
b waste 57.149
c exert effort 42.27

δαπάνη, ης f
expense 57.160

δαρήσομαι
see δέρω

Δαυίδ m
David 93.91

δέ
a and 89.94
b and then 89.87
c but 89.124
see also μέν (τοι) . . . δέ
δέ : unit
νυνὶ δέ
and so 91.4

δέδεχται
scc δέχομαι

δεδεκώς
see δέω

δέδεμαι
see δέω

δέδομαι
see δίδωμι

δέδωκα
scc δίδωμι

δεδώκειν
see δίδωμι

δέη
see δεῖ

δεήθητι
see δέομαι

δέησις, εως *f*
plea *33.171*

δεθῆναι
see δέω

δεῖ
(subj δέη, inf δεῖν,
ptc δέον, impf ἔδει)
a be necessary *71.34*
b should *71.21*

δεῖγμα, τος *n*
example *28.48*

δειγματίζω
disgrace publicly *25.200*

δείκνυμι
(fut δείξω, aor ἔδειξα,
impv δεῖξον, aor pass
ptc δειχθείς)
a make known *28.47*
b explain *33.150*

δεικνύω
see δείκνυμι

δειλία, ας *f*
cowardice *25.266*

δειλιάω
be cowardly *25.267*

δειλός, ή, όν
coward *25.268*

δεῖνα *m, f*
somebody *92.19*

δεινός, ή, όν
severe *22.31*

δεινῶς
terribly *78.24*

δεῖξον
see δείκνυμι

δείξω
see δείκνυμι

δειπνέω
to eat a meal *23.20*

δεῖπνον, ου *n*
a meal *23.22*
b main meal *23.25*

δείρας
see δέρω

δεισιδαιμονία, ας *f*
religion *53.2*

δεισιδαίμων, ον
religious *53.3*

δειχθείς
see δείκνυμι

δέκα
ten *60.19*

δεκαοκτώ
eighteen *60.24*

δεκαπέντε
fifteen *60.23*

Δεκάπολις, εως *f*
Decapolis 93.460

δεκατέσσαρες
fourteen 60.22

δεκάτη, ης *f*
tenth 60.66

δέκατον, ου *n*
tenth part 60.65

δεκατόομαι
give a tenth 57.114

δέκατος, η, ον
tenth 60.57

δεκατόω
collect tithes 57.115

δεκτός, ή, όν
a pleasing 25.85
b welcomed 34.54
c appropriate 66.9

δελεάζω
lure into sin 88.303

δένδρον, ου *n*
tree, bush 3.2

δεξιά, ᾶς *f*
a right hand 8.32
b power 76.4
δεξιά : units
δεξιὰς δίδωμι
make a covenant 34.42
ἐκ δεξιῶν καθίζω
be in high position . . 87.34
καθίζω ἐν δεξιᾷ
be in high position . . 87.36
μὴ γνώτω ἡ ἀριστερά
σου τί ποιεῖ ἡ δεξιά σου
do secretly 28.74

δεξιολάβος, ου *m*
spearman 55.22

δεξιός, ά, όν
right 82.8

δέομαι
(impf ἐδεῖτο, aor ἐδε-
ήθην, impv δεήθητι)
plead 33.170

δέον
see δεῖ

δέος, ους *n*
reverence 53.59

Δερβαῖος, ου *m*
Derbean 93.461

Δέρβη, ης *f*
Derbe 93.462

δέρμα, τος *n*
skin 6.184

δερμάτινος, η, ον
leather 6.185

δέρω
(aor ἔδειρα, ptc δείρας,
fut pass δαρήσομαι)
whip 19.2

δεσμά
see δεσμός

δεσμεύω
bind 18.15

δέσμη, ης *f*
bundle 18.16

δέσμιος, ου *m*
prisoner 37.117

δεσμός, οῦ *m* (*n* in plural)
a chains 6.14
b imprisonment 37.115
c illness 23.156

δεσμοφύλαξ, ακος *m*
prison guard 37.124

δεσμωτήριον, ου *n*
prison 7.24

δεσμώτης, ου *m*
prisoner *37.117*

δεσπότης, ου *m*
a ruler *37.63*
b owner *57.13*

δεῦρο
a (come) here *84.24*
b the present time *67.43*

δεῦτε
(come) here *84.24*

δευτεραῖος, α, ον
on the second day *67.180*

δευτερόπρωτος, ον
the second after the
first *61.12*

δεύτερος, α, ον
a second *60.49*
b afterward *67.50*

δέχομαι
(pf 3 sg δέδεχται)
a receive *57.125*
b welcome *34.53*
c believe *31.51*
d take hold of *18.1*

δέω
(aor ἔδησα, subj δήσω,
pf ptc δεδεκώς, pf pass
δέδεμαι, aor pass inf
δεθῆναι)
a bind *18.13*
b imprison *37.114*
c compel *37.33*
d restrict *37.45*
e prohibit *37.46*
f cause illness *23.157*

δή
then *91.6*

δῆλος, η, ον
evident *28.58*

δηλόω
a make known *28.42*
b make clear *33.152*

Δημᾶς, ᾶ *m*
Demas *93.92*

δημηγορέω
make a speech *33.26*

Δημήτριος, ου *m*
Demetrius *93.93*

δημιουργός, οῦ *m*
builder *45.8*

δῆμος, ου *m*
assembly *11.78*

δημόσιος, α, ον
public *28.66*

δηνάριον, ου *n*
coin *6.75*

δήποτε
ever *67.9*

δήπου
indeed *91.7*

δήσω
see δέω

διά
a by (agent) *90.4*
b by (instrument) *90.8*
c through (means) . . . *89.76*
d on behalf of (bene-
faction) *90.38*
e because of (reason
participant) *90.44*
f on account of (rea-
son) *89.26*
g through (extension) *84.29*
h along (extension) . . . *84.32*
i during (time) *67.136*
j throughout (time) . . *67.140*
διά : units
διὰ βραχέων
briefly *67.106*

δι' ἐτῶν
after years 67.60

δι' ἡμερῶν
a few days later 67.59

δι' ὀλίγων
in a short time 67.106

διὰ παντός
  a regularly 67.15
  b always 67.86

Δία
see Ζεύς 93.94

διαβαίνω
(aor διέβην, ptc διαβάς)
cross over 15.31

διαβάλλω
(aor pass διεβλήθην)
accuse 33.426

διαβεβαιόομαι
state with confidence   33.322

διαβλέπω
see clearly 24.35

διάβολος, ου m
  a Devil 12.34
  b demon 12.37
  c slanderer 33.397
  d wicked person 88.124

διαγγέλλω
(aor pass subj διαγγελῶ)
  a give notice 33.203
  b proclaim 33.207

διαγίνομαι
pass (of time) 67.84

διαγινώσκω
  a examine thoroughly   27.3
  b decide a case 56.21

διάγνωσις, εως f
deciding a case 56.21

διαγογγύζω
grumble 33.383

διαγρηγορέω
become fully awake . . . 23.76

διάγω
behave 41.3

διαδέχομαι
receive from . . . . : 57.130

διάδημα, τος n
diadem crown 6.196

διαδίδωμι
(aor διέδωκα, impv 2
sg διάδος, impf pass
3 sg διεδίδετο)
give out 57.94

διάδοχος, ου m
successor 61.11

διαζώννυμι
(aor διέζωσα, διε-
ζωσάμην, pf pass
ptc διεζωσμένος)
gird 49.14

διαθήκη, ης f
  a making of covenant   34.43
  b covenant 34.44
  c testament 57.124

διαθήσομαι
see διατίθεμαι

διαίρεσις, εως f
  a distribution 57.91
  b variety 58.39

διαιρέω
(aor διεῖλον)
divide 57.91

διακαθαίρω
(aor inf διακαθᾶραι)
clean out 79.51

διακαθαρίζω
(fut διακαθαριῶ)
clean out 79.51

διακατελέγχομαι
refute *33.443*

διακονέω
a serve *35.19*
b take care of *35.37*
c wait upon *46.13*
d be a deacon *53.66*
διακονέω : unit
διακονέω τραπέζαις
   handle finances *57.230*

διακονία, ας *f*
a service *35.19*
b ministry *35.21*
c provision *35.38*
d waiting upon *46.13*
e contribution *57.119*

διάκονος, ου *m, f*
a servant *35.20*
b deacon *53.67*

διακόσιοι, αι, α
two hundred *60.34*

διακούω
hear a legal case *56.13*

διακρίνομαι
(aor διεκρίθην)
a doubt *31.37*
b dispute *33.444*
c criticize *33.412*

διακρίνω
a evaluate carefully . . . *30.109*
b prefer *30.99*
c make a distinction . . *30.113*

διάκρισις, εως *f*
a ability to decide *30.112*
b dispute *33.444*

διακωλύω
prevent *13.146*

διαλαλέω
converse *33.158*

διαλέγομαι
(aor διελέχθην)
a argue *33.446*
b make a speech *33.26*

διαλείπω
(aor διέλιπον)
cease *68.36*

διάλεκτος, ου *f*
language *33.1*

διαλλάσσομαι
(aor impv διαλλάγηθι)
make peace *40.2*

διαλογίζομαι
a reason thoroughly . . *30.10*
b converse *33.158*

διαλογισμός, οῦ *m*
a reasoning *30.10*
b what is reasoned . . . *30.16*
c dispute *33.446*
d doubt *31.37*

διαλύω
scatter *15.136*

διαμαρτύρομαι
a testify *33.223*
b insist *33.319*
c warn *33.425*

διαμάχομαι
protest strongly *39.27*

διαμένω
a associate *34.3*
b continue *68.11*
c continue to exist . . . *13.89*

διαμερίζομαι
spread out *15.140*

διαμερίζω
a distribute *57.89*
b be opposed to *39.14*
c divide *63.23*

διαμερισμός, οῦ *m*
division 39.14

διανέμομαι
(aor διενεμήθην)
become known 28.24

διανέμω
cause to spread 84.2

διανεύω
gesture 33.485

διανόημα, τος *n*
thought 30.15

διάνοια, ας *f*
a mind 26.14
b way of thinking 30.5
c thought 30.15
διάνοια : unit
ἀναζώννυμαι τὰς
ὀσφύας τῆς διανοίας
   be ready to learn . . . 27.55

διανοίγω
(aor pass διηνοίχθην)
a make open 79.110
b explain 33.142
διανοίγω : units
διανοίγω τὴν καρδίαν
   cause to be open-
   minded 27.49
διανοίγω τὸν νοῦν
   cause to be open-
   minded 27.49
ἄρσην διανοίγων μήτραν
   firstborn son 10.45

διανυκτερεύω
spend the night 67.195

διανύω
a finish 68.25
b continue 68.18

διαπαρατριβή, ῆς *f*
constant arguing 33.452

διαπεράω
cross over 15.31

διαπλέω
sail across 54.11

διαπονέομαι
be irked 88.190

διαπορεύομαι
a travel through 15.21
b pass by 15.22

διαπορέω
be perplexed 32.10

διαπραγματεύομαι
earn 57.195

διαπρίομαι
be furious 88.181

διαρήσσω
see διαρρήγνυμι

διαρπάζω
plunder 57.238

διαρρήγνυμι
(aor διέρρηξα)
rip 19.32

διασαφέω
a explain 33.143
b tell in detail 33.200

διασείω
extort 57.245

διασκορπίζω
a scatter 15.136
b squander 57.151

διασπάω
tear apart 19.29

διασπείρω
(aor pass διεσπάρην)
scatter 15.136

διασπορά, ᾶς *f*
diaspora 15.137

διαστάς
see διΐσταμαι

διαστέλλομαι
(aor διεστειλάμην)
command 33.323

διάστημα, τος *n*
interval 67.150

διαστήσας
see διΐσταμαι

διαστολή, ῆς *f*
distinction 58.42

διαστρέφω
(pf pass διέστραμμαι)
a mislead 31.71
b pervert 88.264
c turn away from 13.46

διασῴζω
(aor pass διεσώθην)
a rescue 21.19
b heal 23.136

διαταγή, ῆς *f*
ordinance 33.326

διάταγμα, τος *n*
ordinance 33.326

διαταράσσομαι
(aor διεταράχθην)
be deeply troubled 25.246

διατάσσω
(aor pass ptc δια-
ταγείς, διαταχθείς, pf
pass διατέταγμαι)
a command 33.325
b arrange for 62.8

διατελέω
remain 13.27

διατηρέω
avoid 13.153

διατίθεμαι
(fut διαθήσομαι, aor
διεθέμην)
a make a will 57.123
b make a covenant . . . 34.43
διατίθεμαι : unit
διατίθεμαι βασιλείαν
give right to rule . . . 37.105

διατρίβω
stay 85.61

διατροφή, ῆς *f*
food 5.1

διαυγάζω
shine through 14.43

διαυγής, ές
transparent 79.24

διαφέρω
(aor subj διενέγκω)
a carry through 15.196
b drive about 15.163
c be different 58.41
d be valuable 65.6

διαφεύγω
(aor subj διαφύγω)
escape 15.64

διαφημίζω
spread news 33.214

διαφθείρω
(aor pass διεφθάρην,
pf pass διέφθαρμαι)
a destroy utterly 20.40
b deprave 88.266
c waste away 23.146

διαφθορά, ᾶς *f*
decay 23.205

διάφορος, ον
varied 58.40

διαφυλάσσω
protect 21.21

διεθέμην
see διατίθεμαι

διεῖλον
see διαιρέω

διελεύσομαι
see διέρχομαι

διελέχθην
see διαλέγομαι

διελήλυθα
see διέρχομαι

διεληλυθώς
see διέρχομαι

διελθεῖν
see διέρχομαι

διέλιπον
see διαλείπω

διενέγκω
see διαφέρω

διενθυμέομαι
think seriously about   30.2

διέξοδος, ου f
main street crossing .. 1.102

διερμηνευτής, οῦ m
interpreter 33.146

διερμηνεύω
a translate 33.145
b explain 33.148

διέρχομαι
(fut διελεύσομαι, aor
διῆλθον, inf διελθεῖν,
pf διελήλυθα, ptc
διεληλυθώς)
a move on to 15.17
b travel through 15.21
c cross over 15.31
d penetrate 15.32

διέρχομαι : unit
τὴν ψυχὴν διέρχεται
ῥομφαία
feel pain and sorrow 25.279

διερωτάω
learn about 27.11

διεσπάρην
see διασπείρω

διεστειλάμην
see διαστέλλομαι

διέστην
see διΐσταμαι

διέστραμμαι
see διαστρέφω

διεταράχθην
see διαταράσσομαι

διετής, ές
two years old 67.170

διετία, ας f
two year period 67.169

διεφθάρην
see διαφθείρω

διέφθαρμαι
see διαφθείρω

διήγειρα
see διεγείρω

διηγέομαι
tell fully 33.201

διήγησις, εως f
narration 33.11

διῆλθον
see διέρχομαι

διηνεκής, ές
διηνεκής : unit
εἰς τὸ διηνεκές
always 67.95

διηνοίχθην
see διανοίγω

διθάλασσος, ον
cross-currents *14.32*
διθάλασσος : unit
τόπος διθάλασσος
reef *1.68*

διϊκνέομαι
penetrate *15.32*

διΐσταμαι (+ 2 aor)
(aor διέστην, ptc δια-
στάς, διαστήσας)
a move on *15.12*
b depart from *15.50*
c pass (of time) *67.84*

διϊσχυρίζομαι
insist firmly *33.321*

δικαιοκρισία, ας f
just verdict *56.27*

δίκαιος, α, ον
a righteous *88.12*
b be put right with . . . *34.47*
c proper *66.5*

δικαιοσύνη, ης f
a righteousness *88.13*
b be put right with . . . *34.46*
c religious observances *53.4*
d charity *57.111*

δικαιόω
a be put right with . . . *34.46*
b show to be right *88.16*
c acquit *56.34*
d set free *37.138*
e obey righteous
commands *36.22*

δικαίωμα, τος n
a regulation *33.334*
b righteous act *88.14*
c acquit *56.34*

δικαίως
right *88.15*

δικαίωσις, εως f
a be put right with . . . *34.46*
b acquittal *56.34*

δικαστής, οῦ m
judge *56.28*

δίκη, ης f
a punishment *38.8*
b the goddess Justice *12.27*

δίκτυον, ου n
fishnet *6.11*

δίλογος, ον
hypocritical *88.235*

διό
therefore *89.47*

διοδεύω
travel through *15.21*

Διονύσιος, ου m
Dionysius *93.96*

διόπερ
therefore *89.47*

διοπετές, οῦ n
stone from heaven *2.48*

διόρθωμα, τος n
reform *72.17*

διόρθωσις, εως f
a new order *62.5*
b reformation *62.6*

διορύσσω
(aor pass inf διορυχ-
θῆναι)
break through *19.41*

Διός
see Ζεύς *93.97*

Διόσκουροι, ων m
Dioscuri *93.98*

διότι
  a because 89.26
  b that 90.21

Διοτρέφης, ους *m*
  Diotrephes 93.99

διπλοῦς, ῆ, οῦν
  double 60.75

διπλόω
  to double 59.70

δίς
  twice 60.69
  δίς : units
  ἅπαξ καὶ δίς
    several times 60.70
  δίς ἀποθάνων
    completely dead 23.123

δισμυριάς, άδος *f*
  δισμυριάς : unit
  δισμυριάδες μυριάδων
    countless 60.9

διστάζω
  doubt 31.37

δίστομος, ον
  double-edged 79.94

δισχίλιοι, αι, α
  two thousand 60.40

διϋλίζω
  filter out 46.17

διχάζω
  cause to revolt 39.41

διχοστασία, ας *f*
  discord 39.13

διχοτομέω
  a cut in two 19.19
  b punish severely 38.12

διψάω
  a be thirsty 23.39
  b desire strongly 25.17

δίψος, ους *n*
  thirst 23.39

δίψυχος, ον
  doubleminded 31.38

διωγμός, οῦ *m*
  persecution 39.45

διώκτης, ου *m*
  persecutor 39.46

διώκω
  a pursue 15.158
  b press forward 15.223
  c persecute 39.45
  d strive to 68.66
  διώκω : unit
  κατὰ σκοπὸν διώκω
    strive for a purpose 89.56

δόγμα, τος *n*
  a law 33.333
  b decree 33.332

δογματίζομαι
  obey rules 36.21

δοθείς
  see δίδωμι

δοθήσομαι
  see δίδωμι

δοῖ
  see δίδωμι

δοκεῖ
  seem 31.30

δοκέω
  (aor ἔδοξα)
  a suppose 31.29
  b be disposed to 25.7
  c choose 30.96
  δοκέω : unit
  οἱ δοκοῦντες
    prominent persons 87.42

δοκιμάζω
  a test *27.45*
  b regard as worthwhile *30.98*
  c judge as good *30.114*

δοκιμασία, ας *f*
  testing *27.45*

δοκιμή, ῆς *f*
  a testing *27.45*
  b evidence *72.7*
  c value *65.12*

δοκίμιον, ου *n*
  a testing *27.45*
  b genuineness *73.3*

δόκιμος, ον
  a considered good *30.115*
  b genuine *73.4*
  c honored *87.7*

δοκός, οῦ *f*
  beam (of wood) *7.78*

δόλιος, α, ον
  treacherous *88.155*

δολιόω
  (impf 3 pl ἐδολιοῦσαν)
  deceive *88.154*

δόλος, ου *m*
  treachery *88.154*

δολόω
  cause to be false *72.9*

δόμα, τος *n*
  gift *57.73*

Δονεῖ *m*
  Doni *93.100*

δόξα, ης *f*
  a splendor *79.18*
  b brightness *14.49*
  c amazing might *76.13*
  d praise *33.357*
  e honor *87.4*
  f greatness *87.23*

  g glorious being *12.49*
  h heaven *1.15*
  i pride *25.205*
  δόξα : units
  δίδωμι δόξαν τῷ θεῷ
    promise to tell truth *33.468*
  μεγαλοπρεπὴς δόξα
    Sublime Glory *12.6*

δοξάζομαι
  be wonderful *65.5*

δοξάζω
  a praise *33.357*
  b honor *87.8*
  c glorify *87.24*

Δορκάς, άδος *f*
  Dorcas *93.101*

δός
  see δίδωμι

δόσις, εως *f*
  a giving *57.71*
  b gift *57.73*

δότης, ου *m*
  giver *57.72*

Δουβέριος, ου *m*
  Doberian *93.463*

δουλαγωγέω
  make ready for
  service *35.30*

δουλεία, ας *f*
  subservience *37.26*

δουλεύω
  a be a slave *87.79*
  b be controlled by *37.25*
  c serve *35.27*

δούλη, ης *f*
  slave woman *87.83*

δουλόομαι
  be under obligation . . . *37.24*

δοῦλος, η, ον
subservient to *37.3*

δοῦλος, ου *m*
slave *87.76*

δουλόω
a enslave *87.82*
b make subservient . *37.27*

δοῦναι
see δίδωμι

δούς
see δίδωμι

δοχή, ῆς *f*
banquet *23.27*

δράκων, οντος *m*
dragon *4.54*

δραμών
see τρέχω

δράσσομαι
trap *27.32*

δραχμή, ῆς *f*
coin *6.76*

δρέπανον, ου *n*
sickle . . . . : *6.5*
δρέπανον : units
βάλλω τὸ δρέπανον
    begin to harvest *43.17*
ἀποστέλλω τὸ δρέπανον
    begin to harvest *43.17*
πέμπω τὸ δρέπανον
    begin to harvest *43.17*

δρόμος, ου *m*
a race *50.5*
b mission *42.26*

Δρούσιλλα, ης *f*
Drusilla *93.102*

δύναμαι
(2 sg δύνῃ or δύνασε
or δύνασαι, opt δυναί-
μην, impf ἐδυνάμην
or ἠδυνάμην, aor ἠδυ-
νάσθην or ἠδυνήθην)
be able *74.5*

δύναμις, εως *f*
a ability *74.1*
b power *76.1*
c mighty deed *76.7*
d ruler *37.61*
e supernatural power *12.44*
f meaning *33.134*

δυναμόω
enable *74.6*

δύνασαι
see δύναμαι

δύνασε
see δύναμαι

δυνάστης, ου *m*
official *37.62*

δυνατέω
be able *74.5*

δυνατός, ή, όν
a possible *71.2*
b able *74.2*
c competent *74.4*
δυνατός : units
ὁ δυνατός
    the Mighty One *74.3*
οἱ δυνατοί
    important people . . . *87.43*

δύνῃ
see δύναμαι

δύνω
(aor ἔδυν)
go down *15.113*

δύο, dat δυσίν
two *60.11*

δυσβάστακτος, ον
difficult *22.34*

δυσεντέριον, ου *n*
dysentery *23.160*

δυσερμήνευτος, ον
hard to interpret *33.149*

δύσις, εως *f*
west *82.2*

δύσκολος, ον
difficult *22.32*

δυσκόλως
with difficulty *22.32*

δυσμή, ῆς *f*
west *82.2*

δυσνόητος, ον
difficult to understand *32.22*

δυσφημέω
defame *33.398*

δυσφημία, ας *f*
defame *33.398*

δῶ
see δίδωμι

δώδεκα
twelve *60.21*
δώδεκα : unit
αἱ δώδεκα φυλαί
all God's people *11.15*

δωδέκατος, η, ον
twelfth *60.59*

δωδεκάφυλον, ου *n*
the twelve tribes *10.3*

δώῃ, δώῃ
see δίδωμι

δῶμα, τος *n*
housetop *7.51*
δῶμα : unit
ἐπὶ τῶν δωμάτων
in public *28.64*

δωρεά, ᾶς *f*
gift *57.84*

δωρεάν
a without cost *57.85*
b for no reason *89.20*
c for no purpose *89.63*

δωρέομαι
grant *57.83*

δώρημα, τος *n*
gift *57.84*

δῶρον, ου *n*
a gift *57.84*
b offering box *6.142*

δωροφορία, ας *f*
bringing of gifts *57.86*

δώσω
see δίδωμι

ἔα
ah *88.191*

ἐάν
a if *89.67*
b when *67.32*
c ever *71.8*
ἐάν : units
ἡνίκα ἐάν
whenever *67.36*
ὁσάκις ἐάν
whenever *67.36*

ἐάνπερ
if indeed *89.68*

ἑαυτοῦ, ῆς, οῦ
himself, herself, itself *92.25*
ἑαυτοῦ : units
ἀπέρχομαι πρὸς ἑαυτόν

go back to one's
place *15.92*
τὸν ἑαυτοῦ ἄρτον ἐσθίω
earn a living *57.190*
λέγω ἐν ἑαυτῷ
think to oneself *31.5*

ἑαυτῶν
each other *92.26*

ἐάω
(fut ἐάσω, aor εἴασα,
impf 3 sg εἴα, 3 pl
εἴων, impv 2 pl ἐᾶτε,
pres ptc ἐων)
allow *13.138*
ἐάω : unit
ἐάω ἕως
stop *68.35*

ἔβαλον
see βάλλω

ἑβδομήκοντα
seventy *60.30*

ἑβδομηκοντάκις
a seventy times *60.74*
b seventy multiples . . . *60.77*

ἕβδομος, η, ον
seventh *60.54*

ἐβεβλήμην
see βάλλω

Ἔβερ m
Eber *93.103*

ἐβλήθην
see βάλλω

ἐβουλήθην
see βούλομαι

Ἑβραϊκός, ή, όν
Hebrew *93.104*

Ἑβραῖος, ου m
Hebrew *93.105*

Ἑβραΐς, ΐδος f
Hebrew *93.104*

Ἑβραϊστί
Hebrew language *33.6*

ἐγγίζω
a come near (move-
ment) *15.75*
b come near (time) . . . *67.21*

ἐγγράφω
record *33.62*

ἔγγυος, ου m
guarantor *70.8*

ἐγγύς
a near (place) *83.26*
b near (time) *67.61*

ἐγεγόνει
see γίνομαι

ἐγείρομαι
(fut ἐγερθήσομαι, aor
ἠγέρθην, pf ἐγήγερμαι)
a stand up *17.9*
b wake up *23.74*
c make war against . . . *55.2*

ἐγείρω
(fut ἐγερῶ, aor ἤγειρα,
pf pass ἐγήγερμαι, aor
pass ἠγέρθην, fut pass
ἐγερθήσομαι)
a cause to stand up . . . *17.10*
b stand up *17.9*
c cause to wake up . . . *23.77*
d cause to exist *13.83*
e raise to life *23.94*
f restore *13.65*
g heal *23.140*

ἐγενήθην
see γίνομαι

ἐγενόμην
see γίνομαι

69

ἔγερσις, εως f
resurrection 23.93

ἐγήγερμαι
see ἐγείρομαι

ἔγημα
see γαμέω

ἐγκάθετος, ου m
spy 27.47

ἐγκαίνια, ων n
festival of dedication
of the Temple 51.9

ἐγκαινίζω
cause to exist 13.84

ἐγκακέω
become discouraged . . 25.288

ἐγκαλέω
accuse 33.427

ἐγκαταλείπω
(aor ἐγκατέλ(ε)ιπον)
a leave to exist 13.92
b forsake 35.54
c cease 68.36

ἐγκατέλ(ε)ιπας
alt aor 2 sg of
ἐγκαταλείπω

ἐγκατοικέω
dwell among 85.72

ἐγκαυχάομαι
boast 33.368

ἐγκεντρίζω
graft 43.10

ἔγκλημα, τος n
accusation 56.6

ἐγκομβόομαι
dress 49.9

ἐγκοπή, ῆς f
obstacle 13.148

ἐγκόπτω
(aor ἐνέκοψα)
a prevent 13.147
b irritate 25.185

ἐγκράτεια, ας f
self-control 88.83

ἐγκρατεύομαι
control oneself 88.83

ἐγκρατής, ές
self-controlled 88.84

ἐγκρίνω
classify 58.27

ἐγκρύπτω
(aor ἐνέκρυψα)
put into 85.50

ἔγκυος, ον
pregnant 23.50

ἔγνωκα
see γινώσκω

ἐγνώκειν
see γινώσκω

ἔγνων
see γινώσκω

ἐγνώσθην
see γινώσκω

Ἔγυπτος
see Αἴγυπτος 93.464

ἐγχρίω
rub on 47.15

ἐγώ, (ἐ)μοῦ, (ἐ)μοί, (ἐ)μέ
I 92.1

ἐδαφίζω
a raze 20.57
b kill 20.64

ἔδαφος, ους *n*
ground *1.44*

ἐδεδώκειν
see δίδωμι

ἐδεήθην
see δέομαι

ἔδειξα
see δείκνυμι

ἔδειρα
see δέρω

ἔδησα
see δέω

ἐδιδάχθην
see διδάσκω

ἐδίδοσαν
see δίδωμι

ἐδίδου
see δίδωμι

ἐδίδουν
see δίδωμι

ἐδόθην
see δίδωμι

ἐδολιοῦσαν
see δολιόω

ἔδοξα
see δοκέω

ἑδραῖος, α, ον
firm *31.92*

ἑδραίωμα, τος *n*
support *31.93*

ἔδραμον
see τρέχω

ἔδυν
see δύνω

ἔδωκα
see δίδωμι

Ἐζεκίας, ου *m*
Hezekiah *93.106*

ἔζην
see ζάω

ἐθελοθρησκία, ας *f*
self-imposed religion . . *53.12*

ἔθεντο
see τίθημι

ἔθηκα
see τίθημι

ἐθίζω
(pf pass εἴθισμαι)
be in habit of *41.26*

ἐθνάρχης, ου *m*
official *37.80*

ἐθνικός, ή, όν
heathen *11.38*

ἐθνικῶς
like a heathen *11.39*

ἔθνος, ους *n*
nation *11.55*
ἔθνος : unit
τὰ ἔθνη
heathen *11.37*

ἔθος, ους *n*
custom *41.25*

ἔθου
see τίθημι

ἔθρεψα
see τρέφω

εἰ
a if *89.65*
b because *89.30*
c that, whether *90.26*

εἰ : units
εἰ τύχοι
   probably 71.13
εἰ μή
   except that 89.131
εἰ μήν
   surely 91.8

εἴα
   see ἐάω

εἴασα
   see ἐάω

εἶδα
   see ὁράω

εἰδέα, ας f
   form 58.14

εἰδέναι
   see οἶδα

εἰδήσω
   see οἶδα

εἶδον
   see ὁράω

εἰδός
   see εἰδώς

εἶδος, ους n
   a form 58.14
   b sight 24.1

εἰδυῖα
   see οἶδα

εἰδῶ
   see οἶδα

εἰδωλεῖον, ου n
   temple of an idol 7.19

εἰδωλόθυτον, ου n
   sacrificial meat 5.15

εἰδωλολάτρης, ου m
   worshiper of idols 53.64

εἰδωλολατρία, ας f
   idolatry 53.63

εἴδωλον, ου n
   a idol 6.97
   b false god 12.23

εἰδώς
   see οἶδα

εἴθισμαι
   see ἐθίζω

εἰκῇ
   a without reason 89.20
   b with no result 89.54
   c for no purpose 89.63

εἴκοσι
   twenty 60.25

εἴκω
   (aor εἶξα)
   yield 39.21

εἰκών, όνος f
   a image 6.96
   b likeness 58.35
   c representation 58.61

εἰλάμην
   see αἱρέομαι

εἰλευθέρωσεν
   see ἐλευθερόω

εἴληπται
   see λαμβάνω

εἴληφα
   see λαμβάνω

εἰλικρίνεια, ας f
   sincerity 88.42

εἰλικρινής, ές
   sincere 88.41

εἷλχον
   see ἕλκω

εἵλκυσα
see ἕλκω

εἵλκωμαι
see ἑλκόομαι

εἰμί
(impv ἴσθι, ἔστω,
ἤτω, 3 pl ἔστωσαν,
inf εἶναι, impf ἦν,
ἤμην, fut ἔσομαι)
a be 13.1
b be identical 13.4
c exist 13.69
d happen 13.104
e be in a place 85.1
f be possible 71.1
g belong 58.67
h represent 58.68
εἰμί : units
εἰμὶ ἐν
  continue to do 68.20
εἰμὶ εἰς
  become 13.51
εἰμί τις
  be important 87.49
ἐν βάρει εἰμί
  claim importance . . . 65.56
εἰμὶ εἰς τὸν κόλπον
  be closely associated 34.18
εἰμὶ ὑπὸ ζυγόν
  be a slave 87.80
θέλει εἶναι
  it means 33.136
εἰς χολὴν πικρίας εἰμί
  be terribly envious . . 88.166
τοῦτ' ἔστιν
  that means 89.106
ὅ ἐστιν
  that means 89.106

εἵνεκεν
see ἕνεκεν

εἶξα
see εἴκω

εἶπα
see λέγω

εἰπεῖν
see λέγω

εἴπερ
if indeed 89.66

εἶπον
see λέγω

εἰργασάμην
see ἐργάζομαι

εἴργασμαι
see ἐργάζομαι

εἴρηκα
see λέγω

εἰρήκει
see λέγω

εἴρημαι
see λέγω

εἰρηνεύω
live in peace 88.102

εἰρήνη, ης f
a peace 22.42
b freedom from worry 25.248

εἰρηνικός, ή, όν
free from worry 25.249

εἰρηνοποιέω
make peace 40.4

εἰρηνοποιός, οῦ m
peacemaker 40.5

εἰς
a to (extension) 84.16
b into (extension) 84.22
c on (location) 83.47
d inside (location) 83.13
e among (location) . . . 83.9
f in order to (purpose) 89.57
g so that (result) 89.48
h by (means) 89.76

i with reference to
  (content)......... 90.23
j to the point of (de-
  gree)............ 78.51
k to (change of state) 13.62
l to (experiencer) 90.59
m on behalf of (bene-
  faction)........... 90.41
n by (guarantor) 90.30
o for (time) 67.117
p at (time) 67.160
q until (time)........ 67.119
εἰς : units
εἰς τὸ διηνεκές
  forever 67.95
εἰς τὰ ἄμετρα
  excessive 78.27
εἰμὶ εἰς
  become 13.51
ἀπό . . . εἰς
  from . . . to 13.62
ἐκ . . . εἰς
  completely 78.48
εἰς τὸ πάλιν
  again 67.55
εἰς τὸ παντελές
  a forever 67.95
  b completely 78.47
εἰς τέλος
  completely 78.47
εἰς ἡμέραν αἰῶνος
  forever 67.95
εἰς (τὸν) αἰῶνα (τοῦ
αἰῶνος/τῶν αἰώνων)
  forever 67.95
(εἰς) (παντὰς) τοὺς
αἰῶνας (τῶν αἰώνων)
  forever 67.95
ἐχθὲς καὶ σήμερον καὶ
εἰς τοὺς αἰῶνας
  eternally 67.87
ἐπιβαλὼν τὴν χεῖρα
ἐπ' ἄροτρον καὶ
βλέπων εἰς τὰ ὀπίσω
  start to do and then
  hesitate.......... 68.6
τίθεμαι εἰς τὰ ὦτα
  a listen carefully ... 24.64
  b remember well ... 29.5
ἀποβαίνω εἰς
  result in 89.41

ἔρχομαι εἰς
  result in 89.43
κατέχω εἰς
  head for 54.22
εἰς χολὴν πικρίας εἰμί
  be terribly envious 88.166
εἰς τὸ οὖς
  privately 28.73
ἀπέρχομαι εἰς τὰ ὀπίσω
  no longer follow.... 36.36
εἰς τὸ χεῖρον ἔρχομαι
  become more sick .. 23.150
εἰσφέρω εἰς τὰς ἀκοάς
  a cause to hear..... 24.55
  b speak about 33.92

εἷς, μία, ἕν, gen ἑνός, μιᾶς,
ἑνός
  a one (number) 60.10
  b one (indefinite) 92.22
  c one (unit) 63.4
εἷς : unit
ἀπὸ μιᾶς
  one by one 61.2

εἰσάγω
  (aor εἰσήγαγον)
  a lead into........ 15.173
  b carry in......... 15.194

εἰσακούω
  a listen to 24.60
  b obey 36.15

εἰσδέχομαι
  receive 34.53

εἰσδραμοῦσα
  see εἰστρέχω

εἴσειμι
  (inf εἰσιέναι, pres 3
  pl εἰσίασιν, impf 3 sg
  εἰσῄει)
  move into 15.93

εἰσενεγκεῖν
  see εἰσφέρω

εἰσέρχομαι
(fut εἰσελεύσομαι, aor
εἰσῆλθον, pf εἰσελήλυθα)
a move into 15.93
b happen 13.110
c begin 68.7
d begin to experience 90.70
εἰσέρχομαι : unit
εἰσέρχομαι καὶ ἐξέρχομαι
live with 41.24

εἰσήγαγον
see εἰσάγω

εἰσῄει
see εἴσειμι

εἰσήνεγκον
see εἰσφέρω

εἰσίασιν
see εἴσειμι

εἰσιέναι
see εἴσειμι

εἰσκαλέομαι
invite in 33.316

εἴσοδος, ου f
a coming 15.87
b acceptance 34.56

εἰσπηδάω
rush into 15.237

εἰσπορεύομαι
move into 15.93
εἰσπορεύομαι : unit
εἰσπορεύομαι καὶ
ἐκπορεύομαι
live with 41.24

εἰστήκειν
see ἵσταμαι

εἰστρέχω
(aor ptc f εἰσδραμοῦσα)
run into 15.232

εἰσφέρω
(aor εἰσήνεγκον, inf
εἰσενεγκεῖν)
a bring in 15.194
b cause to 90.93
εἰσφέρω : unit
εἰσφέρω εἰς τὰς ἀκοάς
a cause to hear 24.55
b speak about 33.92

εἶτα
a afterwards 67.44
b furthermore 89.100

εἴτε . . . εἴτε
if . . . if 89.69

εἶτεν
see εἶτα

εἶχον
see ἔχω

εἴωθα
be in habit of 41.26

εἴων
see ἐάω

ἐκ
a out of (extension) . . . 84.4
b because of (reason) 89.25
c by (means) 89.77
d with (instrument) . . 90.12
e with (manner) 89.85
f from (source) 90.16
g from (dissociation) 89.121
h from (derivation) . . . 89.3
i one of (part-whole) 63.20
j from (cessation) 68.54
k when (time) 67.33
l since (time) 67.131
m with (price) 57.163
n of (substance) 89.142
ἐκ : units
ἐκ . . . εἰς
completely 78.48
ἐκ μέρους
in part 63.15

ἐξ ἐναντίας
  a opposite 83.42
  b hostile 39.6
ἐκ μέτρου
  sparingly 78.12
ἐκ περισσοῦ
  extremely 78.20
ἐκ τοῦ αἰῶνος
  since all time 67.133
συνέχομαι ἐκ
  have conflicting
  thoughts 30.18
ἐξέρχομαι ἐκ τῆς
ὀσφύος
  be born of 23.60
ἐκ δεξιῶν καθίζω
  be in high position   87.34
ἐξ ἀριστερῶν καθίζω
  be in less high
  position 87.35

ἕκαστος, η, ον
  each 59.27

ἑκάστοτε
  always .... : 67.88

ἑκατέστησας
  see καθίστημι

ἑκατόν
  one hundred 60.33

ἑκατονταετής, ές
  hundred years 67.173

ἑκατονταπλασίων, ον
  hundred times as much 60.78

ἑκατοντάρχης, ου m
  Roman officer 55.16

ἑκατόνταρχος, ου m
  Roman officer ... 55.16

ἐκβαίνω
  (aor ἐξέβην)
  go out of 15.40

ἐκβάλλω
  (fut ἐκβαλῶ, aor ἐξέβα-
  λον, plpf ἐκβεβλήκειν,
  aor pass ἐξεβλήθην, fut
  pass ἐκβληθήσομαι)
  a throw out 15.220
  b drive out 15.44
  c send out 15.68
  d lead out 15.174
  e exorcise 53.102
  f cause to be 13.68
ἐκβάλλω : unit
ἐκβάλλω τὸ ὄνομα
  slander 33.396

ἔκβασις, εως f
  a end 67.68
  b result 89.39
  c way of escape 21.16

ἐκβολή, ῆς f
  throwing out 15.220

ἔκγονον, ου n
  grandchild 10.48

ἐκδαπανάω
  give oneself completely 42.28

ἐκδέχομαι
  a wait for 85.60
  b expect......... 30.53
  c remain until 13.28

ἔκδηλος, ον
  easily known 28.59

ἐκδημέω
  be absent 85.21
ἐκδημέω : unit
ἐκδημέω ἐκ τοῦ σώματος
  die 23.111

ἐκδίδομαι
  (fut ἐκδώσομαι, aor
  ἐξεδόμην)
  rent out 57.177

ἐκδιηγέομαι
  tell fully 33.201

ἐκδικέω
a give justice *56.35*
b revenge *39.33*
c punish *38.8*

ἐκδίκησις, εως *f*
a give justice *56.35*
b revenge *39.33*
c punishment *38.8*

ἔκδικος, ου *m*
punisher *38.9*

ἐκδιώκω
a pursue and drive out *15.159*
b persecute *39.45*

ἔκδοτος, ον
handed over, betrayed *37.112*

ἐκδοχή, ῆς *f*
expectation *30.53*

ἐκδύω
take off clothes *49.18*

ἐκδώσομαι
see ἐκδίδομαι

ἐκεῖ
there *83.2*

ἐκεῖθεν
from there *84.10*
see also κἀκεῖθεν

ἐκείνης
there *83.2*

ἐκεῖνος, η, ο
that *92.30*

ἐκεῖσε
there *83.2*

ἐκέκραξα
see κράζω

ἐκέρασα
see κεράννυμι

ἐκέρδησα
see κερδαίνω

ἐκζητέω
a seek diligently *27.35*
b bring charges against *56.9*

ἐκζήτησις, εως *f*
a speculation *31.33*
b idle dispute *33.442*

ἐκθαμβέομαι
be astounded *25.210*

ἔκθαμβος, ον
astounded *25.211*

ἐκθαυμάζω
be very amazed *25.214*

ἔκθετος, ον
exposed *85.47*

ἐκκαθαίρω
(aor impv ἐκκαθάρατε)
clean out *79.50*

ἐκκαίομαι
(aor ἐξεκαύθην)
ἐκκαίομαι : unit
ἐκκαίομαι ἐν τῇ ὀρέξει
have a strong desire *25.16*

ἐκκεντέω
pierce *19.14*

ἐκκέχυμαι
see ἐκχέω

ἐκκλάω
break off *19.36*

ἐκκλείω
a not allow *13.143*
b exclude *34.36*

ἐκκλησία, ας *f*
a congregation *11.32*
b church *11.33*
c assembly *11.78*

ἐκκλίνω
a keep away from *34.41*
b turn away from *31.99*
c cease............ *68.41*

ἐκκολυμβάω
swim away.......... *15.247*

ἐκκομίζω
carry out *15.198*

ἐκκόπτω
(aor pass ἐξεκόπην, fut
pass ἐκκοπήσομαι)
a cut down/off *19.18*
b do away with *13.101*

ἐκκρέμαμαι
(impf ἐξεκρεμάμην)
a consider seriously .. *30.34*
b persist in *68.15*

ἐκλαλέω
tell *33.73*

ἐκλάμπω
shine forth *14.38*

ἐκλανθάνομαι
(pf ἐκλέλησμαι)
forget entirely *29.15*

ἔκλαυσα
see κλαίω

ἐκλέγομαι
(aor 2 sg ἐξελέξω)
a select *30.86*
b choose *30.92*

ἐκλείπω
(aor subj ἐκλίπω)
a fail *57.46*
b depart........... *15.58*
c cease (event)...... *68.36*
d cease (state) *13.39*

ἐκλεκτός, ή, όν
chosen *30.93*

ἐκλέλησμαι
see ἐκλανθάνομαι

ἐκλήθην
see καλέω

ἐκλογή, ῆς f
a choice............ *30.92*
b chosen *30.93*

ἐκλύομαι
a become extremely
weary *23.79*
b become discouraged *25.288*

ἐκμάσσω
(aor ἐξέμαξα)
wipe dry *79.83*

ἐκμυκτηρίζω
ridicule *33.409*

ἐκνεύω
slip out............ *15.60*

ἐκνήφω
return to one's right
senses.............. *30.26*

ἑκούσιος, α, ον
willing *25.65*

ἑκουσίως
a willingly.......... *25.65*
b purposely *30.64*

ἔκπαλαι
a long ago *67.24*
b for a long time *67.132*

ἐκπειράζω
a test *27.46*
b try to trap........ *27.31*
c tempt *88.308*

ἐκπέμπω
send out *15.68*

ἐκπερισσῶς
excessive *78.31*

ἐκπετάννυμι
(aor ἐξεπέτασα)
stretch out *16.19*

ἐκπηδάω
rush out *15.236*

ἐκπίπτω
(aor ἐξέπεσον, inf
ἐκπεσεῖν, pf ἐκπέπτωκα)
a fall from *15.120*
b run aground *54.19*
c forsake *34.26*
d worsen *13.59*
e become inadequate　*75.7*
f experience no longer　*90.72*

ἐκπλέω
(aor ἐξέπλευσα, inf
ἐκπλεῦσαι)
sail away from *54.6*

ἐκπληρόω
make happen *13.106*

ἐκπλήρωσις, εως *f*
completion *67.69*

ἐκπλήσσομαι
(aor ἐξεπλάγην)
be greatly astounded . . *25.219*

ἐκπνέω
(aor ἐξέπνευσα)
die *23.103*

ἐκπορεύομαι
depart out of *15.40*
ἐκπορεύομαι : unit
εἰσπορεύομαι καὶ
ἐκπορεύομαι
　live with *41.24*

ἐκπορνεύω
engage in illicit sex . . . *88.271*

ἐκπτύω
reject *34.37*

ἐκρεμάσθην
see κρεμάννυμι

ἐκριζόω
uproot *43.11*

ἐκρίθην
see κρίνω

ἐκρύβην
see κρύπτω

ἔκστασις, εως *f*
a amazement *25.217*
b ecstatic vision *33.489*

ἐκστρέφομαι
(pf ἐξέστραμμαι)
be corrupt *88.265*

ἐκσῶσαι
see ἐξωθέω[b], fn 2

ἐκταράσσω
stir up against *39.44*

ἐκτεθείς
see ἐκτίθεμαι

ἐκτείνω
(fut ἐκτενῶ, aor ἐξέτεινα)
stretch out *16.19*
ἐκτείνω : unit
ἐκτείνω τὰς χεῖρας ἐπί
　arrest *37.110*

ἐκτελέω
complete *68.22*

ἐκτένεια, ας *f*
earnestness *25.70*

ἐκτενής, ές
a continuous *68.12*
b eager *25.71*

ἐκτενῶς
a continuously *68.12*
b eagerly *25.71*

ἐκτίθεμαι
(aor ἐξετέθην, ptc
ἐκτεθείς)
explain *33.151*

ἐκτίθημι
put out of 85.46

ἐκτινάσσω
shake out 16.8

ἕκτος, η, ον
sixth 60.53

ἐκτός
a outside 83.20
b the outside of 83.21
c except 89.138
d independent of 89.121

ἐκτρέπομαι
(fut ἐκτραπήσομαι,
aor ἐξετράπην)
a stray after 31.65
b avoid 13.155

ἐκτρέπω
(aor subj pass ἐκτράπην)
sprain 23.178

ἐκτρέφω
a provide food for 23.6
b rear 35.51

ἔκτρωμα, τος *n*
untimely birth 23.55

ἐκφέρω
(fut ἐξοίσω, aor ἐξή-
νεγκα, inf ἐξενεγκεῖν)
a carry out 15.197
b lead out 15.174
c grow 23.194

ἐκφεύγω
(aor ἐξέφυγον, inf
ἐκφυγεῖν)
a flee from 15.63
b escape 21.14

ἐκφοβέω
terrify 25.257

ἔκφοβος, ον
terrified 25.256

ἐκφύω
sprout leaves 23.195

ἐκχέομαι
(fut ἐκχυθήσομαι, aor
ἐξεχύθην, pf ἐκκέχυμαι)
a flow out 14.18
b plunge into 68.75
c fully experience 90.82
d devote to 41.13

ἐκχέω
(fut ἐκχεῶ, aor ἐξέχεα,
inf ἐκχέαι, pf pass
ἐκκέχυμαι)
a cause to flow out . . . 47.4
b scatter 15.138
c give in abundance . . 59.50
d cause to fully
experience 90.89
ἐκχέω : unit
αἷμα ἐκχέω
murder 20.84

ἐκχύννομαι
ἐκχύννομαι : unit
ἐκχύννεται τὸ αἷμα
die as sacrifice 23.112

ἐκχύννω
ἐκχύννω : unit
αἷμα ἐκχύννω
murder 20.84

ἐκχωρέω
depart 15.41

ἐκψύχω
die 23.99

ἑκών, οὖσα, όν
willing 25.65

ἔλαβον
see λαμβάνω

ἔλαθον
see λανθάνω

ἐλαία, ας *f*
  a olive (tree) *3.9*
  b olive (fruit) *3.39*

ἔλαιον, ου *n*
  olive oil *6.202*

ἐλαιών, ῶνος *m*
  olive orchard *3.12*

Ἐλαμίτης, ου *m*
  Elamite *93.465*

ἐλάσσων, ον
  a fewer *59.3*
  b lesser (status) *87.67*
  c younger *67.116*

ἐλαττονέω
  have too little *57.41*

ἐλαττόομαι
  become less (status) . . . *87.69*

ἐλαττόω
  make less (status) *87.68*

ἐλαύνω
  (pf ἐλήλακα)
  drive along *15.161*

ἐλαφρία, ας *f*
  fickleness *88.99*

ἐλαφρός, ά, όν
  a light *86.2*
  b limited *78.10*
  c easy *22.38*

ἐλάχιστος, η, ον
  a very small *79.125*
  b least important
    (value) *65.57*
  c least important
    (status) *87.66*

ἔλαχον
  see λαγχάνω

Ἐλεάζαρ *m*
  Eleazar *93.107*

ἐλεάω
  show mercy *88.76*

ἐλεγμός, οῦ *m*
  rebuke *33.417*

ἔλεγξις, εως *f*
  rebuke *33.417*

ἔλεγχος, ου *m*
  evidence for *72.8*

ἐλέγχω
  (aor pass ἠλέγχθην)
  rebuke *33.417*

ἐλεεινός, ή, όν
  pitiable *88.79*

ἐλεέω
  see ἐλεάω

ἐλεημοσύνη, ης *f*
  a acts of charity *57.111*
  b donation *57.112*

ἐλεήμων, ον
  merciful *88.77*

ἔλεος, ους *n*
  (show) mercy *88.76*

ἐλευθερία, ας *f*
  freedom *37.133*

ἐλεύθερος, α, ον
  a (be) free *37.134*
  b free person *87.84*

ἐλευθερόω
  (aor ἠλευθέρωσα,
  εἱλευθέρωσα)
  set free *37.135*

ἐλεύκανα
  see λευκαίνω

ἔλευσις, εως *f*
  coming *15.81*

ἐλεύσομαι
see ἔρχομαι

ἐλεφάντινος, η, ον
made of ivory 2.44

ἐλήλακα
see ἐλαύνω

ἐλήλυθα
see ἔρχομαι

ἐλθεῖν
see ἔρχομαι

Ἐλιακίμ m
Eliakim 93.108

ἔλιγμα, τος n
package 79.121

Ἐλιέζερ m
Eliezer 93.109

Ἐλιούδ m
Eliud 93.110

Ἐλισάβετ f
Elizabeth 93.111

Ἐλισαῖος, ου m
Elisha............. 93.112

ἐλίσσω
roll up 79.120

ἐλκόομαι
(pf εἵλκωμαι)
have sores 23.180

ἕλκος, ους n
sore 23.179

ἕλκω
(impf εἷλκον, fut ἑλ-
κύσω, aor εἵλκυσα,
subj 3 sg ἑλκύσῃ)
a pull............. 15.212
b lead by force 15.178

Ἑλλάς, άδος f
Greece 93.466

Ἕλλην, ηνος m
a Greek 11.90
b Gentile 11.40

Ἑλληνικός, ή, όν
Greek............. 11.92

Ἑλληνίς, ίδος f
a Greek woman 11.91
b Gentile woman 11.41

Ἑλληνιστής, οῦ m
Greek-speaking Jew .. 11.93

Ἑλληνιστί
in Greek........... 33.5

ἐλλογάω
see ἐλλογέω

ἐλλογέω
a record........... 33.45
b charge to account... 57.226

Ἐλμαδάμ m
Elmadam........... 93.113

ἑλόμενος
see αἱρέομαι

ἐλπίζω
(fut ἐλπιῶ, aor ἤλπισα,
pf ἤλπικα)
a hope (for) 25.59
b expect........... 30.54

ἐλπίς, ίδος f
a hope 25.59
b what is hoped for ... 25.61
c basis for hope...... 25.62

Ἐλύμας, α m
Elymas............ 93.114

ελωι
my God 12.3

ἔμαθον
  see μανθάνω

ἐμαυτοῦ, ῆς
  myself 92.3

ἐμβαίνω
  (aor ἐνέβην, ptc ἐμβάς,
  inf ἐμβῆναι)
  a embark 15.95
  b step into 15.225

ἐμβάλλω
  (aor inf ἐμβαλεῖν)
  throw in 85.35

ἐμβάπτω
  (aor ptc ἐμβάψας)
  dip in 47.11

ἐμβατεύω
  enter into mysteries . . . 53.15

ἐμβιβάζω
  cause to embark 15.96

ἐμβλέπω
  a look straight at 24.9
  b think about 30.1

ἐμβριμάομαι
  a insist sternly 33.320
  b scold 33.421
  c feel strongly 25.56

ἐμέ
  see ἐγώ

ἔμεινα
  see μένω

ἐμέω
  vomit 23.44

ἔμιξα
  see μίγνυμι

ἐμμαίνομαι
  be enraged 88.182

Ἐμμανουήλ m
  Emmanuel 93.115

Ἐμμαοῦς f
  Emmaus 93.467

ἐμμένω
  (aor ἐνέμεινα)
  a remain 85.55
  b continue 68.11

Ἐμμώρ m
  Hamor 93.116

ἐμνήσθην
  see μιμνήσκομαι

ἐμοί
  see ἐγώ

ἐμός, ή, όν
  mine 92.2

ἐμπαιγμονή, ῆς f
  mock 33.406

ἐμπαιγμός, οῦ m
  mock 33.406

ἐμπαίζω
  (aor ἐνέπαιξα, aor
  pass ἐνεπαίχθην)
  a mock 33.406
  b trick 88.156

ἐμπαίκτης, ου m
  mocker 33.407

ἐμπεριπατέω
  live among 85.81

ἐμπεσοῦμαι
  see ἐμπίπτω

ἐμπί(μ)πλαμαι
  (aor ἐνεπλήσθην, subj
  ἐμπλησθῶ, pf ἐμπέ-
  πλησμαι)
  a become satisfied
    with food 23.18
  b enjoy 25.114

ἐμπί(μ)πλημι
(ptc ἐμπιπλῶν, aor
ἐνέπλησα)
satisfy with food *23.17*

ἐμπί(μ)πρημι
(aor ἐνέπρησα)
set on fire *14.65*

ἐμπιπλάομαι
see ἐμπί(μ)πλαμαι

ἐμπιπλάω
see ἐμπί(μ)πλημι

ἐμπίπτω
(fut ἐμπεσοῦμαι, aor
ἐνέπεσον)
a fall into *15.121*
b experience *90.71*

ἐμπλέκομαι
(aor ptc ἐμπλακείς)
involved in *90.81*

ἐμπλησθῶ
see ἐμπίμπλαμαι

ἐμπλοκή, ῆς f
braiding *49.26*

ἐμπνέω
ἐμπνέω : unit
ἐμπνέω ἀπειλῆς
threaten strongly ... *33.293*

ἐμπορεύομαι
a be in business *57.196*
b cheat *88.148*

ἐμπορία, ας f
business *57.196*

ἐμπόριον, ου n
marketplace *57.206*

ἔμπορος, ου m
merchant *57.203*

ἔμπροσθεν
a in front of *83.33*
b on the front *83.36*
c in the judgment of *90.20*

ἐμπτύω
spit *23.43*

ἐμφανής, ές
a visible *24.22*
b well-known *28.35*

ἐμφανίζω
a make visible *24.19*
b make known *28.36*
c tell *33.208*
d bring charges *56.8*

ἔμφοβος, ον
terrified *25.256*

ἐμφυσάω
breathe on......... *23.185*

ἔμφυτος, ον
established in *85.31*

ἐν
see εἰς

ἐν
a in (location) *83.13*
b among (location) ... *83.9*
c on (location) *83.47*
d at (location) *83.23*
e in (state) *13.8*
f into (extension) *84.22*
g in union with
(association) *89.119*
h with (attendant
circumstances)..... *89.80*
i with (instrument) .. *90.10*
j with (manner) *89.84*
k with regard to
(specification) *89.5*
l of (substance)...... *89.141*
m to (experiencer) *90.56*
n by (agent) *90.6*
o by (guarantor) *90.30*
p by (means) *89.76*
q because (reason).... *89.26*

r so that (result) *89.48*
s when (time) *67.33*
t during (time) *67.136*
u in (content) *90.23*
ἐν : units
ἐν ἀληθείᾳ
    really *70.4*
ἐν παρρησίᾳ
    publicly *28.29*
ἐν τῇ σκοτίᾳ
    privately *28.71*
ἐν (τῷ) κρυπτῷ
    privately *28.71*
ἐν παραβολῇ
    figuratively *33.17*
ἐν βάρει εἰμί
    claim importance ... *65.56*
ἐν γάστρι ἔχω
    be pregnant *23.50*
ἐν μεγάλῳ
    in a long time *67.89*
ἐν μέρει
    with regard to *89.5*
ἐν ὀλίγῳ
    a in a short time ... *67.106*
    b easily *22.41*
ἐν ῥιπῇ ὀφθαλμοῦ
    suddenly *67.114*
ἐν τῷ (καθ)εξῆς
    later *67.52*
ἐν τῷ μεταξύ
    meanwhile *67.138*
ἐν ᾧ
    as long as *67.139*
προβαίνω ἐν ἡμέραις
    be old *67.99*
εἰμί ἐν
    continue to do *68.20*
ἐνδημέω ἐν τῷ σώματι
    be alive *23.91*
(εἰμί) ἐν θανάτοις
    in danger of death *23.117*
ἐν τάχει
    (very) soon *67.56*
καθίζω ἐν δέξιᾳ
    be in high position .. *87.36*
ἔχω μέρος ἐν
    experience together *90.83*

ἐναγκαλίζομαι
    embrace *34.63*

ἐνάλιον, ου *n*
    sea creature *4.58*

ἔναντι
    a in front of *83.33*
    b in the judgment of *90.20*

ἐναντίας
    see ἐκ : units

ἐναντίον
    a in front of *83.33*
    b in the judgment of *90.20*

ἐναντιόομαι
    be hostile toward *39.1*

ἐναντίος, α, ον
    a against *82.11*
    b hostile *39.6*

ἐνάρχομαι
    begin *68.3*

ἔνατος, η, ον
    ninth *60.56*

ἐνγ-
    see ἐγγ-

ἐνδεής, ές
    poor *57.51*

ἔνδειγμα, τος *n*
    proof *28.52*

ἐνδείκνυμαι
    (aor ἐνεδειξάμην)
    a demonstrate *28.51*
    b do to *13.131*

ἔνδειξις, εως *f*
    proof *28.52*

ἔνδεκα
    eleven *60.20*

ἐνδέκατος, η, ον
    eleventh *60.58*

ἐνδέχεται
  be possible 71.4

ἐνδημέω
  be at home 85.20
  ἐνδημέω : unit
  ἐνδημέω ἐν τῷ σώματι
    be alive 23.91

ἐνδιδύσκω
  clothe 49.1

ἔνδικος, ον
  just 88.15

ἐνδοξάζομαι
  be honored 87.9

ἔνδοξος, ον
  a splendid 79.19
  b honored 87.6

ἔνδυμα, τος n
  clothing 6.162
  ἔνδυμα : unit
  ἔρχομαι ἐν ἐνδύμασιν
  προβάτων
    pretend to be good   88.233

ἐνδυναμόομαι
  become able 74.7

ἐνδυναμόω
  cause to be able 74.6

ἐνδύνω
  enter secretly 15.94

ἔνδυσις, εως f
  wear 49.11

ἐνδύω
  clothe 49.1

ἐνδώμησις, εως f
  a building material . . . 7.77
  b foundation 7.41

ἐνέβην
  see ἐμβαίνω

ἐνέγκαι
  see φέρω

ἐνέγκας
  see φέρω

ἐνεγκεῖν
  see φέρω

ἐνεδειξάμην
  see ἐνδείκνυμαι

ἐνέδρα, ας f
  ambush 39.51

ἐνεδρεύω
  a be in ambush 39.51
  b make plans against   30.70

ἐνειλέω
  wrap 79.118

ἔνειμι
  (ptc ἐνών)
  be inside 85.19

ἔνεκα
  see ἕνεκεν

ἕνεκεν
  a on account of 89.31
  b in order that 89.58
  c because of 90.43

ἐνέκρυψα
  see ἐγκρύπτω

ἐνέμεινα
  see ἐμμένω

ἐνενήκοντα
  ninety 60.32

ἐνεός, ά, όν
  speechless 33.108

ἐνέπαιξα
  see ἐμπαίζω

ἐνεπαίχθην
  see ἐμπαίζω

ἐνέπεσον
see ἐμπίπτω

ἐνέπλησα
see ἐμπί(μ)πλημι

ἐνεπλήσθην
see ἐμπί(μ)πλημι

ἐνέπρησα
see ἐμπί(μ)πρημι

ἐνέργεια, ας *f*
function *42.3*

ἐνεργέω
a function *42.3*
b cause to function . . . *42.4*
c bring about *13.9*

ἐνέργημα, τος *n*
deed *42.11*

ἐνεργής, ές
effective *13.124*

ἐνέστηκα
see ἐνίσταμαι

ἐνεστηκώς
see ἐνίσταμαι

ἐνεστώς
see ἐνίσταμαι

ἐνετειλάμην
see ἐντέλλομαι

ἐνετράπην
see ἐντρέπω

ἐνέτυχον
see ἐντυγχάνω

ἐνευλογέω
act kindly toward *88.69*

ἐνεχθείς
see φέρω

ἐνέχομαι
be under control *37.4*

ἐνέχω
a have grudge against *88.169*
b be hostile toward . . . *39.4*

ἐνθάδε
here *83.1*

ἔνθεν
from here *84.9*

ἐνθυμέομαι
think about *30.1*

ἐνθύμησις, εως *f*
thought *30.15*

ἔνι
exist *13.70*

ἐνιαυτός, οῦ *m*
a one year *67.168*
b era *67.146*

ἐνίσταμαι (+ pf act)
(pf ἐνέστηκα, ptc ἐν-
εστηκώς, ἐνεστώς, fut
midd ἐνστήσομαι)
a happen *13.109*
b present (time) *67.41*
c imminent *67.63*

ἐνισχύω
a strengthen *79.66*
b regain strength *79.65*

ἐνχ-
see ἐγχ-

ἐννέα
nine *60.18*

ἐννεύω
gesture *33.485*

ἔννοια, ας *f*
a way of thinking *30.5*
b intention *30.66*

ἔννομος, ον
a legal 33.336
b subject to law 33.342

ἔννυχα
at night 67.193

ἐνοικέω
dwell in 85.73

ἐνορκίζω
put under oath 33.467

ἑνός
see εἷς

ἑνότης, ητος f
unity 63.3

ἐνοχλέομαι
be afflicted 22.17

ἐνοχλέω
afflict 22.24

ἔνοχος, ον
a guilty 88.312
b guilty and deserving 88.313
c subject to 37.5

ἐνπ-
see ἐμπ-

ἐνστήσομαι
see ἐνίσταμαι

ἔνταλμα, τος n
commandment 33.330

ἐνταφιάζω
prepare for burial 52.6

ἐνταφιασμός, οῦ m
preparation for burial 52.6

ἐντέλλομαι
(fut ἐντελοῦμαι, aor
ἐνετειλάμην, ptc ἐντει-
λάμενος, pf ἐντέταλμαι)
command 33.329

ἐντεῦθεν
a from here 84.9
b from this 92.34

ἔντευξις, εως f
intercession 33.347

ἔντιμος, ον
a valuable 65.2
b honored 87.6

ἐντολή, ῆς f
commandment 33.330

ἐντόπιος, ου m
local people 11.60

ἐντός
a among 83.9
b what is inside 83.17

ἐντρέπομαι
(fut ἐντραπήσομαι)
respect 87.11

ἐντρέπω
(aor subj pass ἐντραπῆν)
make ashamed 25.196

ἐντρέφω
train 33.242

ἔντρομος, ον
a trembling 16.6
b fearful 25.261

ἐντροπή, ῆς f
shame 25.195

ἐντρυφάω
carouse 88.253

ἐντυγχάνω
(aor ἐνέτυχον)
a plead 33.169
b intercede 33.347

ἐντυλίσσω
a wrap 79.118
b roll up 79.120

ἐντυπόω
engrave 33.67

ἐνυβρίζω
insult 33.390

ἔνυξα
see νύσσω

ἐνυπνιάζομαι
dream 33.487

ἐνύπνιον, ου *n*
dream 33.486

ἐνφ-
see ἐμφ-

ἐνών
see ἔνειμι

ἐνώπιον
a in front of 83.33
b in the opinion of . . . 90.20

Ἐνώς *m*
Enos 93.117

ἐνωτίζομαι
listen carefully to 24.62

Ἐνώχ *m*
Enoch 93.118

ἐξ
see ἐκ

ἕξ
six 60.15

ἐξαγγέλλω
(aor ἐξήγγειλα)
proclaim throughout . . 33.204

ἐξαγοράζομαι
ἐξαγοράζομαι : unit
ἐξαγοράζομαι τὸν καιρόν
  a make good use of
    opportunity 65.42
  b work urgently . . . 68.73

ἐξαγοράζω
redeem 37.131

ἐξάγω
(aor ἐξήγαγον)
lead out 15.174

ἐξαιρέομαι
(aor ἐξειλάμην, inf
ἐξελέσθαι)
a rescue 21.17
b choose 30.90

ἐξαιρέω
(aor ἐξεῖλον, impv ἔξελε)
take out 85.43

ἐξαίρω
(aor impv 2 pl ἐξάρατε)
exclude 34.36

ἐξαιτέομαι
(aor ἐξῃτησάμην)
ask with success 33.166

ἐξαίφνης
immediately 67.113

ἐξακολουθέω
a follow 36.33
b imitate 41.48

ἐξακόσιοι, αι, α
six hundred 60.38

ἐξαλείφω
a wipe away 47.18
b eliminate 13.102

ἐξάλλομαι
jump up 15.240

ἐξανάστασις, εως *f*
resurrection 23.93

ἐξανατέλλω
sprout leaves 23.195

ἐξανίσταμαι (+ 2 aor)
(aor ἐξανέστην)
stand up 17.11

ἐξανίστημι
(aor ἐξανέστησα)
ἐξανίστημι : unit
ἐξανίστημι σπέρμα
　beget............ *23.59*

ἐξαπατάω
deceive............ *31.12*

ἐξάπινα
immediately........ *67.113*

ἐξαπορέομαι
despair............ *25.237*

ἐξαποστέλλω
(fut ἐξαποστελῶ, aor
ἐξαπέστειλα, aor pass
ἐξαπεστάλην)
a send out.......... *15.68*
b send a message..... *15.67*

ἐξάρατε
see ἐξαίρω

ἐξαρτίζω
a bring to an end *67.71*
b make adequate *75.5*

ἐξαστράπτω
glisten *14.47*

ἐξαυτῆς
immediately........ *67.113*

ἐξέβαλον
see ἐκβάλλω

ἐξέβην
see ἐκβαίνω

ἐξεβλήθην
see ἐκβάλλω

ἐξεγείρω
(fut ἐξεγερῶ, aor ἐξή-
γειρα)
a raise to life *23.94*
b cause to exist *13.83*
c give higher status to *87.38*

ἐξεδόμην
see ἐκδίδομαι

ἐξειλάμην
see ἐξαιρέομαι

ἐξεῖλον
see ἐξαιρέω

ἔξειμι
(inf ἐξιέναι, ptc ἐξιών,
impf 3 pl ἐξήεσαν)
go out of 15.40

ἐξεκαύθην
see ἐκκαίομαι

ἐξεκόπην
see ἐκκόπτω

ἐξεκρεμάμην
see ἐκκρέμαμαι

ἔξελε
see ἐξαιρέω

ἐξελέξω
see ἐκλέγομαι

ἐξελέσθαι
see ἐξαιρέομαι

ἐξελεύσομαι
see ἐξέρχομαι

ἐξελήλυθα
see ἐξέρχομαι

ἐξέλκω
lure away *31.74*

ἐξέμαξα
see ἐκμάσσω

ἐξενεγκεῖν
see ἐκφέρω

ἐξέπεσον
see ἐκπίπτω

ἐξεπέτασα
  see ἐκπετάννυμι

ἐξεπλάγην
  see ἐκπλήσσομαι

ἐξέπλευσα
  see ἐκπλέω

ἐξέπνευσα
  see ἐκπνέω

ἐξέραμα, τος n
  vomit *8.70*

ἐξεραυνάω
  seek diligently *27.35*

ἐξέρχομαι
  (fut ἐξελεύσομαι, aor
  ἐξῆλθον, pf ἐξελήλυθα)
  a go out *15.40*
  b pass away *13.93*
  ἐξέρχομαι : units
  ἐξέρχομαι ἐν τῆς ὀσφύος
    be born of *23.60*
  εἰσέρχομαι καὶ ἐξέρχομαι
    live with *41.24*

ἐξεστακέναι
  see ἐξίστημι

ἐξέστην
  see ἐξίσταμαι

ἐξέστησα
  see ἐξίστημι

ἔξεστι
  (ptc ἐξόν)
  a be possible *71.1*
  b ought to *71.32*

ἐξέστραμμαι
  see ἐκστρέφομαι

ἐξετάζω
  a try to find out *27.37*
  b inquire *33.182*

ἐξετέθην
  see ἐκτίθεμαι

ἐξέτεινα
  see ἐκτείνω

ἐξετράπην
  see ἐκτρέπομαι

ἐξέφυγον
  see ἐκφεύγω

ἐξέχεα
  see ἐκχέω

ἐξεχύθην
  see ἐκχέομαι

ἐξέωσαι
  see ἐξωθέω

ἐξήγαγον
  see ἐξάγω

ἐξήγγειλα
  see ἐξαγγέλλω

ἐξήγειρα
  see ἐξεγείρω

ἐξηγέομαι
  a tell fully *33.201*
  b make fully known . . *28.41*

ἐξήεσαν
  see ἔξειμι

ἐξήκοντα
  sixty *60.29*

ἐξῆλθον
  see ἐξέρχομαι

ἐξήνεγκα
  see ἐκφέρω

ἐξῆς
ἐξῆς : units
τῇ ἐξῆς
   the next day *67.208*
ἐν τῷ ἐξῆς
   see καθεξῆς

ἐξητησάμην
see ἐξαιτέομαι

ἐξηχέομαι
proclaim *33.222*

ἐξιέναι
see ἔξειμι

ἕξις, εως *f*
practice *42.10*

ἐξίσταμαι (+ 2 aor)
(aor ἐξέστην, impf
ἐξιστάμην)
a be greatly astonished *25.218*
b be insane *30.24*

ἐξιστάνω
see ἐξίστημι

ἐξίστημι
(aor ἐξέστησα, pf inf
ἐξεσταχέναι)
astonish greatly *25.220*

ἐξισχύω
be fully able *74.10*

ἐξιών
see ἔξειμι

ἔξοδος, ου *f*
a departure *15.42*
b death *23.101*

ἐξοίσω
see ἐκφέρω

ἐξολεθρεύω
destroy *20.35*

ἐξομολογέομαι
a profess *33.274*
b admit *33.275*
c give thanks *33.351*
d praise *33.359*

ἐξομολογέω
agree *33.278*

ἐξόν
see ἔξεστι

ἐξορκίζω
put under oath *33.467*

ἐξορκιστής, οῦ *m*
exorcist *53.103*

ἐξορύσσω
dig out *19.42*

ἐξουδενέω
ill-treat *88.133*

ἐξουθενέω
despise *88.195*

ἐξουσία, ας *f*
a authority to rule ... *37.35*
b jurisdiction *37.36*
c symbol of authority *37.37*
d ruler *37.38*
e control *37.13*
f power *76.12*
g supernatural power *12.44*
h right to judge *30.122*
ἐξουσία : unit
ἄρχων τῆς ἐξουσίας
τοῦ ἀέρος
   supernatural power *12.44*

ἐξουσιάζω
reign *37.48*

ἐξουσιαστικός, ή, όν
authoritative *37.41*

ἐξοχή, ῆς *f*
high rank *87.19*

ἐξυπνίζω
cause to wake up *23.77*

ἔξυπνος, ον
awakened *23.75*

ἔξω
a outside *83.20*
b away *84.27*
ἔξω : units
ὁ ἔξω
outsider *11.10*
ὁ ἔξω ἄνθρωπος
body *8.3*

ἔξω
see ἔχω

ἔξωθεν
a from outside *84.15*
b outside *83.20*
c the outside of *83.21*
ἔξωθεν : unit
ὁ ἔξωθεν
outsider *11.10*

ἐξωθέω
(aor ἔξωσα, inf
ἐξῶσαι, ἐξέωσαι)
a drive away *15.45*
b run aground *54.17*

ἐξώτερος, α, ον
ἐξώτερος : unit
τὸ σκότος τὸ ἐξώτερον
abode of evil spirits *1.23*

ἔοικα
be like *64.4*

ἑόρακα
see ὁράω

ἑορτάζω
celebrate *51.1*

ἑορτή, ῆς f
festival *51.2*

ἐπαγγελία, ας f
a promise *33.288*
b agreement *33.280*

ἐπαγγέλλομαι
(aor ἐπηγγειλάμην,
pf ἐπήγγελμαι)
a promise *33.286*
b assert *33.219*

ἐπάγγελμα, τος n
promise *33.288*

ἐπάγω
(aor inf ἐπαγαγεῖν,
ptc ἐπάξας)
bring upon *13.9*

ἐπαγωνίζομαι
struggle for *39.30*

ἔπαθον
see πάσχω

ἐπαθροίζομαι
gather together more . . *15.132*

Ἐπαίνετος, ου m
Epaenetus *93.119*

ἐπαινέω
(aor ἐπήνεσα)
praise *33.354*

ἔπαινος, ου m
a praise *33.354*
b what is to be
praised *33.355*

ἐπαίρομαι
a rise up against *39.38*
b be arrogant *88.212*

ἐπαίρω
(aor ἐπῆρα, inf
ἐπᾶραι, ptc ἐπάρας,
aor pass ἐπήρθην)
raise *15.105*
ἐπαίρω : units
ἐπαίρω τὴν κεφαλήν
have courage *25.160*

ἐπαίρω τοὺς ὀφθαλμούς
look 24.34
ἐπαίρω τὴν πτέρναν
oppose 39.3
ἐπαίρω φώνην
speak loudly 33.78

ἐπαισχύνομαι
be ashamed of 25.193

ἐπαιτέω
beg 33.173

ἐπακολουθέω
a devote oneself to . . . 25.79
b happen along 13.113
ἐπακολουθέω : unit
ἐπακολουθέω τοῖς ἴχνεσιν
imitate 41.47

ἐπακούω
listen to 24.60

ἐπακροάομαι
listen to 24.61

ἐπάν
whenever 67.31

ἐπάναγκες
necessary 71.39

ἐπανάγω
(aor inf ἐπαναγαγεῖν)
a return to 15.91
b put out to sea 54.5

ἐπαναμιμνήσκω
remind 29.10

ἐπαναπαύομαι
(fut pass ἐπαναπαήσομαι)
a remain 13.25
b trust in 31.83

ἐπανέρχομαι
(aor inf ἐπανελθεῖν)
return to 15.91

ἐπανίσταμαι
rebel against 39.34

ἐπανόρθωσις, εως f
correcting faults 72.16

ἐπάνω
a on, above 83.49
b more than 78.30
c superior 87.31

ἐπάξας
see ἐπάγω

ἐπᾶραι
see ἐπαίρω

ἐπάρας
see ἐπαίρω

ἐπάρατος, ον
accursed 33.475

ἐπαρκέω
a help 35.1
b provide for 35.32

ἐπαρχεία, ας f
province 1.84

ἔπαυλις, εως f
residence 7.4

ἐπαύριον
ἐπαύριον : unit
τῇ ἐπαύριον
the next day 67.208

Ἐπαφρᾶς, ᾶ m
Epaphras 93.120

ἐπαφρίζω
cause to foam up 14.29

Ἐπαφρόδιτος, ου m
Epaphroditus 93.121

ἐπέβαλον
see ἐπιβάλλω

ἐπέβην
see ἐπιβαίνω

ἐπεγείρω
(aor ἐπήγειρα)
commence 68.9

ἐπέγνωκα
see ἐπιγινώσκω

ἐπέγνων
see ἐπιγινώσκω

ἐπεγνώσθην
see ἐπιγινώσκω

ἐπεδίδου
see ἐπιδίδωμι

ἐπεδόθην
see ἐπιδίδωμι

ἐπέδωκα
see ἐπιδίδωμι

ἐπεθέμην
see ἐπιτίθεμαι

ἐπέθηκα
see ἐπιτίθημι

ἐπεί
because 89.32

ἐπειδή
a because 89.32
b when 67.45

ἐπειδήπερ
because 89.32

ἐπεῖδον
see ἐφοράω

ἐπειθόμην
see πείθω, πείθομαι

ἔπεισα
see πείθω

ἐπεισαγωγή, ῆς f
introduction 68.10

ἐπεισείσαντες
see ἐπισείω

ἐπεισέρχομαι
(fut ἐπεισελεύσομαι)
happen 13.119

ἔπειτα
later 67.44

ἐπέκειλα
see ἐπικέλλω

ἐπέκεινα
beyond 83.55

ἐπεκεκλήμην
see ἐπικαλέομαι

ἐπεκλήθην
see ἐπικαλέω

ἐπεκτείνομαι
a stretch toward 16.20
b try hard to 13.20

ἐπελαβόμην
see ἐπιλαμβάνομαι

ἐπελαθόμην
see ἐπιλανθάνομαι

ἐπελεύσομαι
see ἐπέρχομαι

ἐπέλθοι
see ἐπέρχομαι

ἐπέμεινα
see ἐπιμένω

ἐπενδύομαι
put on garment 49.2

ἐπενδύτης, ου m
cloak 6.172

ἐπενεγκεῖν
see ἐπιφέρω

ἐπεποίθειν
see πείθω

ἐπέρχομαι
(fut ἐπελεύσομαι, aor
ἐπῆλθον, ptc ἐπελθών,
opt 3 sg ἐπέλθοι)
a arrive *15.83*
b assault *39.47*
c happen *13.119*

ἐπερωτάω
a ask *33.180*
b ask for *33.161*
c interrogate *56.14*

ἐπερώτημα, τος *n*
request *33.162*

ἔπεσα
see πίπτω

ἐπέστειλα
see ἐπιστέλλω

ἐπέστην
see ἐφίσταμαι

ἐπεστράφην
see ἐπιστρέφω

ἐπετίθεσαν
see ἐπιτίθημι

ἐπετράπην
see ἐπιτρέπω

ἐπέτυχον
see ἐπιτυγχάνω

ἐπεφάνην
see ἐπιφαίνομαι

ἐπέχω
(aor ἐπέσχον)
a be alert for *27.59*
b hold firmly to *31.47*
c watch *24.33*
d stay on *85.59*

ἐπηγγειλάμην
see ἐπαγγέλλομαι

ἐπήγγελμαι
see ἐπαγγέλλομαι

ἐπήγειρα
see ἐπεγείρω

ἐπῆλθον
see ἐπέρχομαι

ἐπήνεσα
see ἐπαινέω

ἔπηξα
see πήγνυμι

ἐπῆρα
see ἐπαίρω

ἐπηρεάζω
mistreat *88.129*

ἐπήρθην
see ἐπαίρω

ἐπί
a upon (location) *83.46*
b at (location) *83.23*
c among (location) . . . *83.9*
d before (location) *83.35*
e toward (extension) . . *84.17*
f onto (extension) *84.20*
g upon (responsibility) *90.17*
h to (experiencer) *90.57*
i by (instrument) *90.9*
j against (opposition) *90.34*
k for (benefaction) . . . *90.40*
l and (addition) *89.101*
m over (authority) *37.9*
n because of (reason) *89.27*
o in order to (purpose) *89.60*
p concerning (content) *90.23*
q in view of (basis) . . . *89.13*
r up to (degree) *78.51*
s at, when (time) *67.33*
t during (time) *67.136*
u by (agent) *90.5*

ἐπί : units
ἐπ' ἀληθείας
  really *70.4*
ἐπ' εὐλογίαις
  large amount *59.56*
ἐπὶ θύραις
  (very) soon *67.58*
ἐπὶ πολύ
  for a long time *67.89*
ἐφ' ἱκανόν
  for a long time *67.91*
τὴν μέριμναν
ἐπιρίπτω ἐπί
  stop worrying and
  trust *25.250*
ἐπιρίπτω ἐπί
  make responsible for *90.18*
ἐπιστρέφω καρδίας ἐπί
  make friendly toward *25.95*
ἐπὶ τῆς Μωϋσέως
καθέδρας καθίστημι
  be authority on
  Law of Moses *37.44*
ἐπιβάλλω τὴν χεῖρα
ἐπ' ἀροτρὸν καὶ
βλέπω εἰς τὰ ὀπίσω
  start to do and
  then hesitate *68.6*
ἐπιβάλλω τὰς χεῖρας/
τὴν χεῖρα (ἐπί)
  arrest *37.110*
ἐκτείνω τὰς χεῖρας ἐπί
  arrest *37.110*
πίπτω ἐπί τινα
  cause to suffer *24.93*
ὁ ἐπὶ τόπον πλέων
  sea traveller *54.27*
ἐπὶ τὴν κεφαλήν
  responsibility *37.102*
κρεμάννυμι ἐπὶ ξύλου
  crucify *20.76*
ἀναβαίνω ἐπὶ καρδίαν
  begin to think *30.17*

ἐπιβαίνω
(aor ἐπέβην, ptc ἐπι-
βάς, pf ἐπιβέβηκα)
a arrive *15.83*
b go onto *15.97*

ἐπιβάλλω
(fut ἐπιβαλῶ, aor
ἐπέβαλον)
a throw on *15.218*
b put on *85.51*
c splash into *14.21*
d belong to *57.3*
e think about seriously *30.7*
f begin *68.5*
ἐπιβάλλω : units
ἐπιβάλλω τὰς χεῖρας/
τὴν χεῖρα (ἐπί)
  arrest *37.110*
ἐπιβάλλω τὴν χεῖρα
ἐπ' ἄροτρον καὶ
βλέπω εἰς τὰ ὀπίσω
  start to do and
  then hesitate *68.6*
βρόχον ἐπιβάλλω
  impose restrictions *37.2*

ἐπιβαρέω
  be financial burden . . . *57.224*

ἐπιβάς
  see ἐπιβαίνω

ἐπιβέβηκα
  see ἐπιβαίνω

ἐπιβιβάζω
  cause to mount *15.98*

ἐπιβλέπω
a notice *24.12*
b pay attention to *30.45*
c help *35.8*
d pay respect to *87.17*

ἐπίβλημα, τος *n*
  patch *6.157*

ἐπιβουλή, ῆς *f*
  plot *30.71*

ἐπιγαμβρεύω
  marry *34.71*

ἐπίγειος, ον
a on the earth *1.41*
b human *9.7*

ἐπιγίνομαι
(aor ptc ἐπιγενόμενος)
happen 13.107

ἐπιγινώσκω
(fut ἐπιγνώσομαι, aor
ἐπέγνων, subj ἐπι-
γνῶ, ptc ἐπιγνούς, pf
ἐπέγνωκα, aor pass
ἐπεγνώσθην)
a know about 28.2
b understand 32.16
c learn about 27.8
d recognize 27.61
e acknowledge 31.27

ἐπίγνωσις, εως f
a knowledge
(activity) 28.2
b knowledge
(content) 28.18
ἐπίγνωσις : units
εἰς ἐπίγνωσιν ἔρχομαι
a learn about 27.4
b come to under-
stand 32.17
ἔχω ἐν ἐπιγνώσει
acknowledge 31.28

ἐπιγραφή, ῆς f
inscription 33.46

ἐπιγράφω
write on 33.65

ἔπιδε
see ἐφοράω

ἐπιδείκνυμι
(aor impv 2 pl ἐπιδεί-
ξατε)
a cause to be seen 24.25
b show to be true 72.5

ἐπιδέχομαι
a welcome 34.53
b obey 36.14

ἐπιδημέω
live as a foreigner 85.78

ἐπιδιατάσσομαι
add to 59.73

ἐπιδίδωμι
(impf 3 sg ἐπεδίδου,
fut ἐπιδώσω, aor ἐπέ-
δωκα, ptc ἐπιδούς,
subj 3 sg ἐπιδῷ, aor
pass ἐπεδόθην)
a give to 57.75
b yield 39.21

ἐπιδιορθόω
put into order 62.4

ἐπιδύω
go down (upon) 15.114

ἐπιείκεια, ας f
gentleness 88.62

ἐπιεικής, ές
gentle 88.63

ἐπιζητέω
a try to find out 27.42
b desire 25.9

ἐπιθανάτιος, ον
sentenced to die 23.116

ἐπιθεῖναι
see ἐπιτίθημι

ἐπιθείς
see ἐπιτίθημι

ἐπίθες
see ἐπιτίθημι

ἐπίθεσις, εως f
laying on 85.51

ἐπιθήσω
see ἐπιτίθημι

ἐπιθυμέω
a desire greatly 25.12
b lust 25.20

ἐπιθυμητής, οῦ m
one who greatly
desires 25.13

ἐπιθυμία, ας f
a deep desire 25.12
b lust 25.20

ἐπιθῶ
see ἐπιτίθημι

ἐπικαθίζω
sit upon 17.15

ἐπικαλέομαι
(pf ἐπικέκλημαι, plpf
ἐπεκεκλήμην)
a ask for help 33.176
b appeal to a higher
court 56.15
ἐπικαλέομαι : unit
ἐπικαλέομαι τὸ ὄνομά
τινος ἐπί τινα
be people of 11.28

ἐπικαλέω
(aor pass ἐπεκλήθην)
call 33.131

ἐπικάλυμμα, τος n
pretext 28.56

ἐπικαλύπτω
forgive 40.11

ἐπικατάρατος, ον
accursed 33.475

ἐπίκειμαι
a lie on 85.4
b press against 19.43
c be in force 76.17
d keep on 68.16
e exist 13.73

ἐπικέκλημαι
see ἐπικαλέομαι

ἐπικέλλω
(aor ἐπέκειλα)
run aground 54.18

Ἐπικούρειος, η, ον
Epicurean 11.96

ἐπικουρία, ας f
help 35.7

ἐπικράνθην
see πικραίνω

ἐπικρίνω
decide 30.75

ἐπιλαμβάνομαι
(aor ἐπελαβόμην)
a take hold of 18.2
b arrest 37.110
c trap 27.32
d help 35.1
e be concerned for . . . 30.42
f experience 90.63

ἐπιλανθάνομαι
(aor ἐπελαθόμην,
inf ἐπιλαθέσθαι,
pf ἐπιλέλησμαι)
a forget 29.14
b neglect 29.17

ἐπιλέγομαι
choose 30.88

ἐπιλέγω
name 33.129

ἐπιλείπω
fail 13.41

ἐπιλείχω
lick 23.42

ἐπιλέλησμαι
see ἐπιλανθάνομαι

ἐπιλησμονή, ῆς f
forgetting 29.14

ἐπίλοιπος, ον
remaining 63.21

ἐπίλυσις, εως f
explanation 33.141

ἐπιλύω
  a explain *33.141*
  b resolve *30.81*

ἐπιμαρτυρέω
  witness *33.262*

ἐπιμέλεια, ας *f*
  taking care of *35.44*

ἐπιμελέομαι
  a take care of *35.44*
  b think about *30.40*

ἐπιμελῶς
  carefully *30.41*

ἐπιμένω
  (aor ἐπέμεινα, inf
  ἐπιμεῖναι)
  a remain *85.55*
  b continue *68.11*

ἐπινεύω
  agree *33.279*

ἐπίνοια, ας *f*
  intention *30.66*

ἔπιον
  see πίνω

ἐπιορκέω
  a break an oath *33.464*
  b swear falsely *33.465*

ἐπίορκος, ου *m*
  perjurer *33.466*

ἐπιοῦσα, ης *f*
  ἐπιοῦσα : unit
  τῇ ἐπιούσῃ
    on the next day *67.208*

ἐπιούσιος, ον
  a daily *67.183*
  b today *67.206*

ἐπιπίπτω
  (aor ἐπέπεσον, pf ἐπι-
  πέπτωκα)
  a press against *19.43*
  b happen *13.122*
  ἐπιπίπτω : unit
  ἐπιπίπτω ἐπὶ τὸν τρά-
  χηλον
    embrace *34.64*

ἐπιπλήσσω
  rebuke *33.420*

ἐπιποθέω
  a deeply desire *25.18*
  b have great affection
    for *25.47*

ἐπιπόθησις, εως *f*
  deep desire *25.18*

ἐπιπόθητος, ον
  longed for *25.48*

ἐπιποθία, ας *f*
  deep desire *25.18*

ἐπιπορεύομαι
  arrive *15.83*

ἐπιράπτω
  sew on *48.5*

ἐπιράσθην
  see πειράζω

ἐπιρίπτω
  throw on *15.219*
  ἐπιρίπτω : units
  τὴν μέριμναν ἐπιρίπτω ἐπί
    stop worrying and
    trust *25.250*
  ἐπιρίπτω ἐπί
    make responsible for *90.18*

ἐπισείω
  (aor ptc ἐπεισείσαντες)
  start a riot *39.44*

ἐπίσημος, ον
  well known *28.31*

ἐπισιτισμός, οῦ *m*
food *5.1*

ἐπισκέπτομαι
a select carefully *30.102*
b visit *34.50*
c take care of *35.39*
d be present *85.11*

ἐπισκευάζομαι
get ready *77.8*

ἐπισκηνόω
take up residence *85.75*

ἐπισκιάζω
cast a shadow upon . . . *14.62*

ἐπισκοπεύω
see ἐπισκοπέω

ἐπισκοπέω
a take care of *35.39*
b guard against *30.46*
c minister unto *53.70*

ἐπισκοπή, ῆς *f*
a visitation *34.51*
b office as a church
leader *53.69*
c position of
responsibility *35.40*

ἐπίσκοπος, ου *m*
a guardian *35.43*
b church leader *53.71*

ἐπισπάομαι
conceal circumcision . . *53.52*

ἐπισπείρω
sow on top of *43.8*

ἐπίσταμαι
a know *28.3*
b understand *32.3*

ἐπιστάς
see ἐφίσταμαι

ἐπίστασις, εως *f*
a anxiety *25.239*
b rebellion *39.34*
c responsibility for . . . *35.42*

ἐπιστάτης, ου *m*
master *87.50*

ἐπιστέλλω
(aor ἐπέστειλα, inf
ἐπιστεῖλαι)
write a letter *33.49*

ἐπιστῇ
see ἐφίσταμαι

ἐπίστηθι
see ἐφίσταμαι

ἐπιστήμων, ον
intelligent *32.27*

ἐπιστηρίζω
strengthen *74.19*

ἐπιστολή, ῆς *f*
a letter (object) *6.63*
b letter (content) *33.48*

ἐπιστομίζω
put to silence *33.124*

ἐπιστρέφομαι
(aor ptc ἐπιστραφείς)
turn around *16.13*

ἐπιστρέφω
(aor ἐπέστρεφα, aor pass
ἐπεστράφην)
a return *15.90*
b change one's beliefs *31.60*
c cause to change
beliefs *31.61*
d change one's ways   *41.51*
ἐπιστρέφω : unit
ἐπιστρέφω καρδίας ἐπί
make friendly
toward *25.95*

ἐπιστροφή, ῆς *f*
  a change of one's
    beliefs *31.60*
  b change of one's
    ways *41.51*

ἐπιστῶ
  see ἐφίσταμαι

ἐπισυνάγομαι
  come together *15.124*

ἐπισυνάγω
  (aor inf ἐπισυναγαγεῖν
  and ἐπισυνάξαι)
  cause to come together *15.126*

ἐπισυναγωγή, ῆς *f*
  a gathering together . . *15.126*
  b assembling *15.128*

ἐπισυντρέχω
  run together to a place *15.134*

ἐπισφαλής, ές
  dangerous *21.3*

ἐπισχύω
  persist in *68.71*

ἐπισωρεύω
  increase greatly *59.65*

ἐπιταγή, ῆς *f*
  a ordinance *33.326*
  b authority *37.42*

ἐπιτάσσω
  command *33.325*

ἐπιτελέω
  a complete *68.22*
  b bring about *13.108*
  c erect *45.2*

ἐπιτήδειος, α, ον
  needed *57.48*

ἐπιτίθεμαι
  (fut ἐπιθήσομαι, aor
  ἐπεθέμην)
  a give *57.78*
  b attack *39.47*

ἐπιτίθημι
  (3 pl ἐπιτιθέασιν, impv
  ἐπιτίθει, impf 3 pl
  ἐπετίθεσαν, fut ἐπιθήσω,
  aor ἐπέθηκα, impv
  ἐπίθες, subj ἐπιθῶ, inf
  ἐπιθεῖναι, ptc ἐπιθείς)
  a place on *85.51*
  b add *59.72*
  c subject to *90.87*
  ἐπιτίθημι : units
  ἐπιτίθημι ὄνομα
    give a name to *33.128*
  ἐπιτίθημι ζυγὸν ἐπὶ
  τὸν τράχηλον
    load down with
    obligations *22.27*

ἐπιτιμάω
  a rebuke *33.419*
  b command *33.331*

ἐπιτιμία, ας *f*
  punishment *38.6*

ἐπιτρέπω
  (aor pass ἐπετράπην)
  allow *13.138*

ἐπιτροπή, ῆς *f*
  authority *37.40*

ἐπίτροπος, ου *m*
  a foreman *37.86*
  b guide *36.5*

ἐπιτυγχάνω
  (aor ἐπέτυχον, inf
  ἐπιτυχεῖν)
  a acquire *57.60*
  b experience *90.61*

ἐπιφαίνομαι
  (aor ἐπεφάνην)
  appear *24.21*

ἐπιφαίνω
(aor inf ἐπιφᾶναι)
illuminate *14.39*

ἐπιφάνεια, ας *f*
appearance *24.21*

ἐπιφανής, ές
wonderful *79.22*

ἐπιφαύσκω
(fut ἐπιφαύσω)
illuminate *14.39*

ἐπιφέρω
(aor inf ἐπενεγκεῖν)
cause to experience . . . *90.94*

ἐπιφωνέω
cry out *33.77*

ἐπιφώσκω
dawn *14.41*

ἐπιχειρέω
try *68.59*

ἐπιχέω
pour on *47.6*

ἐπιχορηγέω
a provide for *35.31*
b add *59.74*

ἐπιχορηγία, ας *f*
provision *35.31*

ἐπιχρίω
rub on *47.15*

ἐπλάσθην
see πλάσσω

ἐπλήγην
see πλήσσω

ἔπλησα
see πίμπλημι

ἐπλήσθην
see πίμπλημι

ἔπνευσα
see πνέω

ἐποικοδομέω
a build upon *45.5*
b make more able *74.15*

ἐπονομάζομαι
call oneself *33.132*

ἐποπτεύω
watch *24.45*

ἐπόπτης, ου *m*
eyewitness *24.46*

ἔπος, ους *n*
ἔπος : unit
ὡς ἔπος εἰπεῖν
so to speak *33.139*

ἐπουράνιος, ον
a in the sky *1.8*
b heavenly *1.12*
c from God *12.17*
ἐπουράνιος : units
σῶμα ἐπουράνιον
heavenly body *1.26*
τὰ πνευματικὰ τῆς πονη-
ρίας ἐν τοῖς ἐπουρανίοις
supernatural powers *12.44*

ἐπράθην
see πιπράσκω

ἐπρήσθησαν
see ἐπρίσθησαν

ἐπρίσθησαν
see πρίζω

ἑπτά
seven *60.16*

ἑπτάκις
seven times *60.73*

ἑπτακισχίλιοι, αι, α
seven thousand *60.44*

ἐπυθόμην
see πυνθάνομαι

Ἔραστος, ου *m*
Erastus *93.122*

ἐραυνάω
try to learn *27.34*

ἐργάζομαι
(aor ἠργασάμην, εἰργα-
σάμην, pf εἴργασμαι)
a work *42.41*
b do business *57.198*
c perform *90.47*
d bring about *13.9*

ἐργασία, ας *f*
a behavior *41.20*
b business *57.198*
c profit *57.193*
ἐργασία : unit
δίδωμι ἐργασίαν
do one's best *68.62*

ἐργάτης, ου *m*
a worker *42.43*
b doer *41.21*

ἔργον, ου *n*
a act *42.11*
b work............ *42.42*
c workmanship...... *42.12*

ἐρεθίζω
a make resentful *88.168*
b cause *90.55*

ἐρείδω
become fixed *15.5*

ἐρεύγομαι
announce *33.192*

ἐρημία, ας *f*
lonely place *1.86*

ἐρημόομαι
be destroyed *20.41*

ἔρημος, ον
a uninhabited *85.84*
b lonely place *1.86*
c forsaken *35.55*
ἔρημος : unit
ἔρημος τόπος
lonely place *1.86*

ἐρήμωσις, εως *f*
be destroyed *20.41*
ἐρήμωσις : unit
τὸ βδέλυγμα τῆς ἐρη-
μώσεως
horrible thing which
defiles *53.38*

ἐρίζω
quarrel............. *33.447*

ἐριθεία, ας *f*
a selfish ambition *88.167*
b hostility *39.7*

ἔριον, ου *n*
a wool (body part) ... *8.15*
b wool (artifact)...... *6.171*

ἔρις, ιδος *f*
a strife............. *39.22*
b quarrel *33.447*

ἐρίφιον, ου *n*
he-goat............. *4.19*

ἔριφος, ου *m*
he-goat............. *4.19*

ἔριψα
see ῥίπτω

Ἑρμᾶς, ᾶ *m*
Hermas *93.123*

ἑρμηνεία, ας *f*
interpretation *33.147*

ἑρμηνεύω
translate............ *33.145*

Ἑρμῆς, οῦ *m*
Hermes *93.124*

Ἑρμογένης, ους *m*
Hermogenes *93.125*

ἑρπετόν, οῦ *n*
reptile *4.51*

ἔρραμαι
see ῥαίνω

ἐρραντισμένος
see ῥαντίζω

ἐρρέθην
see λέγω

ἔρρηξα
see ῥήγνυμι

ἐρρίζωμαι
see ῥιζόομαι

ἔρριμμαι
see ῥίπτω

ἐρρυσάμην
see ῥύομαι

ἐρρύσθην
see ῥύομαι

ἔρρωσθε
see ῥώννυμαι

ἔρρωσο
see ῥώννυμαι

ἐρυθρός, ά, όν
red *79.30*

ἔρχομαι
(impf ἠρχόμην, fut
ἐλεύσομαι, aor ἦλθον,
ἦλθα, inf ἐλθεῖν, pf
ἐλήλυθα)
a go, come *15.7*
b come *15.81*
c become *13.50*
d happen to *13.117*
ἔρχομαι : units
ἔρχομαι εἰς
result in *89.43*

εἰς τὸ χεῖρον ἔρχομαι
become more sick . . *23.150*
ἔρχομαι ἐν ἐνδύμασιν
προβάτων
pretend to be good *88.233*
εἰς ἐπίγνωσιν ἔρχομαι
a learn about *27.4*
b come to under-
stand *32.17*

ἐρῶ
see λέγω

ἐρωτάω
a ask *33.180*
b ask for *33.161*

ἔσβεσα
see σβέννυμι

ἐσήμανα
see σημαίνω

ἐσθής, ῆτος *f*
clothing *6.162*

ἐσθήσεσι
see ἐσθής

ἐσθίω
(fut φάγομαι, aor ἔφαγον
inf φαγεῖν)
a eat *23.1*
b destroy *20.44*
ἐσθίω : unit
τὸν ἑαυτοῦ ἄρτον ἐσθίω
earn a living *57.190*

ἔσκυλμαι
see σκύλλω

Ἐσλί *m*
Esli *93.126*

ἐσμυρνισμένον
see σμυρνίζω

ἔσομαι
see εἰμί

ἔσοπτρον, ου *n*
mirror *6.221*

ἔσπαρμαι
  see σπείρω

ἑσπέρα, ας *f*
  evening 67.191

Ἐσρώμ *m*
  Hezron 93.127

ἑσσόομαι
  (aor ἡσσώθην)
  be treated worse 88.134

ἐστάθην
  see ἵσταμαι

ἑστάναι
  see ἵσταμαι

ἕστηκα
  see ἵσταμαι

ἑστηκώς
  see ἵσταμαι

ἔστην
  see ἵσταμαι

ἔστησα
  see ἵστημι

ὅ ἐστιν
  that means 89.106

ἐστράφην
  see στρέφω

ἐστρωμένος
  see στρώννυμι

ἔστρωσα
  see στρώννυμι

ἔστω
  see εἰμί

ἑστώς
  see ἵσταμαι

ἔστωσαν
  see εἰμί

ἔσχατος, η, ον
  a final(ly) 61.13
  b least important 87.66

ἐσχάτως
  ἐσχάτως : unit
  ἐσχάτως ἔχω
    be very sick 23.151

ἔσχηκα
  see ἔχω

ἔσχον
  see ἔχω

ἔσω
  inside 83.13
  ἔσω : units
  ὁ ἔσω
    insider 11.11
  ὁ ἔσω (ἄνθρωπος)
    inner being 26.1

ἔσωθεν
  a from inside 84.14
  b within 83.16
  c the inner being 26.2

ἐσώτερος, α, ον
  inner 83.15

ἑταῖρος, ου *m*
  companion 34.16

ἐταράχθην
  see ταράσσω

ἐτάφην
  see θάπτω

ἐτέθην
  see τίθημι

ἔτεκον
  see τίκτω

ἑτερόγλωσσος, ον
  speaking a strange
  language 33.4

ἑτεροδιδασκαλέω
teach a different
doctrine *33.235*

ἑτεροζυγέω
be mismatched *34.9*

ἕτερος, α, ον
a different *58.36*
b another *58.37*
ἕτερος : units
τῇ ἑτέρᾳ
the next day *67.208*
ἀπέρχομαι ὀπίσω
σαρκὸς ἑτερός
have homosexual
intercourse *88.279*

ἑτέρως
differently *58.36*

ἐτέχθην
see τίκτω

ἔτι
a still *67.128*
b in addition *59.75*
c nevertheless *89.135*

ἐτίθει
see τίθημι

ἐτίθεσαν
see τίθημι

ἐτίθουν
see τίθημι

ἑτοιμάζω
make ready *77.3*

ἑτοιμασία, ας f
readiness *77.1*

ἕτοιμος, η, ον
ready *77.2*

ἑτοίμως
ready *77.2*

ἔτος, ους n
year *67.167*
ἔτος : units
ἔτη τεσσεράκοντα
very long time *67.94*
δι' ἐτῶν
after years *67.60*

ἐτύθην
see θύω

εὖ
a good (moral) *88.6*
b good (value) *65.23*

Εὕα, ας f
Eve *93.128*

εὐαγγελίζω
tell the good news *33.215*

εὐαγγέλιον, ου n
the good news *33.217*

εὐαγγελιστής, οῦ m
evangelist *53.76*

εὐαρεστέω
cause to be pleased . . . *25.93*

εὐάρεστος, ον
pleasing *25.94*

εὐαρέστως
pleasing *25.94*

Εὔβουλος, ου m
Eubulus *93.129*

εὖγε
good (value) *65.23*

εὐγενής, ές
a important *87.27*
b open-minded *27.48*

εὐδία, ας f
fair weather *14.1*

εὐδοκέω
a   be pleased with *25.87*
b   enjoy *25.113*
c   prefer *30.97*

εὐδοκία, ας *f*
a   what pleases *25.88*
b   desire *25.8*

εὐεργεσία, ας *f*
good deed *88.7*

εὐεργετέω
do good *88.7*

εὐεργέτης, ου *m*
benefactor *35.15*

εὔθετος, ον
a   suitable *66.3*
b   useful *65.32*

εὐθέως
immediately, then *67.53*

εὐθυδρομέω
sail a straight course . . *54.3*

εὐθυμέω
be encouraged *25.146*

εὔθυμος, ον
encouraged *25.147*

εὐθύμως
encouraged *25.147*

εὐθύνω
a   make straight *79.89*
b   pilot a ship *54.21*

εὐθύς, εῖα, ύ
a   straight *79.88*
b   upright *88.17*
εὐθύς : unit
εὐθεῖα ὁδός
    just way of life *88.18*

εὐθύς (adv)
immediately, then *67.53*

εὐθύτης, ητος *f*
righteousness *88.19*

εὐκαιρέω
a   have time to *67.4*
b   spend time *67.80*

εὐκαιρία, ας *f*
opportunity *67.5*

εὔκαιρος, ον
favorable time *67.6*

εὐκαίρως
favorable time *67.6*

εὔκοπος, ον
easy *22.39*

εὐλάβεια, ας *f*
reverence *53.7*

εὐλαβέομαι
a   show reverence for   *53.7*
b   obey *36.13*

εὐλαβής, ές
pious *53.8*

εὐλογέω
a   praise *33.356*
b   bless *33.470*
c   act kindly toward . . . *88.69*

εὐλογητός, ή, όν
to be praised *33.362*

εὐλογία, ας *f*
a   praise *33.356*
b   flattery *33.366*
c   blessing *33.470*
d   benefit *88.70*
e   gift *57.105*
εὐλογία : unit
ἐπ' εὐλογίαις
    large amount *59.56*

εὐμετάδοτος, ον
generous *57.97*

Εὐνίκη, ης *f*
Eunice 93.130

εὐνοέω
a consider favorably . . 30.23
b agree with 31.20
c settle a case 56.3

εὔνοια, ας *f*
eagerness 25.72

εὐνουχίζω
a makc a cunuch 9.26
b be a celibate 9.27

εὐνοῦχος, ου *m*
a eunuch 9.25
b impotent male 9.28
c celibate 9.29
d court official 37.85

εὐξαίμην
see εὔχομαι

Εὐοδία, ας *f*
Euodia 93.131

εὐοδόομαι
a get along well 22.47
b gain in business 57.64
c complete 68.30

εὐπάρεδρον, ου *n*
devotion 53.68

εὐπειθής, ές
easily persuaded 33.305

εὐπερίσπαστος, ον
easily distracting 30.32

εὐπερίστατος, ον
controlling tightly 37.6

εὐποιΐα, ας *f*
good deed 88.7

εὐπορέομαι
be rich 57.27

εὐπορία, ας *f*
a prosperity 57.32
b good business 57.201

εὐπρέπεια, ας *f*
beauty 79.13

εὐπρόσδεκτος, ον
a quite pleasing 25.86
b truly favorable 22.44

εὐπροσωπέω
make good showing . . . 88.236

Εὐρακύλων, ωνος *m*
northeast wind 14.9

εὑρίσκομαι
(aor εὑρέθην, fut
εὑρεθήσομαι)
be found to be 13.7

εὑρίσκω
(impf εὑ-, ηὑ-, fut
εὑρήσω, aor εὗρον, opt
3 pl εὕροιεν, pf εὕρηκα,
aor pass εὑρέθην, fut
pass εὑρεθήσομαι)
a discover 27.27
b learn 27.1
c attain 13.17
d begin to experience 90.70

Εὐρυκλύδων, ωνος *m*
see Εὐρακύλων . . . . . . 14.9 *fn* 4

εὐρύχωρος, ον
broad 81.18

εὐσέβεια, ας *f*
a religion 53.1
b piety 53.5

εὐσεβέω
a worship 53.53
b fulfill one's duties . . 71.29

εὐσεβής, ές
religious 53.6

εὐσεβῶς
religious 53.6

εὔσημος, ον
intelligible 32.19

εὔσπλαγχνος, ον
compassionate 25.51

εὐσχημόνως
a with propriety 88.50
b properly 66.4

εὐσχημοσύνη, ης f
attractiveness 79.13

εὐσχήμων, ον
a attractive 79.15
b honored 87.33

εὐτόνως
vigorously 78.18

εὐτραπελία, ας f
vulgar speech 33.34

Εὔτυχος, ου m
Eutychus 93.132

εὐφημία, ας f
praise 33.356

εὔφημος, ον
worthy of praise 33.360

εὐφορέω
produce much fruit . . . 23.204

εὐφραίνομαι
(aor ηὐφράνθην, inf
εὐφρανθῆναι)
a rejoice 25.122
b celebrate 51.3

εὐφραίνω
make glad 25.131

Εὐφράτης, ου m
Euphrates 93.468

εὐφροσύνη, ης f
joyfulness 25.121

εὐχαριστέω
a thank 33.349
b be thankful 25.100

εὐχαριστία, ας f
thanksgiving 33.349

εὐχάριστος, ον
a thankful 25.99
b thanking 33.352

εὐχή, ῆς f
a prayer 33.178
b vow 33.469

εὔχομαι
(aor opt εὐξαίμην)
a pray 33.178
b desire 25.6

εὔχρηστος, ον
useful 65.31

εὐψυχέω
be encouraged 25.146

εὐωδία, ας f
fragrance 79.46

εὐώνυμος, ον
left 82.7

ἐφ'
see ἐπί

ἔφαγον
see ἐσθίω

ἐφάλλομαι
(aor ἐφαλόμην)
jump on 15.239

ἐφάνην
see φαίνομαι

ἐφάπαξ
a once *60.67*
b once and for all *60.68*
c at the same time *67.34*

Ἐφέσιος, α, ον
Ephesian *93.469*

Ἐφέσιος, ου m
Ephesian *93.470*

Ἔφεσος, ου f
Ephesus *93.471*

ἐφέστηκα
see ἐφίσταμαι

ἐφεστώς
see ἐφίσταμαι

ἐφευρετής, οῦ m
inventor *30.69*

ἔφη
see φημί

ἐφημερία, ας f
work group *11.47*

ἐφήμερος, ον
daily *67.183*

ἐφικνέομαι
(aor inf ἐφικέσθαι)
arrive *15.84*

ἐφίσταμαι (+ 2 aor, pf,
plpf act)
(aor ἐπέστην, subj ἐπι-
στῶ, impv ἐπίστηθι, ptc
ἐπιστάς, pf ἐφέστηκα,
ptc ἐφεστώς)
a stand at *17.5*
b be near *85.13*
c happen *13.119*
d attack *39.47*
e be imminent *67.63*
f begin *68.7*
g continue *68.14*

ἐφοράω
(aor ἐπεῖδον, impv ἔπιδε)
pay attention to *30.45*

Ἐφραίμ m
Ephraim *93.472*

ἔφυγον
see φεύγω

εφφαθα
be opened *79.111*

ἐχάρην
see χαίρω

ἐχθές
yesterday *67.203*
ἐχθές : unit
ἐχθὲς καὶ σήμερον καὶ
εἰς τοὺς αἰῶνας
always *67.87*

ἔχθρα, ας f
enmity *39.10*

ἐχθρός, ά, όν
be enemy of *39.11*

ἔχιδνα, ης f
a snake *4.53*
b evil person *88.123*

ἐχόμενος, η, ον
neighboring *83.29*
ἐχόμενος : unit
τῇ ἐχομένῃ
the next day *67.208*

ἔχω
(impf εἶχον, fut ἕξω,
aor ἔσχον, subj βχῶ,
pf ἔσχηκα)
a possess *57.1*
b hold on to *18.6*
c hold a view *31.1*
d wear *49.13*
e be able to *74.12*
f experience *90.65*
g be *13.2*
h cause *90.51*
i content marker *90.27*

ἔχω : units
καλῶς ἔχω
  be healthy 23.129
κακῶς ἔχω
  be sick 23.148
ἐσχάτως ἔχω
  be very sick 23.151
ἐν γάστρι ἔχω
  be pregnant 23.50
κοίτην ἔχω
  be pregnant 23.50
κατὰ κεφαλῆς ἔχω
  have one's head
  covered 49.16
ἔχω ἐν ἐπιγνώσει
  acknowledge 31.28
ἔχω κοινός
  share mutually 57.99
ἔχω πνεῦμα πύθωνα
  be a fortuneteller . . . 33.285
ἔχω οὖς
  be able to hear 24.59
ἔχω μέρος ἐν
  experience together 90.83

ἐῶν
  see ἐάω

ἑώρακα
  see ὁράω

ἑώρων
  see ὁράω

ἕως
  a until 67.119
  b while 67.139
  c as far as 84.19
  d to the point of 78.51
  e as much as 59.21
ἕως : units
ἐάω ἕως
  stop 68.35
ἕως ὅτου
  a until 67.119
  b while 67.139
ἕως οὗ
  a until 67.119
  b while 67.139

Ζαβουλών m
  a Zebulun (person) . . . 93.133
  b Zebulun (place) 93.473

Ζακχαῖος, ου m
  Zacchaeus 93.134

Ζάρα m
  Zerah 93.135

Ζαχαρίας, ου m
  Zechariah 93.136

ζάω
  (contracted ζῶ, impf
  ἔζην)
  a live 23.88
  b live again 23.93
  c behave 41.2

Ζεβεδαῖος, ου m
  Zebedee 93.137

ζεστός, ή, όν
  hot 79.71

ζεῦγος, ους n
  pair 60.79

ζευκτηρία, ας f
  bands 6.19

Ζεύς, gen Διός, acc Δία, m
  Zeus 93.138

ζέω
  ζέω : unit
  ζέω τῷ πνεύματι
  show enthusiasm . . . 25.73

ζηλεύω
  set one's heart on 25.76

ζῆλος, ου m, ους n
  a earnest concern 25.46
  b jealousy 88.162
  c extremely 78.25

ζηλόω
a set one's heart on . . . *25.76*
b have deep concern
for *25.46*
c covet *25.21*
d be jealous *88.163*

ζηλωτής, οῦ *m*
a enthusiast *25.77*
b nationalist *11.88*

ζημία, ας *f*
suffer loss *57.69*

ζημιόομαι
a suffer loss *57.69*
b undergo punishment *38.7*

Ζηνᾶς ᾶν *m*
Zenas *93.139*

ζητέω
a try to find *27.41*
b seek information . . . *27.34*
c desire *25.9*
d demand *33.167*
e try *68.60*
f try to obtain *57.59*
g attempt to find *13.19*
ζητέω : unit
ζητέω τὴν ψυχήν
want to kill *20.66*

ζήτημα, τος *n*
dispute *33.440*

ζήτησις, εως *f*
a seek information . . . *27.34*
b dispute *33.440*

ζιζάνιον, ου *n*
darnel *3.30*

Ζοροβαβέλ *m*
Zerubbabel *93.140*

ζόφος, ου *m*
gloom *14.57*
ζόφος : unit
ὁ ζόφος τοῦ σκότους
gloomy hell *1.24*

ζυγός, οῦ *m*
a yoke *6.8*
b balance scale *6.214*
ζυγός : units
εἰμὶ ὑπὸ ζυγόν
be a slave *87.80*
ἐπιτίθημι ζυγὸν ἐπὶ
τὸν τράχηλον
load down with
obligations *22.27*

ζύμη, ης *f*
a yeast *5.11*
b pretense *88.237*

ζυμόω
use yeast *5.12*

ζῶ
see ζάω

ζωγρέω
control *37.1*

ζωή, ῆς *f*
life *23.88*
ζωή : unit
ψυχὴ ζωῆς
living creature *4.1*

ζώνη, ης *f*
belt *6.178*

ζώννυμι
(impf 2 sg ἐζώννυες,
fut ζώσω, aor midd
impv ζῶσαι)
a gird *49.14*
b dress *49.8*

ζωννύω
see ζώννυμι

ζῳογονέω
a keep alive *23.89*
b make live *23.92*

ζῷον, ου *n*
a animal *4.2*
b living being *12.32*

ζωοποιέω
make live *23.92*

ζῶσαι
see ζώννυμι

ζώσω
see ζώννυμι

ἡ
see ὁ

ἤ
a or *89.139*
b than *64.18*
see also πρὶν ἤ

ἤ . . . ἤ
either . . . or *89.140*

ἤγαγον
see ἄγω

ἤγγειλα
see ἀγγέλλω

ἤγειρα
see ἐγείρω

ἡγεμονεύω
be governor *37.60*

ἡγεμονία, ας *f*
government *37.58*

ἡγεμών, όνος *m*
a ruler *37.59*
b governor *37.83*

ἡγέομαι
a be of opinion *31.1*
b guide *36.1*
c govern *37.58*

ἡγέρθην
see ἐγείρω

ἤδε
see ὅδε

ᾔδειν
see οἶδα

ἡδέως
gladly *25.129*

ἤδη
already *67.20*
ἤδη : unit
ἤδη ποτέ
now at last *67.40*

ἤδιστα
gladly *25.129*

ἡδονή, ῆς *f*
a pleasure *25.111*
b passion *25.27*

ἠδυνάμην
see δύναμαι

ἠδυνάσθην
see δύναμαι

ἠδυνήθην
see δύναμαι

ἡδύοσμον, ου *n*
mint *3.23*

ἤθελον
see θέλω

ἦθος, ους *n*
custom *41.25*

ἥκω
(pres 3 pl ἥκασιν)
a arrive *15.84*
b be here *85.10*
c happen *13.112*

ἡλάμην
see ἅλλομαι

ἠλέγχθην
see ἐλέγχω

ἦλθα
see ἔρχομαι

ἦλθον
 see ἔρχομαι

ηλι
 my God *12.3*

Ἠλί *m*
 Heli *93.141*

Ἠλίας, ου *m*
 Elijah *93.142*

ἡλικία, ας *f*
 a lifetime *67.151*
 b mature *67.156*
 c stature *81.4*

ἡλίκος, η, ον
 a how extensive *79.127*
 b intense *78.13*

ἥλιος, ου *m*
 sun *1.28*

ἧλος, ου *m*
 nail *6.22*

ἤλπικα
 see ἐλπίζω

ἤλπισα
 see ἐλπίζω

ἡμάρτηκα
 see ἁμαρτάνω

ἥμαρτον
 see ἁμαρτάνω

ἡμεῖς, ἡμῶν
 we *92.4*

ἡμέρα, ας *f*
 a day *67.178*
 b daylight period *67.186*
 c period *67.142*
 d daylight *14.40*
 e court of justice *56.1*
 ἡμέρα : units
 υἱοὶ τῆς ἡμέρας
  God's people *11.14*

εἰς ἡμέραν αἰῶνος
 forever *67.95*
ἀφ' ἡμερῶν ἀρχαίων
 long ago *67.26*
δι' ἡμερῶν
 a few days later *67.59*
προβαίνω ἐν ἡμέραις
 be old *67.99*
ἡμέρα ἐξ ἡμέρας
 day after day *67.92*
ἡμέρας τεσσεράκοντα
καὶ νύκτας τεσσεράκοντα
 long time *67.93*
ἡμέρα σφαγῆς
 day of condemnation *56.33*

ἡμέτερος, α, ον
 our *92.5*

ἤμην
 see εἰμί

ἡμιθανής, ές
 half dead *23.122*

ἥμισυς, εια, υ
 one half *60.62*

ἡμίωρον, ου *n*
 half an hour *67.200*

ἠμφίεσμαι
 see ἀμφιέννυμι

ἦν
 see εἰμί

ἤνεγκα
 see φέρω

ἠνέχθην
 see φέρω

ἠνέῳγμαι
 see ἀνοίγω

ἠνέῳξα
 see ἀνοίγω

ἠνεῴχθην
 see ἀνοίγω

ἡνίκα
  ἡνίκα : unit
  ἡνίκα ἄν /ἐάν
    whenever 67.36

ἡνοίγην
  see ἀνοίγω

ἡνοίχθην
  see ἀνοίγω

ἡντληκώς
  see ἀντλέω

ἤπερ
  than 64.19

ἤπερ
  see ὅσπερ

ἤπιος, α, ον
  gentle 88.61

Ἢρ m
  Er 93.143

ἦρα
  see αἴρω

ἤρεμος, ον
  quiet 88.104

ἤρεσα
  see ἀρέσκω

ἤρθην
  see αἴρω

ἦρκα
  see αἴρω

ἦρμαι
  see αἴρω

ἡρπάγην
  see ἁρπάζω

ἡρχόμην
  see ἔρχομαι

Ἡρῴδης, ου m
  Herod 93.144

Ἡρῳδιανοί, ῶν m
  Herodians 11.87

Ἡρῳδιάς, άδος f
  Herodias 93.145

Ἡρῳδίων, ωνος m
  Herodion 93.146

Ἠσαΐας, ου m
  Isaiah 93.147

Ἠσαῦ m
  Esau 93.148

ἡσσώθητε
  see ἑσσόομαι

ἥσσων, ον
  a less 78.38
  b worse 65.29

ἡσυχάζω
  a rest 23.82
  b live quiet life 88.103
  c remain quiet 33.119

ἡσυχία, ας f
  a quiet circumstances 22.43
  b silence 33.119
  c quiet living 88.103

ἡσύχιος, ον
  quiet 88.104

ἥτις
  see ὅστις

ἤτοι . . . ἤ
  either . . . or 89.140

ἡττάομαι
  (perf ἥττημαι)
  be defeated 39.61

ἥττημα, τος n
  failure 13.22

ἤτω
see εἰμί

ηὐξήθην
see αὐξάνω

ηὔξησα
see αὐξάνω

ηὐφράνθην
see εὐφραίνω

ἤφιεν
see ἀφίημι

ἠχέω
make a noise 14.80

ἤχθην
see ἄγω

ἦχος, ου m or ους n
a sound 14.75
b information 33.211
ἦχος : unit
χαλκὸς ἠχῶν
brass gong 6.95

ἠψάμην
see ἅπτω

θα
come 15.82

Θαδαῖος
see Θαδδαῖος 93.149

Θαδδαῖος, ου m
Thaddaeus 93.150

θάλασσα, ης f
a sea 1.69
b lake 1.70

θάλπω
take care of 35.36

Θαμάρ f
Tamar 93.151

θαμβέομαι
be amazed 25.209

θάμβος, ους n
astonishment 25.208

θανάσιμον, ου n
deadly 23.115

θανατηφόρος, ον
deadly 23.115

θάνατος, ου m
a death 23.99
b plague 23.158
θάνατος : unit
(εἰμὶ) ἐν θανάτοις
in danger of death . . 23.117

θανατόω
a execute 20.65
b stop completely 68.48

θάπτω
(aor pass ἐτάφην)
bury 52.4
θάπτω : units
θάπτω τὸν πατέρα μου
take care of one's
father until death . . . 35.46
ἄφες τοὺς νεκροὺς θάψαι
τοὺς ἑαυτῶν νεκρούς
that is not the issue 33.137

Θάρα m
Terah 93.152

θαρρέω
have courage 25.156

θαρσέω
have courage 25.156

θάρσος, ους n
θάρσος : unit
λαμβάνω θάρσος
take courage 25.157

θαῦμα, τος n
a amazement 25.212
b miracle 25.216

θαυμάζω
  be amazed 25.213
  θαυμάζω : unit
  θαυμάζω πρόσωπον
    flatter 33.365

θαυμάσιος, α, ον
  marvelous 25.215

θαυμαστός, ή, όν
  marvelous 25.215

θεά, ᾶς f
  goddess 12.25

θεάομαι
  a look at 24.14
  b visit 34.50

θεατρίζω
  shame publicly 25.201

θέατρον, ου n
  a theater 7.54
  b spectacle 24.15

θεῖναι
  see τίθημι

θεῖον, ου n
  a divine being 12.13
  b sulfur 2.26
  θεῖον : unit
  λίμνη τοῦ πυρὸς (καὶ
  θεῖου)
    hell 1.22

θεῖος, α, ον
  divine 12.14

θειότης, ητος f
  divine being 12.13

θείς
  see τίθημι

θειώδης, ες
  sulfureous yellow 79.36

θέλημα, τος n
  a desire 25.2
  b purpose 30.59
  θέλημα : unit
  σαρκὸς θέλημα
    sexual desires 25.29

θέλησις, εως f
  desire 25.1

θέλω
  (impf ἤθελον)
  a purpose . . . 30.58
  b be of an opinion 31.4
  c desire 25.1
  d enjoy 25.102
  θέλω : unit
  θέλει εἶναι
    it means 33.136

θεμέλιον, ου n
  a foundation 7.41
  b basis 89.12

θεμέλιος, ου m
  a foundation 7.41
  b foundation stone . . . 7.43

θεμελιόω
  a lay a foundation 7.42
  b establish belief 31.94

θεοδίδακτος, ον
  taught by God 33.228

θεομάχος, ον
  fighting against God . . 39.32

θεόπνευστος, ον
  inspired by God 33.261

θεός, οῦ m, f
  a God 12.1
  b god 12.22
  c goddess 12.25
  θεός : units
  υἱὸς τοῦ θεοῦ
    Son of God 12.15
  ὁ θεὸς τοῦ αἰῶνος τούτου
    the Devil 12.24

δίδωμι δόξαν τῷ θεῷ
  promise to tell truth *33.468*

θεοσέβεια, ας *f*
  religion *53.1*

θεοσεβής, ές
  religious *53.6*

θεοστυγής, ές
  hating God *88.205*

θεότης, ητος *f*
  divine being *12.13*

Θεόφιλος, ου *m*
  Theophilus *93.153*

θεραπεία, ας *f*
  a healing *23.139*
  b household servants   *46.6*

θεραπεύω
  a heal *23.139*
  b serve *35.19*

θεράπων, οντος *m*
  servant *35.20*

θερίζω
  reap *43.14*

θερισμός, οῦ *m*
  a reaping *43.14*
  b harvest *43.15*

θεριστής, οῦ *m*
  reaper *43.16*

θερμαίνομαι
  warm oneself *79.73*

θέρμη, ης *f*
  heat *79.70*

θέρος, ους *n*
  summer *67.163*

θέσθε
  see τίθημι

Θεσσαλονικεύς, έως *m*
  Thessalonian *93.474*

Θεσσαλονίκη, ης *f*
  Thessalonica *93.475*

θέτε
  see τίθημι

Θευδᾶς, ᾶ *m*
  Theudas *93.154*

θεωρέω
  a look at *24.14*
  b understand *32.11*
  c experience *90.79*

θεωρία, ας *f*
  spectacle *24.15*

θήκη, ης *f*
  receptacle *6.119*

θηλάζω
  a nurse (of a baby) . . . *23.7*
  b nurse a baby *23.8*

θῆλυς, εια, υ
  female *79.103*

θήρα, ας *f*
  a trap *6.24*
  b control *37.15*

θηρεύω
  catch in mistake *27.30*

θηριομαχέω
  be in serious conflict . . *39.28*

θηρίον, ου *n*
  a animal *4.3*
  b quadruped *4.4*
  c wicked person *88.119*

θησαυρίζω
  a treasure up *65.11*
  b cause to happen *13.135*

θησαυρός, οῦ *m*
a storeroom *7.32*
b treasure box *6.140*
c treasure *65.10*

θήσω
see τίθημι

θιγγάνω
a touch *24.74*
b kill *20.75*

θλίβομαι
suffer hardship *22.15*

θλίβω
(pf pass ptc τεθλιμμένος)
a crowd against *19.44*
b cause trouble to *22.21*

θλῖψις, εως *f*
trouble *22.2*

θνήσκω
(pf τέθνηκα)
die *23.99*

θνητός, ή, όν
mortal *23.124*

θορυβάζομαι
be upset *25.234*

θορυβέομαι
be upset *25.234*

θορυβέω
start a riot *39.44*

θόρυβος, ου *m*
a clamor *14.79*
b riot *39.42*

θραύω
oppress *22.22*

θρέμμα, τος *n*
livestock *4.5*

θρηνέω
a wail *25.141*
b sing funeral songs . . *33.115*
c lament *52.2*

θρῆνος, ου *m*
song of grief. *33.116*

θρησκεία, ας *f*
religion *53.1*

θρησκός, όν
religious. *53.6*

θριαμβεύω
a triumph over *39.59*
b cause to triumph . . . *39.60*

θρίξ, τριχός *f*
hair *8.12*

θροέομαι
be alarmed *25.262*

θρόμβος, ου *m*
clot of blood *8.65*

θρόνος, ου *m*
a throne *6.112*
b ruler *37.70*
c supernatural power *12.44*
d authority to rule . . . *37.71*
e place of ruling *37.72*

θρύπτω
break into pieces *19.37*

Θυάτειρα, ων *n*
Thyatira *93.476*

Θυάτιρα, ων *n*
Thyatira *93.476*

θυγάτηρ, τρός *f*
a daughter (own) *10.46*
b daughter (address) . . *9.47*
c female descendant . . *10.31*
d female inhabitant . . . *11.65*
θυγάτηρ : unit
θυγάτηρ Σιών
people of Jerusalem *11.66*

θυγάτριον, ου *n*
little daughter *10.47*

θύελλα, ης *f*
windstorm *14.6*

θύϊνος, η, ον
made of citron wood . . *3.63*

θυμίαμα, τος *n*
a incense *6.211*
b incense offering *53.25*

θυμιατήριον, ου *n*
incense altar *6.116*

θυμιάω
offer incense *53.25*

θυμομαχέω
a be furious *88.180*
b quarrel angrily *33.453*

θυμόομαι
be extremely angry . . . *88.179*

θυμός, οῦ *m*
a fury *88.178*
b intense desire *25.19*

θύρα, ας *f*
a door *7.49*
b entrance *7.39*
θύρα : units
ἐπὶ θύραις
soon *67.58*
πρὸ θυρῶν
soon *67.58*
ἀνοίγω θύραν
make possible *71.9*

θυρεός, οῦ *m*
shield *6.40*

θυρίς, ίδος *f*
window *7.47*

θυρωρός, οῦ *m*
doorkeeper *46.8*

θυσία, ας *f*
sacrifice *53.20*

θυσιαστήριον, ου *n*
altar *6.114*

θύω
(aor pass ἐτύθην)
a sacrifice *53.19*
b slaughter *20.72*

θῶ
see τίθημι

Θωμᾶς, ᾶ *m*
Thomas *93.155*

θώραξ, ακος *m*
a breastplate *6.39*
b chest *8.38*

Ἰάϊρος, ου *m*
Jairus *93.156*

Ἰακώβ *m*
Jacob *93.157*

Ἰάκωβος, ου *m*
James *93.158*

ἴαμα, τος *n*
power to heal *23.138*

Ἰαμβρῆς *m*
Jambres *93.159*

Ἰανναί *m*
Jannai *93.160*

Ἰάννης *m*
Jannes *93.161*

ἰάομαι
a heal *23.136*
b renew *13.66*

Ἰάρετ *m*
Jared *93.162*

ἴασις, εως f
   healing 23.136

ἴασπις, ιδος f
   jasper 2.30

Ἰάσων, ονος m
   Jason 93.163

ἰατρός, οῦ m
   physician 23.141

ἴδε
   look! 91.13

ἴδετε
   see ὁράω

ἴδιος, α, ον
   a one's own 57.4
   b peculiar 58.47
   c individually 92.21
   ἴδιος : units
   κατ᾽ ἰδίαν
     privately 28.67
   τῷ ἰδίῳ κυρίῳ στήκει
   ἢ πίπτει
     honor depends on
     master's judgment . . 87.56
   οἱ ἴδιοι
     his own people 10.12

ἰδιώτης, ου m
   layman 27.26

ἰδού
   a look! 91.13
   b indeed 91.10

Ἰδουμαία, ας f
   Idumea 93.477

ἱδρώς, ῶτος m
   sweat 8.72

ἰδών
   see ὁράω

ἰδώς
   see οἶδα

Ἰεζάβελ f
   Jezebel 93.164

Ἱεράπολις, εως f
   Hierapolis 93.478

ἱερατεία, ας f
   priesthood 53.86

ἱεράτευμα, τος n
   priesthood 53.86

ἱερατεύω
   be a priest 53.85

Ἱερεμίας, ου m
   Jeremiah 93.165

ἱερεύς, έως m
   priest 53.87

Ἱεριχώ f
   Jericho 93.479

ἱερόθυτος, ον
   sacrificed to a deity . . . 53.21

ἱερόν, οῦ n
   temple 7.16
   ἱερόν : unit
   στρατηγὸς τοῦ ἱεροῦ
     commander of the
     Temple guard 37.91

ἱεροπρεπής, ές
   religious 53.6

ἱερός, ά, όν
   holy 53.9

Ἱεροσόλυμα f and ων n
   Jerusalem 93.480

Ἱεροσολυμίτης, ου m
   inhabitant of Jerusalem 93.481

ἱεροσυλέω
   a rob temples 57.241
   b commit sacrilege . . . 53.104

ἱερόσυλος, ου m
   a temple robber 57.242
   b desecrator 53.105

ἱερουργέω
be a priest 53.85

Ἰερουσαλήμ f
Jerusalem 93.480

ἱερωσύνη, ης f
priesthood 53.86

Ἰεσσαί m
Jesse 93.166

Ἰεφθάε m
Jephthah 93.167

Ἰεχονίας, ου m
Jechoniah 93.168

Ἰησοῦς, οῦ m
Jesus 93.169

ἱκανόν, οῦ n
bail 57.169

ἱκανός, ή, όν
a enough (degree) 78.50
b intense 78.14
c adequate 75.2
d enough (quantity) . . 59.44
e many 59.2
f large 59.12
ἱκανός : units
ποιέω τὸ ἱκανόν
   act in a pleasing
   manner 25.96
ἐφ᾽ ἱκανόν
   for a long time 67.91

ἱκανότης, ητος f
adequacy 75.1

ἱκανόω
make adequate 75.3

ἱκετηρία, ας f
supplication 33.172

ἱκμάς, άδος f
moisture 2.9

Ἰκόνιον, ου n
Iconium 93.482

ἱλαρός, ά, όν
happy 25.117

ἱλαρότης, ητος f
happiness 25.116

ἱλάσκομαι
a forgive 40.9
b show mercy 88.75

ἱλασμός, οῦ m
means of forgiveness . . 40.12

ἱλαστήριον, ου n
a means of forgiveness 40.12
b place of forgiveness 40.13

ἵλεως, ων
merciful 88.77
ἵλεως : unit
ἵλεώς σοι
   God forbid 88.78

Ἰλλυρικόν, οῦ n
Illyricum 93.483

ἱμάς, άντος m
a strap 6.20
b whipping 19.9

ἱματίζω
clothe 49.1

ἱμάτιον, ου n
a clothing 6.162
b coat 6.172

ἱματισμός, οῦ m
clothing 6.162

ἵνα
a in order to 89.59
b as a result 89.49
c that 90.22
d namely 91.15

ἱνατί
why? 89.38

Ἰόππη, ης f
Joppa, Jaffa 93.484

Ἰορδάνης, ου m
Jordan River 93.485

ἰός, οῦ m
a venom 8.74
b rust 2.60

Ἰουδαία, ας f
Judea 93.486

Ἰουδαία, ης f
Jewess 93.170

ἰουδαΐζω
live as a Jew 41.32

Ἰουδαϊκός, ή, όν
Jewish 93.171

Ἰουδαϊκῶς
Jewish 93.171

Ἰουδαῖος, α, ον
Judean 93.487

Ἰουδαῖος, ου m
Jew 93.172
Ἰουδαῖος : unit
ἄρχων τῶν Ἰουδαίων
member of the
Council 37.95

Ἰουδαϊσμός, οῦ m
practice of Judaism . . . 41.33

Ἰούδας, α m
a Judah or Judas
(person) 93.173
b Judah (tribe) 93.174
c Judah (land) 93.488

Ἰουλία, ας f
Julia 93.175

Ἰούλιος, ου m
Julius 93.176

Ἰουνία, ας f
Junia 93.177

Ἰουνιᾶς, ᾶ m
Junias 93.178

Ἰοῦστος, ου m
Justus 93.179

ἱππεύς, έως m
horseman 55.21

ἱππικόν, οῦ n
horseman 55.21

ἵππος, ου m
horse 4.29

ἴρις, ιδος f
circle of light 1.38

Ἰσαάκ m
Isaac 93.180

ἰσάγγελος, ον
like an angel 12.29

ἴσασι
see οἶδα

ἴσθι
see εἰμί

Ἰσκαριώθ
Iscariot 93.181

Ἰσκαρ(ι)ώτης, ου m
see Ἰσκαριώθ 93.181

ἴσος, η, ον
equal 58.33

ἰσότης, ητος f
equality 58.32

ἰσότιμος, ον
equal to 58.34

ἰσόψυχος, ον
similarly minded 26.5

Ἰσραήλ *m*
Israel *93.182*
 Ἰσραήλ : units
 οἶκος Ἰσραήλ
  people of Israel *11.58*
 υἱοὶ Ἰσραήλ
  people of Israel *11.58*

Ἰσραηλίτης, ου *m*
Israelite *93.183*

Ἰσσαχάρ *m*
Issachar *93.184*

ἵσταμαι (+ 2 aor, pf, plpf act)
 (fut στήσομαι, σταθήσο-
 μαι, aor ἔστην, ἐστάθην,
 impv στῆθι, inf στῆναι,
 σταθῆναι, ptc στάς, στα-
 θείς, pf ἕστηκα, inf
 ἑστάναι, ptc ἑστηκώς,
 ἑστώς, plpf εἱστήκειν)
 a stand *17.1*
 b stand up *17.6*
 c be in a place *85.8*
 d cease *68.42*
 e continue to be *13.90*
 f remain firmly *13.29*
 ἵσταμαι : unit
 ἵσταμαι ἐν τῇ καρδίᾳ
  continue one's
  opinion *31.7*

ἱστάνω
see ἵστημι
ἴστε
see οἶδα

ἵστημι (for 2 aor, pf, plpf
act, see ἵσταμαι)
 (fut στήσω, aor ἔστησα)
 a put *85.40*
 b maintain *76.20*
 c establish *76.21*
 d pay *57.158*
 e select *30.87*
 f propose *33.343*

ἱστορέω
visit and get informa-
tion *34.52*

ἰσχυρός, ά, όν
 a powerful *76.11*
 b strong *79.63*
 c intense *78.16*
 d great *87.44*

ἰσχύς, ύος *f*
 a capability *74.8*
 b strength *79.62*

ἰσχύω
 a be capable of *74.9*
 b be strong *79.64*
 c be healthy *23.130*

ἴσως
probably *71.11*

Ἰταλία, ας *f*
Italy *93.489*

Ἰταλικός, ή, όν
Italian *93.490*

Ἰτουραῖος, α, ον
Ituraean *93.491*

ἰχθύδιον, ου *n*
little fish *4.60*

ἰχθύς, ύος *m*
fish *4.59*

ἴχνος, ους *n*
 ἴχνος : units
 ἐπακολουθέω τοῖς ἴχνεσιν
  imitate *41.47*
 στοιχέω τοῖς ἴχνεσιν
  imitate *41.47*
 περιπατέω τοῖς ἴχνεσιν
  imitate *41.47*

Ἰωαθάμ *m*
Jotham *93.185*

Ἰωακείμ *m*
Jehoiakim *93.186*

Ἰωανάν *m*
Joanan *93.187*

Ἰωανᾶς, α *m*
see Ἰωάννης *93.189*

Ἰωάννα, ας *f*
Joanna *93.188*

Ἰωαννᾶς
see Ἰωάννης *93.189*

Ἰωάννης, ου *m*
John *93.190*

Ἰώβ *m*
Job *93.191*

Ἰωβήδ *m*
Obed *93.192*

Ἰωδά *m*
Joda *93.193*

Ἰωήλ *m*
Joel *93.194*

Ἰωνάθας, ου *m*
Jonathas *93.195*

Ἰωνάμ *m*
Jonam *93.196*

Ἰωνᾶς, ᾶ *m*
Jonah *93.197*

Ἰωράμ *m*
Joram *93.198*

Ἰωρίμ *m*
Jorim *93.199*

Ἰωσαφάτ *m*
Jehoshaphat *93.200*

Ἰωσῆς, ῆ or ῆτος *m*
Joses *93.201*

Ἰωσήφ *m*
Joseph *93.202*

Ἰωσήχ *m*
Josech *93.203*

Ἰωσίας, ου *m*
Josiah *93.204*

ἰῶτα *n*
smallest letter *33.36*

κἀγώ (= καί + ἐγώ)
see καί and ἐγώ

καθά
just as *64.14*

καθαίρεσις, εως *f*
a tearing down *20.54*
b making less able *74.16*

καθαιρέω
(fut καθελῶ, aor καθ-
εῖλον, ptc καθελών)
a lower *15.110*
b take down *15.199*
c tear down *20.54*
d destroy *20.42*
e do away with *13.38*

καθαίρω
a make clean *79.49*
b prune *43.12*

καθάπερ
just as *64.15*

καθάπτω
(aor καθῆψα)
fasten on to *18.7*

καθαρίζω
(fut καθαριῶ)
a make clean *79.49*
b purify *53.28*
c heal *23.137*

καθαρισμός, οῦ *m*
purification *53.28*

καθαρός, ά, όν
a clean *79.48*
b pure *53.29*

καθαρότης, ητος *f*
purification 53.28

καθέδρα, ας *f*
chair. 6.111
καθέδρα : unit
ἐπὶ τῆς Μωϋσέως
καθέδρας καθίστημι
be authority on
Law of Moses. 37.44

καθέζομαι
sit (down). 17.12

καθεῖλον
see καθαιρέω

καθελῶ
see καθαιρέω

καθελών
see καθαιρέω

καθεξῆς
one after another 61.1
καθεξῆς : unit
ἐν τῷ (καθ)εξῆς
later 67.52

καθεύδω
a sleep. 23.66
b be dead. 23.104

καθηγητής, οῦ *m*
teacher 33.245

καθῆκα
see καθίημι

καθήκει
be fitting 66.1

κάθημαι
(2 sg κάθη, impv
κάθου)
a sit (down). 17.12
b reside 85.63

καθημερινός, ή, όν
daily. 67.183

καθῆψα
see καθάπτω

καθίζω
a sit (down). 17.12
b cause to sit (down) . . 17.17
c remain 85.63
d appoint. 37.104
καθίζω : units
ἐκ δεξιῶν καθίζω
be in high position 87.34
καθίζω ἐν δεξιᾷ
be in high position 87.36
ἐξ ἀριστερῶν καθίζω
be in less high
position 87.35

καθίημι
(pass ptc καθιέμενος,
aor καθῆκα)
let down. 15.111

καθιστάνω
bring down 15.175

καθίστημι
(fut καταστήσω, aor
κατέστησα, ἐκατέστησα,
pr pass καθίσταμαι, aor
pass κατεστάθην, fut
pass κατασταθήσομαι)
a appoint. 37.104
b cause to be 13.9
καθίστημι : unit
ἐπὶ τῆς Μωϋσέως
καθέδρας καθίστημι
be authority on
Law of Moses. 37.44

καθό
a just as 64.14
b to the degree that . . . 78.53

καθόλου
complete(ly). 78.44

καθοπλίζω
arm fully 55.1

καθοράω
learn about 27.7

καθότι
a because *89.33*
b to the degree that ... *78.53*

κάθου
see κάθημαι

καθώς
a to the degree that ... *78.53*
b inasmuch as *89.34*
c just as *64.14*
d when *67.33*
e how *89.86*

καθώσπερ
just as *64.15*

καί
a and *89.92*
b and then *89.87*
c also *89.93*
d yet *91.12*

καί . . . καί
both . . . and *89.102*

Καϊάφας, α *m*
Caiaphas *93.205*

Κάϊν *m*
Cain *93.206*

Καϊνάμ *m*
Cainan *93.207*

καινός, ή, όν
a new (time) *67.115*
b new (class) *58.71*
c previously unknown *28.33*

καινότερον
latest *67.28*

καινότης, ητος *f*
a newness (time) *67.101*
b newness (class) *58.70*

καίπερ
although *89.71*

καιρός, οῦ *m*
a occasion *67.1*
b period of time *67.78*
c era *67.145*
d opportunity *22.45*
καιρός : units
πρὸς καιρὸν (ὥρας)
for a while *67.109*
ἐξαγοράζομαι τὸν
καιρόν
a make good use
of opportunity ... *65.42*
b work urgently ... *68.73*

Καῖσαρ, ος *m*
a Caesar *93.208*
b Emperor *37.74*

Καισάρεια, ας *f*
Caesarea *93.492*

καίτοι
although *89.72*

καίτοιγε
although *89.72*

καίω
(pf pass κέκαυμαι, fut
pass καυθήσομαι and
καυθήσωμαι)
a burn *14.63*
b ignite *14.65*

κἀκεῖ (= καί + ἐκεῖ)
see καί and ἐκεῖ

κἀκεῖθεν (= καί + ἐκεῖθεν)
see also καί and ἐκεῖθεν
a (and) from there *84.10*
b then *67.47*

κἀκεῖνος (= καί + ἐκεῖνος)
see καί and ἐκεῖνος

κακία, ας *f*
a badness *88.105*
b difficulties *22.5*
c hateful feeling *88.199*

κακοήθεια, ας *f*
malice *88.113*

κακολογέω
revile *33.399*

κακοπάθεια, ας *f*
suffering distress *24.89*

κακοπαθέω
suffer distress *24.89*

κακοποιέω
a do evil *88.112*
b injure *20.12*

κακοποιός, οῦ *m*
evildoer *88.114*

κακός, ή, όν
a bad (moral) *88.106*
b bad (value) *65.26*
c harmed *20.18*
d incorrect *72.22*

κακοῦργος, ου *m*
evildoer *88.114*

κακουχέω
mistreat *88.126*

κακόω
injure *20.12*
κακόω : unit
κακόω τὴν ψυχὴν κατά
cause to dislike *88.200*

κακῶς
a evil *88.106*
b harm *20.18*
c incorrect *72.22*
d severely *78.17*
κακῶς : unit
κακῶς ἔχω
be ill *23.148*

κάκωσις, εως *f*
injury *20.12*

καλάμη, ης *f*
straw *3.58*

κάλαμος, ου *m*
a reed (plant) *3.19*
b reed (stalk) *3.55*
c pen *6.56*
d measuring rod *6.213*

καλέω
(pf κέκληκα, aor pass
ἐκλήθην, fut pass
κληθήσομαι)
a name *33.129*
b call *33.131*
c summon *33.307*
d call to a task *33.312*
e invite *33.315*

καλλιέλαιος, ου *f*
cultivated olive tree . . . *3.10*

κάλλιον
see καλῶς[f] *78.21*

καλοδιδάσκαλος, ου *m, f*
teacher of what is good *33.249*

Καλοὶ Λιμένες *m*
Fair Havens *93.493*

καλοποιέω
do good *88.5*

καλός, ή, όν
a good (moral) *88.4*
b good (value) *65.22*
c advantageous *65.43*
d fitting *66.2*
e beautiful *79.9*
f important *87.25*

κάλυμμα, τος *n*
veil *6.177*

καλύπτω
a cover *79.114*
b keep secret *28.79*

καλῶς
a good (moral) *88.4*
b good (value) *65.23*
c accurate *72.12*
d important *87.25*

e please *33.177*
f certainly *78.21*
καλῶς : unit
καλῶς ἔχω
    be healthy *23.129*

κάμέ (= καί + με)
see καί and ἐγώ

κάμηλος, ου *m, f*
camel *4.30*

κάμινος, ου *f*
furnace *7.73*

καμμύω
καμμύω : unit
καμμύω τοὺς ὀφθαλμούς
    refuse to learn *27.50*

κάμνω
be sick *23.142*
κάμνω : unit
κάμνω τῇ ψυχῇ
    become discouraged *25.291*

κάμοί (= καί + μοι)
see καί and ἐγώ

κάμπτω
κάμπτω : unit
κάμπτω τὸ γόνυ
    worship *53.61*

κἄν (= καί + ἐάν)
even if *89.73*

Κανά *f*
Cana *93.494*

Καναναῖος, ου *m*
nationalist *11.88*

Κανδάκη, ης *f*
a the Candace *37.77*
b Candace *93.209*

κανών, όνος *m*
a rule *33.335*
b area *80.2*

καπηλεύω
peddle for profit *57.202*

καπνός, οῦ *m*
smoke *1.37*

Καππαδοκία, ας *f*
Cappadocia *93.495*

καρδία, ας *f*
a inner self *26.3*
b inside *83.14*
καρδία : units
ἀναβαίνω ἐπὶ καρδίαν
    begin to think *30.17*
διανοίγω τὴν καρδίαν
    cause to be open-
    minded *27.49*
ἵσταμαι ἐν τῇ καρδίᾳ
    continue one's opin-
    ion *31.7*
πληρόω τὴν καρδίαν
    cause to think *30.29*
βάλλω εἰς τὴν καρδίαν
    cause to think *30.29*
τίθημι ἐν τῇ καρδίᾳ
    make up mind *30.76*
τίθεμαι ἐν τῇ καρδίᾳ
    treasure up in mind *29.2*
πηρόω τὴν καρδίαν
    make unable to learn *27.53*
πείθω τὴν καρδίαν
    be assured *25.166*
πλατύνω τὴν καρδίαν
    show affection for . . *25.53*
ἐπιστρέφω καρδίας ἐπί
    make friendly toward *25.95*
κατανύσσομαι τὴν
καρδίαν
    be greatly troubled *25.281*
συνθρύπτω τὴν καρδίαν
    cause great sorrow . . *25.282*
ἀπερίτμητος καρδίαις
καὶ τοῖς ὠσίν
    obstinate *88.224*
ῥαντίζομαι τὴν καρδίαν
    be purified *88.31*

καρδιογνώστης, ου *m*
knower of hearts *28.12*

Κάρπος, ου *m*
Carpus 93.210

καρπός, οῦ *m*
a fruit 3.33
b harvest 43.15
c deed 42.13
καρπός : units
καρπὸν (ἀπο)δίδωμι
  bear fruit 23.199
καρπὸν βλαστάνω
  bear fruit 23.199
καρπὸς τῆς κοιλίας
  child 10.38
καρπὸς τῆς ὀσφύος
  offspring 10.34
καρπὸς παραδίδωσι
  harvest is ripe 23.200
ποιέω καρπόν
  a produce fruit 23.199
  b cause results 13.86
καρπὸν φέρω
  bear fruit 23.199

καρποφορέω
a bear fruit 23.199
b cause results 13.86

καρποφόρος, ον
fruitful 23.201

καρτερέω
persevere 25.178

Καρυῶτος
Carioth, Kerioth 93.496

κάρφος, ους *n*
splinter, speck 3.66

κατά
a down, toward (ex-
  tension) 84.21
b along (extension) . . . 84.30
c throughout (exten-
  sion) 84.31
d facing toward (lo-
  cation) 83.45
e among (location) . . . 83.12
f opposite (location) . . 83.44
g when (time) 67.33

h about (time) 67.35
i in name of
  (guarantor) 90.29
j against (opposition) 90.31
k in accordance with
  (isomorphic) 89.8
l from . . . to (dis-
  tributive) 89.90
m with regard to
  (specification) 89.4
n with (association) . . . 89.113
κατά : units
κατ' ἀλήθειαν
  really 70.4
κατ' ἰδίαν
  privately 28.67
κατὰ βάθους
  extremely 78.22
κατὰ μέρος
  in detail 63.16
κατὰ μόνας
  alone 58.51
κατ' ὀφθαλμούς
  in presence of 83.34
κατὰ πρόσωπον
  a in front of 83.34
  b in person 83.38
τὰ κατὰ πρόσωπον
  outward appearance 31.31
κατὰ λόγον ἀνέχομαι
  accept a complaint . . 56.10
κατὰ κεφαλῆς ἔχω
  have one's head
  covered 49.16
κακόω τὴν ψυχὴν κατά
  cause to dislike 88.200
κατὰ σκοπὸν διώκω
  strive for a purpose 89.56

καταβαίνω
(fut καταβήσομαι, aor
κατέβην, impv κατά-
βηθι, κατάβα, inf κα-
ταβῆναι, ptc κατα-
βάς, pf καταβέβηκα)
move down 15.107

καταβάλλομαι
put down 85.49

καταβάλλω
a knock down *19.10*
b hurt badly *20.21*

καταβαπτίζω
wash *53.31*

καταβαρέω
cause undue hardship *22.26*

καταβαρύνομαι
καταβαρύνομαι : unit
ἦσαν οἱ ὀφθαλμοὶ
καταβαρυνόμενοι
be very sleepy *23.69*

κατάβασις, εως *f*
slope *15.109*

καταβιβάζω
make go down *15.108*

καταβολή, ῆς *f*
creation *42.37*
καταβολή : unit
καταβολὴ σπέρματος
conceive *23.49*

καταβραβεύω
disqualify *30.121*

καταγαγεῖν
see κατάγω

καταγγελεύς, έως *m*
proclaimer *33.205*

καταγγέλλω
(aor κατήγγειλα, aor
pass κατηγγέλην)
proclaim throughout *33.204*

καταγεινώσκω
see καταγινώσκω

καταγελάω
(impf κατεγέλων)
laugh at *33.410*

καταγινώσκω
(pf pass κατέγνωσμαι)
condemn *30.118*

κατάγνυμι
(fut κατεάξω, aor κατέ-
αξα, aor pass κατεάγην,
subj 3 pl κατεαγῶσιν)
break *19.35*

καταγράφω
write down *33.63*

κατάγομαι
(aor κατήχθην, ptc
καταχθείς)
arrive at land *54.15*

κατάγω
(aor κατήγαγον, inf
καταγαγεῖν)
a lead down *15.175*
b bring to shore *54.16*

καταγωνίζομαι
conquer *39.52*

καταδέω
wrap *79.118*

κατάδηλος, ον
easily understood *32.20*

καταδικάζω
condemn *56.31*

καταδίκη, ης *f*
condemnation *56.31*

καταδιώκω
seek for *27.43*

καταδουλόω
make subservient *37.27*

καταδυναστεύω
oppress *22.22*

κατάθεμα, τος *n*
cursed *33.474*

καταθεματίζω
curse 33.472

καταθέσθαι
see κατατίθεμαι

καταισχύνω
put to shame 25.194

κατακαίω
(fut κατακαύσω, aor
inf κατακαῦσαι, aor
pass κατεκάην, fut
pass κατακαήσομαι
and κατακαυθήσομαι)
burn down 14.66

κατακαλύπτομαι
cover one's head 49.16

κατακαυχάομαι
(impv 2 sg κατακαυχῶ)
a boast against 33.370
b despise 88.194
c have more power . . . 74.11

κατάκειμαι
a lie down 17.27
b recline to eat 17.23
c eat a meal 23.21

κατακλάω
break into pieces 19.38

κατακλείω
put into prison 37.125

κατακληρονομέω
make someone receive
a valuable gift 57.135

κατακλίνομαι
(aor κατεκλίθην)
recline to eat 17.23

κατακλίνω
cause to recline to eat 17.24

κατακλύζω
flood 14.34

κατακλυσμός, οῦ m
flood 14.34

κατακολουθέω
follow along behind . . 15.145

κατακόπτω
cut 19.21

κατακρημνίζω
throw down a cliff 15.221

κατάκριμα, τος n
condemnation 56.31

κατακρίνω
(aor pass κατεκρίθην)
condemn 56.31

κατάκρισις, εως f
condemnation 56.31

κατακύπτω
stoop down 17.30

κατακυριεύω
a rule 37.50
b overpower 39.55

καταλαλέω
slander 33.387

καταλαλιά, ᾶς f
slander 33.387

κατάλαλος, ου m
slanderer 33.388

καταλαμβάνομαι
(aor κατελαβόμην)
a learn about 27.10
b happen 13.119

καταλαμβάνω
(aor κατέλαβον, pf
κατείληφα, pf pass
κατείλημμαι, aor
pass κατελήμφθην)
a acquire 57.56
b attack 39.48
c seize 37.108

d overpower *37.19*
e understand *32.18*

καταλέγω
put on a list *33.44*

καταλείπω
(aor κατέλιπον, κατέλειφα, pf pass καταλέλειμμαι)
a leave *15.57*
b leave behind *85.65*
c leave to exist *13.92*
d neglect *30.51*
e no longer relate to . . *34.40*
f leave without help . . *35.17*

καταλιθάζω
stone to death *20.79*

καταλλαγή, ῆς *f*
reconciliation *40.1*

καταλλάσσω
(aor pass κατηλλάγην, ptc καταλλαγείς)
reconcile *40.1*

κατάλοιπος, ον
remaining *63.21*

κατάλυμα, τος *n*
a inn *7.11*
b room *7.30*

καταλύω
a tear down *20.54*
b destroy *20.55*
c put an end to *13.100*
d make invalid *76.23*
e be a guest *34.61*

καταμανθάνω
(aor impv 2 pl καταμάθετε)
consider *30.30*

καταμαρτυρέω
witness against *33.269*

καταμένω
remain *85.55*

καταναλίσκω
destroy completely . . . *20.48*

καταναρκάω
be financial burden . . . *57.224*

κατανεύω
gesture *33.485*

κατανοέω
a consider closely *30.4*
b be concerned about *30.43*
c understand completely *32.12*
d notice *24.51*

καταντάω
a reach *15.84*
b attain *13.16*
c come upon *13.121*

κατάνυξις, εως *f*
bewilderment *30.19*

κατανύσσομαι
(aor κατενύγην)
κατανύσσομαι : unit
κατανύσσομαι τὴν καρδίαν
be greatly troubled *25.281*

καταξιόω
regard as worthy *65.18*

καταπατέω
a trample on *19.52*
b despise *88.196*

κατάπαυσις, εως *f*
rest *23.81*

καταπαύω
a rest *23.81*
b cause to rest *23.85*
c cause to cease *68.46*

καταπέτασμα, τος *n*
curtain *6.160*

καταπίμπρημι
(aor κατέπρησα)
burn to ashes *14.66*

καταπίνω
(aor κατέπιον, inf κα-
ταπιεῖν, καταπεῖν, κα-
ταπῖν, subj 3 sg κατα-
πίει, καταπίη, aor
pass κατεπόθην, subj
καταποθῶ)
a swallow *23.45*
b destroy *20.52*
c cause end of *13.43*
καταπίνω : unit
καταπίνομαι λύπη
be overcome with
grief *25.285*

καταπίπτω
(aor κατέπεσον, ptc
καταπεσών)
a fall *15.118*
b fall down *15.119*

καταπλέω
(aor κατέπλευσα)
sail toward shore *54.13*

καταποθῶ
see καταπίνω

καταπονέομαι
be distressed *25.230*

καταπονέω
mistreat *88.126*

καταποντίζομαι
sink *15.116*

καταποντίζω
cause to sink *15.117*

κατάρα, ας *f*
a curse (activity) *33.471*
b curse (content) *33.473*
c cursed *33.474*

καταράομαι
(aor 2 sg κατηράσω,
pf κατήραμαι)
curse *33.471*

καταργέομαι
a be freed *37.136*
b cease *13.162*

καταργέω
a put an end to *13.100*
b put a stop to *13.163*
c invalidate *76.26*

καταριθμέομαι
belong to *34.33*

καταρτίζω
a make adequate *75.5*
b produce *13.130*
c create *42.36*

κατάρτισις, εως *f*
adequacy *75.5*

καταρτισμός, οῦ *m*
adequacy *75.5*

κατασείω
give a signal *33.478*

κατασκάπτω
tear down *20.56*

κατασκευάζω
a make ready *77.6*
b build *45.1*
κατασκευάζω : unit
κατασκευάζω τὴν ὁδόν
make ready *77.7*

κατασκηνόω
make a nest *6.147*

κατασκήνωσις, εως *f*
nest *6.146*

κατασκιάζω
cast a shadow upon . . . *14.62*

κατασκοπέω
observe secretly *24.50*

κατάσκοπος, ου *m*
spy *27.47*

κατασοφίζομαι
exploit with cunning   *88.147*

κατασταθήσομαι
see καθίστημι

καταστέλλω
(aor ptc καταστείλας,
pf pass κατέσταλμαι)
bring under control . . . *37.31*

κατάστημα, τος *n*
behavior *41.8*

καταστήσω
see καθίστημι

καταστολή, ῆς *f*
manner of dress *49.12*

καταστρέφω
turn over *16.18*

καταστρηνιάω
have lust *25.30*

καταστροφή, ῆς *f*
a harm *20.17*
b destruction *20.49*

καταστρώννυμι
(aor pass κατεστρώθην)
kill *20.63*

κατασύρω
drag off forcefully *15.179*

κατασφάζω
slaughter *20.72*

κατασφραγίζω
seal *6.55*

κατάσχεσις, εως *f*
a possession *57.1*
b taking possession . . . *57.57*

κατάσχω
see κατέχω

κατατίθεμαι
(aor inf καταθέσθαι)
experience *90.62*

κατατομή, ῆς *f*
mutilation *19.22*

κατατρέχω
(aor κατέδραμον)
run down to *15.233*

καταφάγομαι
see κατεσθίω

καταφέρομαι
(aor ptc κατενεχθείς)
καταφέρομαι : units
καταφέρομαι ὕπνῳ
   get sleepier *23.68*
καταφέρομαι ἀπὸ τοῦ
ὕπνου
   be sound asleep *23.71*

καταφέρω
(aor κατήνεγκα)
cause to happen *13.133*
καταφέρω : unit
καταφέρω ψῆφον
   vote against *30.103*

καταφεύγω
(aor κατέφυγον, ptc
καταφυγών)
a flee *15.62*
b take refuge *21.15*

καταφθείρω
(pf pass κατέφθαρμαι)
deprave *88.266*

καταφιλέω
kiss *34.62*

καταφρονέω
despise *88.192*

καταφρονητής, οῦ *m*
scoffer *88.193*

καταχέω
(aor 3 sg κατέχεεν)
pour over *47.5*

καταχθείς
see κατάγομαι

καταχθόνιος, ον
world below *1.17*

καταχράομαι
a make use of *90.13*
b be fully occupied . . . *41.6*

καταψύχω
make cool *79.76*

κατεάγην
see κατάγνυμι

κατεαγῶσιν
see κατάγνυμι

κατέαξα
see κατάγνυμι

κατεάξω
see κατάγνυμι

κατέβην
see καταβαίνω

κατεγέλων
see καταγελάω

κατέγνωσμαι
see καταγινώσκω

κατέδραμον
see κατατρέχω

κατείδωλος, ον
full of idols *6.98*

κατείλημμαι
see καταλαμβάνω

κατείληφα
see καταλαμβάνω

κατεκάην
see κατακαίω

κατεκρίθην
see κατακρίνω

κατελαβόμην
see καταλαμβάνομαι

κατέλαβον
see καταλαμβάνω

κατελήμφθην
see καταλαμβάνω

κατελθεῖν
see κατέρχομαι

κατέλιπον
see καταλείπω

κατέναντι
a opposite *83.42*
b in the judgment of *90.20*

κατενεχθείς
see καταφέρομαι

κατενύγην
see κατανύσσομαι

κατενώπιον
a in front of *83.33*
b in the judgment of *90.20*

κατεξουσιάζω
reign *37.48*

κατέπεσον
see καταπίπτω

κατεπέστησαν
see κατεφίστημι

κατέπιον
see καταπίνω

κατέπλευσα
see καταπλέω

κατεπόθην
see καταπίνω

κατέπρησα
see καταπίμπρημι

κατεργάζομαι
a accomplish........ *42.17*
b do............... *90.47*
c result in *13.9*
d prepare.......... *77.6*

κατέρχομαι
(aor κατῆλθον, inf
κατελθεῖν)
a move down *15.107*
b arrive at land *54.15*

κατεσθίω
(fut καταφάγομαι, aor
κατέφαγον)
a eat up *23.11*
b destroy utterly *20.45*
c rob *57.247*
d waste *57.150*
e exploit completely *88.145*

κατέσθω
see κατεσθίω

κατεστάθην
see καθίστημι

κατέσταλμαι
see καταστέλλω

κατέστησα
see καθίστημι

κατεστρώθην
see καταστρώννυμι

κατευθύνω
(aor opt 3 sg κατευθύ-
ναι, inf κατευθῦναι)
guide *36.1*
κατευθύνω : unit
κατευθύνω τοὺς πόδας
guide behavior *41.17*

κατευλογέω
bless *33.470*

κατέφαγον
see κατεσθίω

κατέφθαρμαι
see καταφθείρω

κατεφίσταμαι (+ 2 aor act)
(aor 3 pl κατεπέστησαν)
attack *39.47*

κατέφυγον
see καταφεύγω

κατέχεεν
see καταχέω

κατέχω
(aor subj κατάσχω)
a prevent.......... *13.150*
b continue belief..... *31.48*
c possess *57.1*
d control *37.17*
e occupy *85.9*
κατέχω : unit
κατέχω εἰς
head for *54.22*

κατήγαγον
see κατάγω

κατήγγειλα
see καταγγέλλω

κατηγγέλην
see καταγγέλλω

κατηγορέω
accuse *33.427*

138

κατηγορία, ας *f*
accusation *33.428*

κατήγορος, ου *m*
accuser *33.429*

κατήγωρ, ορος *m*
accuser *33.429*

κατῆλθον
see κατέρχομαι

κατηλλάγην
see καταλλάσσω

κατήνεγκα
see καταφέρω

κατήραμαι
see καταράομαι

κατηράσω
see καταράομαι

κατήφεια, ας *f*
depression *25.296*

κατηχέω
a teach *33.225*
b inform *33.190*

κατήχθην
see κατάγομαι

κατιόομαι
(pf 3 sg κατίωται)
become rusty *2.61*

κατισχύω
a be fully able *74.10*
b be strong enough . . . *79.64*
c defeat *39.56*

κατοικέω
(aor κατῴκησα)
dwell *85.69*

κατοίκησις, εως *f*
dwelling place *85.70*

κατοικητήριον, ου *n*
dwelling place *85.70*

κατοικία, ας *f*
dwelling place *85.70*

κατοικίζω
(aor κατῴκισα)
cause to dwell *85.82*

κατοπτρίζομαι
a see by reflection *24.44*
b reflect *14.52*

κάτω
a below (location) *83.53*
b down to (direction) *84.26*

κατῴκησα
see κατοικέω

κατῴκισα
see κατοικίζω

κατώτερος, α, ον
lower *83.54*

κατωτέρω
lesser *59.16*

Καῦδα
Cauda *93.497*

καυθήσομαι
see καίω

καυθήσωμαι
see καίω

καῦμα, τος *n*
scorching heat *14.67*

καυματίζω
harm by heat *14.68*

καῦσις, εως *f*
burning *14.63*

καυσόομαι
burn *14.63*

καυστηριάζομαι
καυστηριάζομαι : unit
καυστηριάζομαι τὴν
συνείδησιν
    be insensitive to *27.54*

καύσων, ωνος *m*
    scorching heat *14.67*

καυχάομαι
    boast *33.368*

καύχημα, τος *n*
    a boast............ *33.368*
    b what one boasts
      about *33.371*
    c the right to boast ... *33.372*
    d basis of pride *25.203*

καύχησις, εως *f*
    a boasting *33.368*
    b what one boasts
      about *33.371*
    c pride *25.204*

Καφαρναούμ *f*
    Capernaum *93.498*

Κεγχρεαί, ῶν *f*
    Cenchreae *93.499*

Κεδρών *m*
    Kidron............ *93.500*

κεῖμαι
    a recline *17.26*
    b be in a place *85.3*
    c exist *13.73*

κειρία, ας *f*
    strip of cloth *6.156*

κείρω
    cut hair *19.23*

κέκαυμαι
    see καίω

κεκέρασμαι
    see κεράννυμι

κέκληκα
    see καλέω

κέκλικα
    see κλίνω

κεκόρεσμαι
    see κορέννυμι

κέκραγα
    see κράζω

κέκρικα
    see κρίνω

κέκρυμμαι
    see κρύπτω

κέλευσμα, τος *n*
    call of command *33.324*

κελεύω
    command........... *33.323*

κενοδοξία, ας *f*
    cheap pride *88.221*

κενόδοξος, ον
    falsely proud *88.222*

κενός, ή, όν
    a without anything ... *57.42*
    b foolish *32.60*
    c without result *89.53*
    d without purpose ... *89.64*
    e untrue *72.10*

κενοφωνία, ας *f*
    foolish talk......... *33.376*

κενόω
    a cause to lose power *76.27*
    b empty oneself *87.70*

κέντρον, ου *n*
    a stinger *8.45*
    b goad *6.9*
    c power to kill....... *20.69*
    d power to hurt...... *24.86*

κέντρον : unit
πρὸς κέντρα λακτίζω
   hurt by resistance... *39.19*

κεντυρίων, ωνος *m*
Roman officer *55.16*

κενῶς
for no purpose *89.64*

κεραία, ας *f*
part of letter *33.37*

κεραμεύς, έως *m*
potter *6.129*

κεραμικός, ή, όν
made of potter's clay .. *2.19*

κεράμιον, ου *n*
jar *6.128*

κέραμος, ου *m*
tile *6.224*

κεράννυμι
(aor ἐκέρασα, pf pass
κεκέρασμαι)
a mix............... *63.9*
b pour *47.3*

κέρας, ατος *n*
a horn *8.17*
b corner *79.105*
c power *76.16*

κεράτιον, ου *n*
carob pod.......... *3.46*

κερδαίνω
(fut κερδήσω, aor ἐκέρ-
δησα, subj κερδήσω,
κερδάνω, inf κερδῆσαι)
a make profit *57.189*
b avoid *13.137*

κέρδος, ους *n*
profit *57.192*

κέρμα, τος *n*
coin *6.71*

κερματιστής, οῦ *m*
moneychanger *57.205*

κεφάλαιον, ου *n*
a summary *33.12*
b price............ *57.162*

κεφαλή, ῆς *f*
a head *8.10*
b superior *87.51*
κεφαλή : units
κεφαλὴ γωνίας
   cornerstone *7.44*
κατὰ κεφαλῆς ἔχω
   have one's head
   covered........ *49.16*
τὴν κεφαλὴν κλίνω
   lie down to rest *23.83*
ἐπαίρω τὴν κεφαλήν
   have courage *25.160*
ἐπὶ τὴν κεφαλήν
   responsibility *37.102*
σωρεύω ἄνθρακας πυ-
ρὸς ἐπὶ τὴν κεφαλήν
   cause to be ashamed *25.199*

κεφαλιόω
beat on the head *19.13*

κεφαλίς, ίδος *f*
section of a scroll..... *6.67*

κημόω
muzzle............. *44.6*

κῆνσος, ου *m*
tax *57.180*

κῆπος, ου *m*
garden *1.97*

κηπουρός, οῦ *m*
gardener *43.20*

κηρίον, ου *n*
honeycomb *5.21*

κήρυγμα, τος *n*
preaching.......... *33.258*

κῆρυξ, υχος *m*
preacher 33.259

κηρύσσω
a announce 33.206
b tell 33.207
c preach 33.256

κῆτος, ους *n*
big fish 4.61

Κηφᾶς, ᾶ *m*
Cephas 93.211

κιβωτός, οῦ *f*
a boat 6.44
b box 6.139

κιθάρα, ας *f*
lyre 6.83

κιθαρίζω
play the lyre 6.84

κιθαρῳδός, οῦ *m*
harpist 6.85

Κιλικία, ας *f*
Cilicia 93.501

κινδυνεύω
a be in danger 21.2
b run a risk 21.6

κίνδυνος, ου *m*
danger 21.1

κινέω
a move 15.1
b cause to move 15.3
c shake 16.2
d start a riot 39.44
e cause 90.53

κίνησις, εως *f*
movement 16.1

κιννάμωμον, ου *n*
cinnamon 5.24

Κίς *m*
Kish 93.212

κίχρημι
(aor impv χρῆσον)
lend 57.214

Κλάδιν
see Κλαῦδα 93.502

κλάδος, ου *m*
branch 3.49

κλαίω
(aor ἔκλαυσα)
weep 25.138

κλάσις, εως *f*
breaking 19.34

κλάσμα, τος *n*
piece 19.40

Κλαῦδα
Clauda 93.502

Κλαύδη
see Κλαῦδα 93.502

Κλαυδία, ας *f*
Claudia 93.213

Κλαύδιον
see Κλαῦδα 93.502

Κλαύδιος, ου *m*
Claudius 93.214

κλαυθμός, οῦ *m*
weeping 25.138

κλάω
break 19.34
κλάω : unit
ἄρτον κλάω
have a meal 23.20

κλείς, κλειδός *f*
a key 6.220
b means of 57.63

κλείω
  close............... *79.112*
  κλείω : unit
  κλείω τὰ σπλάγχνα
    refuse to show
    compassion *25.55*

κλέμμα, τος *n*
  theft.............. *57.232*

Κλεοπᾶς, ᾶ *m*
  Cleopas *93.215*

κλέος, ους *n*
  honor............. *87.5*

κλέπτης, ου *m*
  thief.............. *57.233*

κλέπτω
  steal.............. *57.232*

κληθήσομαι
  see καλέω

κλῆμα, τος *n*
  branch *3.50*

Κλήμης, ενος *m*
  Clement........... *93.216*

κληρονομέω
  a receive *57.131*
  b inherit *57.138*

κληρονομία, ας *f*
  a possession *57.132*
  b inheritance....... *57.140*

κληρονόμος, ου *m*
  a receiver *57.133*
  b heir............. *57.139*

κλῆρος, ου *m*
  a lot.............. *6.219*
  b possession *57.88*
  c ministry *37.101*
  d responsibility..... *35.49*
  e part *63.18*

κλῆρος : unit
ὁ κλῆρος πίπτει ἐπί τινα
  choose by lot *30.107*

κληρόω
  choose *30.105*

κλῆσις, εως *f*
  a call *33.312*
  b calling *33.313*
  c role............. *87.2*

κλητός, ή, όν
  a called *33.314*
  b invited *33.318*

κλίβανος, ου *m*
  oven *7.74*

κλίμα, τος *n*
  region *1.79*

κλινάριον, ου *n*
  cot *6.107*

κλίνη, ης *f*
  bed............... *6.106*
  κλίνη : unit
  βάλλω εἰς κλίνην
    cause illness *23.152*

κλινίδιον, ου *n*
  cot *6.107*

κλίνω
  (pf κέκλικα)
  a bow *16.16*
  b put to flight *15.65*
  c draw to a close *67.118*
  d begin to end *68.51*
  κλίνω : units
  τὴν κεφαλὴν κλίνω
    lie down to rest *23.83*
  κλίνω τὸ πρόσωπον
  εἰς τὴν γήν
    prostrate oneself ... *17.21*

κλισία, ας *f*
  eating group *11.5*

κλοπή, ῆς f
  theft 57.232

κλύδων, ωνος m
  wave 14.25

κλυδωνίζομαι
  be tossed about by
  waves 16.12

Κλωπᾶς, ᾶ m
  Clopas 93.217

κνήθομαι
  κνήθομαι : unit
  κνήθομαι τὴν ἀκοήν
    desirous of hearing　25.11

Κνίδος, ου f
  Cnidus 93.503

κοδράντης, ου m
  coin 6.78

κοιλία, ας f
  a belly 8.67
  b womb 8.69
  c feelings 26.11
  d desires 25.28
  κοιλία : units
  καρπὸς τῆς κοιλίας
    child 10.38
  ἡ κοιλία βαστάζει
    be pregnant with . . . 23.51

κοιμάομαι
  a sleep 23.66
  b be dead 23.104

κοίμησις, εως f
  sleep 23.66

κοινός, ή, όν
  a mutual 57.9
  b defiled 53.39
  c worthless 65.15
  d in common 89.118
  κοινός : unit
  ἔχω κοινός
    share mutually 57.99

κοινόω
  a defile 53.33
  b regard as defiled . . . 53.40

κοινωνέω
  a share 57.98
  b do together with . . . 42.16
  κοινωνέω : unit
  κοινωνέω αἵματος καὶ
  σαρκός
    be a person 9.15

κοινωνία, ας f
  a fellowship 34.5
  b share 57.98
  c willing contribution　57.101

κοινωνικός, ή, όν
  ready sharing 57.100

κοινωνός, οῦ m
  partner 34.6

κοίτη, ης f
  a bed 6.108
  b sexual life 23.62
  c sexual immorality . . 88.273
  κοίτη : unit
  κοίτην ἔχω
    be pregnant 23.50

κοιτών, ῶνος m
  bedroom 7.29

κόκκινον, ου n
  scarlet cloth 6.170

κόκκινος, η, ον
  scarlet 79.29

κόκκος, ου m
  seed 3.35

κολάζω
  punish 38.2

κολακεία, ας f
  flattering talk 33.367

κόλασις, εως f
  punishment 38.2

κολαφίζω
a strike with fist *19.7*
b cause harm *20.27*

κολλάομαι
a join *34.22*
b cling to *18.21*
κολλάομαι : unit
κολλάομαι ἄχρι τοῦ
οὐρανοῦ
   increase greatly *59.66*

κολλούριον, ου *n*
eye salve *6.203*

κολλυβιστής, οῦ *m*
moneychanger *57.205*

κολοβόω
reduce in number *59.71*

Κολοσσαί, ῶν *f*
Colossae *93.504*

κόλπος, ου *m*
a lap *8.39*
b fold *6.181*
c bay *1.74*
κόλπος : units
κόλπος ’Αβραάμ
heaven *1.16*
εἰμὶ εἰς τὸν κόλπον
be closely associated *34.18*
ἀνάκειμαι ἐν τῷ κόλπῳ
dine in place of
honor *17.25*

κολυμβάω
swim *15.246*

κολυμβήθρα, ας *f*
pool *7.58*

κολωνία, ας *f*
colony *1.90*

κομάω
wear long hair *49.25*

κόμη, ης *f*
hair *8.14*

κομίζομαι
(fut κομίσομαι,
κομιοῦμαι)
a receive *57.126*
b receive back *57.136*

κομίζω
a carry to *15.191*
b cause to experience *90.92*

κομψότερον
be in better health *23.135*

κονιάω
whitewash *45.12*
κονιάω : unit
τοῖχος κεχονιαμένος
impostor *88.234*

κονιορτός, οῦ *m*
dust *2.15*

κοπάζω
cease *68.42*

κοπετός, οῦ *m*
lamentation *52.1*

κοπή, ῆς *f*
slaughter *20.74*

κοπιάω
a labor *42.47*
b be tired *23.78*
c lose heart *25.289*

κόπος, ου *m*
a labor *42.47*
b trouble *22.7*

κοπρία, ας *f*
dung heap *8.77*

κόπριον, ου *n*
dung *8.76*

κόπτομαι
mourn *52.1*

κόπτω
cut *19.17*

κόραξ, ακος *m*
crow, raven *4.43*

κοράσιον, ου *n*
girl *9.40*

κορβᾶν
gift to God *53.22*

κορβανᾶς, ᾶ *m*
treasury *7.33*

Κόρε *m*
Korah *93.218*

κορέννυμι
(pf pass κεκόρεσμαι,
aor pass ptc κορεσθείς)
a be content *25.80*
b have enough *57.22*

Κορίνθιος, ου *m*
Corinthian *93.505*

Κόρινθος, ου *f*
Corinth *93.506*

Κορνήλιος, ου *m*
Cornelius *93.219*

κόρος, ου *m*
cor *81.21*

κοσμέω
beautify *79.12*

κοσμικός, ή, όν
a earthly *1.40*
b worldly *41.39*

κόσμιος, ον
a modest *88.48*
b proper *66.10*

κοσμοκράτωρ, ορος *m*
a world ruler *37.73*
b supernatural power *12.44*

κόσμος, ου *m*
a universe *1.1*
b earth *1.39*

c world system *41.38*
d people *9.23*
e adorning *79.12*
f adornment *6.188*
g tremendous amount *59.55*
κόσμος : unit
αἰὼν τοῦ κόσμου τούτου
supernatural power *12.44*

Κούαρτος, ου *m*
Quartus *93.220*

κουμ
stand up *17.8*

κουστωδία, ας *f*
guard *55.13*

κουφίζω
make less heavy *86.3*

κόφινος, ου *m*
large basket *6.150*

κράβαττος, ου *m*
cot *6.107*

κράζω
(aor ἐκέκραξα, pf
κέκραγα)
shout *33.83*

κραιπάλη, ης *f*
drunken dissipation . . *88.286*

κρανίον, ου *n*
skull *8.11*

κράσπεδον, ου *n*
a fringe *6.180*
b tassel *6.194*

κραταιόομαι
a become strong *23.134*
b become powerful . . . *76.10*

κραταιός, ά, όν
powerful *76.9*

κρατέω
a hold on to *18.6*

b control *37.16*
c arrest *37.110*
d keep *13.34*
e accomplish *68.29*

κράτιστος, η, ον
most excellent *87.55*

κράτος, ους n
a power *76.6*
b mighty deed *76.7*

κραυγάζω
shout *33.83*

κραυγή, ῆς f
a shout *33.84*
b weeping *25.138*

κρέας, κρέατος/κρέως, acc pl
κρέα n
meat *5.14*

κρείσσων
see κρείττων

κρείττων, ον
a better (value) *65.21*
b greater (status) *87.28*

κρέμαμαι
a hang from *18.22*
b depend upon *89.2*

κρεμάννυμι
(aor ptc κρεμάσας,
aor pass ἐκρεμάσθην,
ptc κρεμασθείς)
cause to hang *18.23*
κρεμάννυμι : unit
κρεμάννυμι ἐπὶ ξύλου
crucify *20.76*

κρημνός, οῦ m
steep slope *1.50*

Κρής, ητός m
Cretan *93.507*

Κρήσκης, εντος m
Crescens *93.221*

Κρήτη, ης f
Crete *93.508*

κριθή, ῆς f
barley *3.44*

κριθῆναι
see κρίνω

κριθήσομαι
see κρίνω

κρίθινος, η, ον
made of barley *3.45*

κρίμα, τος n
a legal decision *56.20*
b authority to judge . . *56.22*
c verdict *56.24*
d condemnation *56.30*
e lawsuit *56.2*
f judgment *30.110*

κρίνον, ου n
wild flower *3.32*

κρίνω
(pf κέκρικα, aor pass
ἐκρίθην, inf κριθῆναι,
fut pass κριθήσομαι)
a decide *30.75*
b prefer *30.99*
c evaluate *30.108*
d hold a view *31.1*
e make legal decision *56.20*
f condemn *56.30*
g rule *37.49*

κρίσις, εως f
a legal decision *56.20*
b authority to judge . . *56.22*
c court of justice *56.1*
d verdict *56.24*
e condemnation *56.30*
f justice *56.25*
g judgment *30.110*
h basis for judgment *30.111*
i punishment *38.1*
κρίσις : unit
ὑπὸ κρίσιν πίπτω
be condemned *56.32*

Κρίσπος, ου *m*
  Crispus 93.222

κριτήριον, ου *n*
  a court of justice 56.1
  b lawsuit 56.2

κριτής, οῦ *m*
  judge 56.28

κριτικός, ή, όν
  able to judge 56.23

κρούω
  knock 19.12

κρυβῆναι
  see κρύπτω

κρύπτη, ης *f*
  secret place 28.78

κρυπτός, ή, όν
  secret 28.69
  κρυπτός : units
  ὁ ἐν τῷ κρυπτῷ (ἄν-
  θρωπος)
    inner being 26.1
  τὰ κρυπτά
    secret knowledge . . . 28.75
  ἐν (τῷ) κρυπτῷ
    secretly 28.71

κρύπτω
  (pf pass κέκρυμμαι,
  aor pass ἐκρύβην,
  inf κρυβῆναι)
  a keep safe 21.12
  b made invisible 24.29
  c hide 24.30
  d keep secret 28.79

κρυσταλλίζω
  shine like crystal 2.47

κρύσταλλος, ου *m*
  a crystal 2.46
  b ice 2.11

κρυφαῖος, α, ον
  in secret 28.72

κρυφῇ
  secretly 28.71

κτάομαι
  acquire 57.58
  κτάομαι : units
  σκεῦος κτάομαι
    sexual life 23.63
  κτάομαι τὴν ψυχήν
    protect oneself 21.20

κτῆμα, τος *n*
  property 57.15

κτῆνος, ους *n*
  beast of burden 4.6

κτήτωρ, ορος *m*
  owner 57.11

κτίζω
  create 42.35

κτίσις, εως *f*
  a creation 42.35
  b creature 42.38
  c universe 1.4
  d institution 42.39
  e authority 37.43

κτίσμα, τος *n*
  creature 42.38

κτίστης, ου *m*
  creator 42.40

κυβεία, ας *f*
  trickery 88.157

κυβέρνησις, εως *f*
  guidance 36.3

κυβερνήτης, ου *m*
  captain of a ship 54.28

κυκλεύω
  surround 15.147

κυκλόθεν
  a around 83.19
  b (on) the outside 83.22

κυκλόω
  a go around........ 15.146
  b surround 15.147

κύκλῳ
  around 83.19

κυλίομαι
  roll about 16.17

κυλισμός, οῦ m
  rolling about 16.17

κυλλός, ή, όν
  crippled 23.176

κῦμα, τος n
  wave 14.25

κύμβαλον, ου n
  cymbals 6.94

κύμινον, ου n
  cummin 3.25

κυνάριον, ου n
  house dog 4.35

Κύπριος, ου m
  Cyprian 93.509

Κύπρος, ου f
  Cyprus........... 93.510

κύπτω
  stoop down 17.29

Κυρηναῖος, ου m
  Cyrenian 93.511

Κυρήνη, ης f
  Cyrene........... 93.512

Κυρήνιος, ου m
  Quirinius.......... 93.223

κυρία, ας f
  lady 87.54

κυριακός, ή, όν
  belonging to the Lord 12.10

κυριεύω
  rule 37.50

κύριος, ου m
  a Lord........... 12.9
  b owner.......... 57.12
  c ruler 37.51
  d sir 87.53
  κύριος : units
  ὀνομάζω τὸ ὄνομα κυρίου
    say that one belongs
    to the Lord 53.62
  τῷ ἰδίῳ κυρίῳ στήκει
  ἢ πίπτει
    honor depends on
    master's judgment .. 87.56

κυριότης, ητος f
  a ruling power 37.52
  b supernatural power 12.44

κυρόω
  a validate 76.18
  b show something to
     be real 70.6

κύων, κυνός, dat pl κυσί m
  a dog........... 4.34
  b bad person 88.122
  c pervert 88.282

κῶλον, ου n
  corpse 8.8

κωλύω
  prevent 13.146

κώμη, ης f
  a village 1.92
  b people of a village .. 11.62

κωμόπολις, εως f
  town 1.91

κῶμος, ου m
  orgy 88.287

κώνωψ, ωπος m
  gnat 4.48

Κώς, Κῶ *f*
Cos 93.513

Κωσάμ *m*
Cosam 93.224

κωφός, ή, όν
  a mute 33.106
  b deaf 24.68

λαβεῖν
  see λαμβάνω

λάβοι
  see λαμβάνω

λαβών
  see λαμβάνω

λαγχάνω
  (aor ἔλαχον, subj
  λάχω, ptc λαχών)
  a receive 57.127
  b choose by lot 30.104
  c be chosen by lot 30.106

Λάζαρος, ου *m*
Lazarus 93.225

λαθεῖν
  see λανθάνω

λάθρᾳ
  secretly 28.71

λαῖλαψ, απος *f*
  windstorm 14.6

λακάω
  burst open 19.30

λακτίζω
  λακτίζω : unit
  πρὸς κέντρα λακτίζω
    hurt by resistance . . 39.19

λαλέω
  speak 33.70

λαλέω : unit
πρὸς τὸ οὖς λαλέω
  whisper 33.91

λαλιά, ᾶς *f*
  a utterance 33.101
  b accent 33.102

λαμβάνω
  (fut λήμψομαι, aor
  ἔλαβον, inf λαβεῖν,
  ptc λαβών, opt 3 sg
  λάβοι, pf εἴληφα, pf
  pass 3 sg εἴληπται)
  a take hold of 18.1
  b acquire 57.55
  c receive 57.125
  d collect 57.65
  e select 30.86
  f come to believe . . . 31.50
  g exploit by deception 88.146
  h experience 90.63
  i cause to experience 90.85
  j put on (clothes) 49.10
  k do 90.48
  λαμβάνω : units
  λαμβάνω θάρσος
    take courage 25.157
  λαμβάνω τὸν σταυρόν
    suffer (unto death) 24.83
  λαμβάνω βασιλείαν
    become a king 37.65
  πεῖραν λαμβάνω
    attempt 68.58
  λαμβάνω πρόσωπον
    show favoritism 88.238

Λάμεχ *m*
Lamech 93.226

λαμπάς, άδος *f*
  a torch 6.102
  b lamp 6.104

λαμπρός, ά, όν
  a shining 14.50
  b sparkling 79.25
  c glamorous 79.20

λαμπρότης, ητος *f*
  brightness 14.49

λαμπρῶς
luxuriously 88.255

λάμπω
shine 14.37

λανθάνω
(aor ἔλαθον, inf λαθεῖν)
a escape notice 28.83
b forget 29.13
c not know 28.14

λαξευτός, ή, όν
hewn out of rock   19.26

Λαοδίκεια, ας f
Laodicea 93.514

Λαοδικεύς, έως m
Laodicean 93.515

λαός, οῦ m
a nation 11.55
b people of God 11.12
c crowd 11.1
d common people 87.64

λάρυγξ, γγος m
throat 8.26

Λασαία, ας f
Lasea 93.516

λατομέω
hew out rock 19.25

λατρεία, ας f
worship 53.14

λατρεύω
worship 53.14

λάχανον, ου n
garden plant 3.29

λάχω
see λαγχάνω

λαχών
see λαγχάνω

Λεββαῖος, ου m
Lebbaeus 93.227

Λεββεδαῖος, ου m
Lebbedaeus 93.228

λεγιών, ῶνος f
army unit 55.8

Λεγιών, ῶνος m
Legion 93.229

λέγω
(fut ἐρῶ, aor εἶπον, εἶπα,
inf εἰπεῖν, pf εἴρηκα,
plpf 3 sg εἰρήκει, pf
pass εἴρημαι, aor pass
ἐρρέθην, ptc ῥηθείς)
a speak 33.69
b name 33.129
c call 33.131
d mean 33.138
e imply 33.140
λέγω : units
ὡς ἔπος εἰπεῖν
so to speak 33.139
λέγω ἐν ἑαυτῷ
think to oneself 31.5

λεῖμμα, τος n
remnant 63.22

λεῖος, α, ον
smooth 79.86

λείπω
a be in need 57.43
b not possessed 57.44
c ought to 71.33

λειτουργέω
a serve 35.22
b perform religious
duties 53.13

λειτουργία, ας f
a service 35.22
b ministry 35.25
c performance of
religious duties 53.13

151

λειτουργικός, ή, όν
serving 35.24

λειτουργός, οῦ *m*
servant 35.23

λεμα
why 89.38

λέντιον, ου *n*
towel 6.161

λεπίς, ίδος *f*
flake 8.57

λέπρα, ας *f*
leprosy 23.161

λεπρός, οῦ *m*
leper 23.162

λεπτόν, οῦ *n*
small coin 6.79

λευδορέω
see λοιδορέω

Λευεί
see Λευί 93.230

Λευή(ς)
see Λευί 93.230

Λευί, acc ίν *m*
Levi 93.231

Λευίς
see Λευί 93.232

Λευίτης, ου *m*
Levite 53.91

Λευιτικός, ή, όν
Levitical 53.92

λευκαίνω
(aor ἐλεύχανα, inf
λευχᾶναι)
make white 79.28

λευκός, ή, όν
a white 79.27
b radiant 14.50

λέων, οντος *m*
lion 4.14

λήθη, ης *f*
forgetting 29.13

λῆμψις, εως *f*
receiving 57.125

λήμψομαι
see λαμβάνω

ληνός, οῦ *f*
wine press 7.66

λῆρος, ου *m*
pure nonsense 33.380

ληστής, οῦ *m*
a robber 57.240
b rebel 39.37

λίαν
very 78.1

λίβα
see λίψ

λίβανος, ου *m*
frankincense 6.212

λιβανωτός, οῦ *m*
censer 6.138

Λιβερτῖνος, ου *m*
free man 87.86

Λιβύη, ης *f*
Libya 93.517

λιθάζω
stone to death 20.79

λίθινος, η, ον
made out of stone 2.25

λιθοβολέω
stone to death *20.79*

λίθος, ου *m*
  a stone (substance) ... *2.23*
  b stone (piece) *2.24*
  λίθος : unit
  λίθος τίμιος
    gem *2.29*

λιθόστρωτον, ου *n*
The Stone Pavement *7.71*

λικμάω
crush *19.47*

λιμήν, ένος *m*
harbor *1.75*

λίμνη, ης *f*
  lake *1.72*
  λίμνη : unit
  λίμνη τοῦ πυρός (καὶ
  θείου)
    hell *1.22*

λιμός, οῦ *m, f*
  a famine *23.33*
  b hunger *23.31*

λίνον, ου *n*
  a linen garment *6.165*
  b wick *6.158*

Λίνος, ου *m*
Linus *93.233*

λιπαρός, ά, όν
luxurious *79.21*

λίτρα, ας *f*
pound *86.4*

λίψ, acc λίβα *m*
southwest *82.6*

λογεία, ας *f*
collection *57.66*

λόγια, ων *n*
sayings *33.97*

λογίζομαι
  a reason about *30.9*
  b keep mental record *29.4*
  c hold a view *31.1*
  d charge to account... *57.227*

λογικός, ή, όν
true to real nature *73.5*

λόγιος, α, ον
  a eloquent *33.32*
  b learned *27.20*

λογισμός, οῦ *m*
  a reasoning *30.9*
  b false reasoning *30.11*

λογομαχέω
argue about words *33.454*

λογομαχία, ας *f*
arguing about words .. *33.454*

λόγος, ου *m*
  a statement *33.98*
  b speech *33.99*
  c gospel........... *33.260*
  d treatise *33.51*
  e Word *33.100*
  f account *57.228*
  g reason *89.18*
  h event *13.115*
  i appearance........ *30.13*
  j accusation *56.7*
  λόγος : units
  λόγος τρέχει
    message spreads *28.25*
  λόγου ποιοῦμαι
    be of opinion *31.2*
  κατὰ λόγον ἀνέχομαι
    accept a complaint .. *56.10*

λόγχη, ης *f*
spear *6.34*

λοιδορέω
slander *33.393*

λοιδορία, ας *f*
slander *33.393*

λοίδορος, ου *m*
  slanderer 33.395

λοιμός, οῦ *m*
  a plague 23.158
  b troublemaker 22.6

(τὸ) λοιπόν
  a from now on 67.134
  b still 67.128
  c at last 61.14
  d furthermore 89.98

λοιπός, ή, όν
  remaining 63.21

Λουκᾶς, ᾶ *m*
  Luke 93.234

Λούκιος, ου *m*
  Lucius 93.235

λουτρόν, οῦ *n*
  washing 53.43

λούω
  wash 47.12

Λύδδα, ας *f*
  Lydda 93.518

Λυδία, ας *f*
  Lydia 93.236

Λυκαονία, ας *f*
  Lycaonia 93.519

Λυκαονιστί
  in Lycaonian 33.8

Λυκία, ας *f*
  Lycia 93.520

λύκος, ου *m*
  a wolf 4.11
  b fierce person 88.121

λυμαίνομαι
  a injure severely 20.24
  b destroy 20.31

λυπέομαι
  be sad 25.274

λυπέω
  make sad 25.275

λύπη, ης *f*
  a regret 25.272
  b sadness 25.273
  λύπη : unit
  καταπίνομαι λύπη
    be overcome with
    grief 25.285

Λυσανίας, ου *m*
  Lysanias 93.237

Λυσίας, ου *m*
  Lysias 93.238

λύσις, εως *f*
  divorce 34.78

λυσιτελεῖ
  be advantageous 65.44

Λύστρα *f, n*
  Lystra 93.521

λύτρον, ου *n*
  ransom 37.130

λυτρόομαι
  liberate 37.128

λύτρωσις, εως *f*
  liberation 37.128

λυτρωτής, οῦ *m*
  liberator 37.129

λυχνία, ας *f*
  lampstand 6.105

λύχνος, ου *m*
  lamp 6.104

λύω
  a untie 18.18
  b set free 37.127
  c destroy 20.53

d dismiss 15.139
e transgress 36.30
f permit 37.47
g do away with 13.38
h put an end to 13.100

Λωΐς, ΐδος f
Lois 93.239

Λώτ m
Lot 93.240

Μάαθ m
Maath 93.241

Μαγαδά
see Μαγαδάν 93.522

Μαγαδάν f
Magadan 93.522

Μαγδαλά f
Magdala 93.523

Μαγδαλάν f
Magdala, Magadan . . . 93.524

Μαγδαληνή, ῆς f
Magdalene 93.242

Μαγεδά
see Μαγαδάν 93.525

Μαγεδάλ f
Magdala, Magadan . . . 93.524

Μαγεδάν
see Μαγαδάν 93.522

μαγεία, ας f
magic 53.96

μαγεύω
practice magic 53.96

μάγος, ου m
a wise man and priest 32.40
b magician 53.97

Μαγώγ m
Magog 93.243

Μαδιάμ m
Midian 93.526

μαθεῖν
see μανθάνω

μαθητεύω
a follow 36.31
b make followers 36.37

μαθητής, οῦ m
a follower 36.38
b pupil 27.16

μαθήτρια, ας f
woman disciple 36.41

Μαθθαῖος, ου m
Matthew 93.244

Μαθθάτ m
Matthat 93.245

Μαθθίας, ου m
Matthias 93.246

Μαθουσαλά m
Methuselah 93.247

μαίνομαι
be insane 30.24

μακαρίζω
regard as happy 25.120

μακάριος, α, ον
happy 25.119

μακαρισμός, οῦ m
happiness 25.118

Μακεδονία, ας f
Macedonia 93.527

Μακεδών, όνος m
Macedonian 93.528

μάχελλον, ου *n*
meat market 57.208

μακράν
far (away) 83.30

μακρόθεν
far (away) 83.30

μακροθυμέω
a be patient 25.168
b delay in 67.126

μακροθυμία, ας *f*
patience 25.167

μακροθύμως
patiently 25.169

μακρός, ά, όν
a long (time) 67.89
b far (away) 81.14

μακροχρόνιος, ον
long (time) 67.89

μαλακία, ας *f*
sickness 23.154

μαλακός, ή, όν
a soft 79.100
b homosexual 88.281

Μαλελεήλ *m*
Maleleel 93.248

μάλιστα
especially 78.7

μᾶλλον
a more (than) 78.28
b instead 89.126
μᾶλλον : unit
ἀλλὰ μᾶλλον
but 89.125

Μάλχος, ου *m*
Malchus 93.249

μάμμη, ης *f*
grandmother 10.19

μαμωνᾶς, ᾶ *m*
worldly wealth 57.34

Μαναήν *m*
Manaen 93.250

Μανασσῆς, ῆ *m*
Manasseh 93.251

μανθάνω
(aor ἔμαθον, inf μαθεῖν,
pf μεμάθηκα)
a be taught 27.12
b come to realize 27.15
c understand 32.14

μανία, ας *f*
insanity 30.24

μάννα *n*
manna 5.22

μαντεύομαι
tell fortunes 33.284

μαραίνομαι
(fut μαρανθήσομαι)
fade away 13.94

μαρανα
our Lord 12.11

μαργαρίτης, ου *m*
pearl 2.43

Μάρθα, ας *f*
Martha 93.252

Μαρία, ας *f*
Mary 93.253

Μαριάμ *f*
Mary 93.254

Μᾶρκος, ου *m*
Mark 93.255

μάρμαρος, ου *m*
marble 2.45

μαρτυρέω
a witness *33.262*
b speak well of *33.263*

μαρτυρία, ας *f*
a witness *33.262*
b testimony *33.264*
c reputation *33.265*

μαρτύριον, ου *n*
a witness *33.262*
b testimony *33.264*

μαρτύρομαι
a testify *33.223*
b insist *33.319*

**μάρτυς, μάρτυρος, dat pl μάρ-
τυσιν** *m*
a witness *33.270*
b martyr *20.67*

μασάομαι
bite *23.40*

μαστιγόω
a beat with a whip . . . *19.9*
b punish *38.11*

μαστίζω
beat with a whip *19.9*

μάστιξ, ιγος *f*
a flogging *19.9*
b disease *23.153*

μαστός, οῦ *m*
breast *8.37*

ματαιολογία, ας *f*
idle discussions *33.377*

ματαιολόγος, ου *m*
empty talker *33.378*

ματαιόομαι
be futile *65.38*

μάταιος, α, ον
futile *65.37*

ματαιότης, ητος *f*
futility *65.37*

μάτην
in vain *89.54*

Ματθαῖος, ου *m*
Matthew *93.244*

Ματθάν *m*
Matthan *93.256*

Ματθάτ *m*
Matthat *93.245*

Ματθίας, ου *m*
Matthias *93.246*

Ματταθά *m*
Mattatha *93.257*

Ματταθίας, ου *m*
Mattathias *93.258*

μάχαιρα, ης *f*
a sword *6.33*
b war *55.6*
c death *20.68*
d discord *39.25*
μάχαιρα : unit
φορέω τὴν μάχαιραν
have power to punish *38.3*

μάχη, ης *f*
severe clash *39.23*

μάχομαι
clash severely *39.23*

με
see ἐγώ

μεγαλεῖον, ου *n*
mighty act *76.8*

μεγαλειότης, ητος *f*
a prominence *87.21*
b mighty power *76.2*

μεγάλη/οι
see μέγας

μεγαλοπρεπής, ές
very wonderful *79.14*
μεγαλοπρεπής : unit
μεγαλοπρεπής δόξα
   Sublime Glory *12.6*

μεγαλύνω
a make large *79.124*
b praise greatness of . . *33.358*
c honor highly *87.15*

μεγάλως
greatly *78.2*

μεγαλωσύνη, ης f
a prominence *87.21*
b Majesty *12.5*

μέγας, μεγάλη, μέγα
a great (quantity) *59.22*
b great (degree) *78.2*
c large *79.123*
d important *87.22*
e surprising *25.207*
μέγας : units
ἐν μεγάλῳ
   in a long time *67.89*
οἱ μεγάλοι
   important persons . . *87.40*

μέγεθος, ους n
greatness *78.2*

μεγιστάν, ᾶνος m
very important
person *87.41*

μέγιστος, η, ον
very important *65.53*

μεθερμηνεύω
translate *33.145*

μέθη, ης f
drunkenness *88.283*

μεθίσταμαι
cease *68.38*

μεθιστάνω
see μεθίστημι

μεθίστημι
(aor μετέστησα, ptc
μεταστήσας, aor pass
subj μετασταθῶ)
a cause to move *15.9*
b cause change *13.64*
c mislead *31.73*

μεθοδεία, ας f
scheming *88.158*

μεθύσκομαι
get drunk *88.285*

μέθυσος, ου m
drunkard *88.288*

μεθύω
a be drunk *88.283*
b drink a lot *23.37*

μείζων, ον
a more *78.28*
b superior to *87.28*
c older *67.102*

μεῖναι
see μένω

μεῖνον
see μένω

μέλαν, ανος n
ink *6.57*

μέλας, αινα, αν
black *79.26*

Μελεά m
Melea *93.259*

Μελεγαδά
Magdala, Magadan . . . *93.524*

μέλει
a think about *30.39*
b be anxious about . . . *25.223*

μελετάω
a keep thinking about *30.20*
b plot............ *30.60*
c continue to do *68.20*

μέλι, ιτος *n*
honey............ *5.20*

μελίσσιος, ον
of bees *4.50*

Μελίτη, ης *f*
Malta *93.529*

μέλλω
a be about to *67.62*
b must be *71.36*
c wait *67.121*

τὸ μέλλον
future............ *67.135*

μέλος, ους *n*
a body part *8.9*
b member *63.17*

Μελχί *m*
Melchi *93.260*

Μελχισέδεκ *m*
Melchizedek *93.261*

μεμάθηκα
see μανθάνω

μεμβράνα, ης *f*
a parchment sheet ... *6.59*
b books made of
parchment *6.66*

μεμενήκεισαν
see μένω

μεμίαμμαι
see μιαίνω

μέμιγμαι
see μίγνυμι

μέμνημαι
see μιμνήσχομαι

μέμφομαι
blame............. *33.431*

μεμψίμοιρος, ον
blaming *33.432*

μέν
a and............. *91.3*
b indeed *91.6*

μέν . . . ἀλλά
on the one hand . . .
on the other hand *89.136*

μέν . . . δέ
a some . . . others *89.104*
b on the one hand . . .
on the other hand .. *89.136*

μέν . . . πλήν
on the one hand . . .
on the other hand *89.136*

Μεννά *m*
Menna *93.262*

μενοῦν
a on the contrary *89.128*
b therefore *89.50*
c surely *91.8*

μενοῦνγε
on the contrary *89.128*

μέντοι
nevertheless *89.130*
μέντοι : unit
ὅμως μέντοι
nevertheless *89.75*

μέντοι . . . δέ
on the one hand . . .
on the other hand *89.136*

μένω
(aor ἔμεινα, impv μεῖ-
νον, inf μεῖναι, plpf 3
pl μεμενήκεισαν)
a stay............. *85.55*
b wait for *85.60*

c continue to exist ... *13.89*
d keep on *68.11*

μερίζω
a divide *63.23*
b distribute *57.89*
c give part *57.90*
d assign responsibility *37.100*

μέριμνα, ης *f*
anxiety *25.224*
μέριμνα : unit
τὴν μέριμναν ἐπιρίπτω ἐπί
  stop worrying and
  trust *25.250*

μεριμνάω
be anxious about *25.225*

μερίς, ίδος *f*
a portion *63.13*
b district *1.85*

μερισμός, οῦ *m*
a division *63.24*
b distribution *57.89*

μεριστής, οῦ *m*
divider *63.25*

μέρος, ους *n*
a part *63.14*
b side *79.108*
c region *1.79*
d group *11.8*
e business *57.199*
f to some degree *78.49*
μέρος : units
ἀνὰ μέρος
  in succession *61.4*
ἀπὸ μέρους
  a in part *63.15*
  b temporary *67.109*
ἐκ μέρους
  in part *63.15*
ἐν μέρει
  with regard to *89.5*
κατὰ μέρος
  in detail *63.16*
ἔχω μέρος ἐν
  experience together *90.83*

μεσημβρία, ας *f*
a noon *67.74*
b south *82.4*

μεσιτεύω
cause agreement *31.21*

μεσίτης, ου *m*
a mediator *31.22*
b reconciler *40.6*

μεσονύκτιον, ου *n*
midnight *67.75*

Μεσοποταμία, ας *f*
Mesopotamia *93.530*

μέσος, η, ον
a among *83.9*
b in the middle *83.10*
μέσος : unit
ἀνὰ μέσον
  a among *83.9*
  b in the middle *83.10*
  c between *89.143*

μεσότοιχον, ου *n*
dividing wall *7.62*

μεσουράνημα, τος *n*
high in the sky *1.10*

μεσόω
half over *67.137*

Μεσσίας, ου *m*
Messiah *53.82*

μεστός, ή, όν
a very full *59.39*
b completely *78.45*
c constantly engaged in *68.77*

μεστόω
cause to bulge *59.40*

μετά
a with (association) *89.108*
b with (accompanying
  object) *89.109*
c with (combinative) *89.123*

d with (attendant
circumstances) *89.79*
e with (experiencer) . . *90.60*
f against (opposition) *90.32*
g after (time) *67.48*
h among (location) . . . *83.9*
i beyond (location) . . . *83.56*
j with (benefaction) . . *90.42*
k with (means) *89.78*

μεταβαίνω
(fut μεταβήσομαι, aor
μετέβην, impv μετάβα,
μετάβηθι, ptc μεταβάς,
pf μεταβέβηκα)
a depart. *15.2*
b become. *13.51*

μεταβάλλομαι
(aor ptc μεταβαλόμενος)
change one's mind . . . *31.58*

μετάγω
guide *15.186*

μεταδίδωμι
(inf μεταδιδόναι, ptc
μεταδιδούς, aor subj
μεταδῶ, impv 3 sg
μεταδότω, inf μετα-
δοῦναι)
share *57.96*

μετάθεσις, εως *f*
a departure *15.2*
b change *13.52*

μεταίρω
(aor μετῆρα)
depart *15.35*

μετακαλέομαι
summon *33.311*

μετακινέω
cause to cease. *13.42*

μεταλαμβάνω
(aor inf μεταλαβεῖν)
a receive share in *57.129*
b experience *90.63*

μετάλημψις, εως *f*
receiving share in *57.129*

μεταλλάσσω
(aor μετήλλαξα)
a exchange *57.142*
b cease and start *68.50*

μεταμέλομαι
a feel sad about *25.270*
b change one's mind *31.59*

μεταμορφόομαι
a change *13.53*
b change appearance *58.16*

μετανοέω
repent *41.52*

μετάνοια, ας *f*
repentance *41.52*

μεταξύ
a between (location) . . *83.11*
b between (associa-
tion) *89.115*
c next *67.54*
μεταξύ : unit
ἐν τῷ μεταξύ
meanwhile *67.138*

μεταπέμπομαι
(aor impv μετάπεμψαι)
send for *15.73*

μετασταθῶ
see μεθίστημι

μεταστήσας
see μεθίστημι

μεταστρέφω
(fut pass μεταστραφή-
σομαι)
change *13.64*

μετασχηματίζω
a change appearance *58.18*
b apply to *89.11*

μετατίθεμαι
μετατίθεμαι : unit
μετατίθεμαι ἀπό
abandon loyalty to .. *34.27*

μετατίθημι
(aor μετέθηκα, aor
pass μετετέθην)
a depart............ *15.2*
b change *13.64*

μετατρέπω
(aor pass impv 3 sg
μετατραπήτω)
change *13.64*

μετέβην
see μεταβαίνω

μετέπειτα
afterwards *67.44*

μετέστησα
see μεθίστημι

μετέχω
(aor μετέσχον, pf
μετέσχηκα)
a share in *57.6*
b eat, drink *23.2*
c belong to *34.31*
μετέχω : unit
τραπέζης μετέχω
belong to a religious
group *34.32*

μετεωρίζομαι
be anxious about *25.232*

μετήλλαξα
see μεταλλάσσω

μετῆρα
see μεταίρω

μετοικεσία, ας *f*
deportation *85.83*

μετοικίζω
(fut μετοικιῶ, aor
μετῴκισα)
deport *85.83*

μετοχή, ῆς *f*
partnership *34.7*

μέτοχος, ου *m*
companion.......... *34.8*

μετρέω
a measure *81.2*
b give a measure *57.92*

μετρητής, οῦ *m*
measure *81.22*

μετριοπαθέω
deal gently with *88.65*

μετρίως
moderately *78.11*

μέτρον, ου *n*
measure *81.1*
μέτρον : unit
ἐκ μέτρου
sparingly *78.12*

μετῴκισα
see μετοικίζω

μέτωπον, ου *n*
forehead........... *8.16*

μέχρι
a until *67.119*
b as far as *84.19*
c to the degree that ... *78.51*

μέχρις
to the degree that..... *78.51*
μέχρις : unit
μέχρις οὗ
until *67.119*

μή
a not *69.3*
b marker of question *69.15*
c so that not *89.62*

μή
μή : units
εἰ μή
  except that *89.131*
μή πως
  see μήπως

μήγε
not *69.10*

μηδαμῶς
by no means *69.6*

μηδέ
a and not *69.7*
b not even *69.8*

μηδείς, μηδεμία, μηδέν
no one, nothing *92.23*

μηδέποτε
never *67.10*

μηδέπω
not yet *67.129*

Μῆδος, ου *m*
Mede *93.531*

μηθέν
see μηδέν

μηκέτι
no longer *67.130*

μῆκος, ους *n*
length *81.12*

μηκύνομαι
grow *23.190*

μηλωτή, ῆς *f*
sheepskin *6.187*

μήν
μήν : unit
εἰ μήν
  surely *91.8*

μήν, μηνός *m*
month *67.174*

μηνύω
inform *33.209*

μήποτε
a never *67.10*
b can be *71.18*
c so that not *89.62*

μήπω
not yet *67.129*

μήπως, (μή πως)
so that not *89.62*

μηρός, οῦ *m*
thigh *8.48*

μήτε
nor *69.9*

μήτηρ, τρός *f*
a mother *10.16*
b archetype *58.64*

μήτι
marker of question . . . *69.16*

μήτιγε
how much more *91.9*

μήτρα, ας *f*
womb *8.69*
μήτρα : unit
ἄρσην διανοίγων μήτραν
  firstborn son *10.45*

μητρολῴας, ου *m*
one who murders his
mother *20.87*

μία
see εἷς
μία : unit
ἀπὸ μιᾶς
  one by one *61.2*

μιαίνω
(pf pass μεμίαμμαι,
aor pass subj μιανθῶ)
a defile (morally) *88.260*
b defile (ritually) *53.34*

μιᾶς
see εἷς

μίασμα, τος n
defilement 88.259

μιασμός, οῦ m
defilement 88.259

μίγμα, τος n
mixture 63.11

μίγνυμι
(aor ἔμιξα, pf pass
μέμιγμαι)
mix 63.10

μικρός, ά, όν
a little (quantity)..... 59.15
b little (size) 79.125
c little (degree) 78.9
d short (time) 67.106
e short (measurement) 81.13
f young 67.116
g unimportant 87.58
μικρός : unit
μικρὸν ὅσον ὅσον
very soon 67.107

Μίλητος, ου f
Miletus 93.532

μίλιον, ου n
(Roman) mile........ 81.29

μιμέομαι
imitate 41.44

μιμητής, οῦ m
imitator 41.45

μιμνῄσκομαι
(aor ἐμνήσθην, impv
μνήσθητι, fut μνησθή-
σομαι, pf μέμνημαι)
a remember 29.7
b remember and re-
spond 29.16

μισέω
hate 88.198

μισθαποδοσία, ας f
reward 38.17

μισθαποδότης, ου m
rewarder 38.18

μίσθιος, ου m
hired worker 57.174

μισθόομαι
hire 57.172

μισθός, οῦ m
a wages 57.173
b reward 38.14

μίσθωμα, τος n
rented 57.175

μισθωτός, οῦ m
hired worker 57.174

Μιτυλήνη, ης f
Mitylene 93.533

Μιχαήλ m
Michael 93.263

μνᾶ, ᾶς f
monetary unit 6.81

Μνάσων, ωνος m
Mnason 93.264

μνεία, ας f
a remembrance 29.7
b remember and
mention 29.18

μνῆμα, τος n
grave 7.75

μνημεῖον, ου n
a grave 7.75
b monument 7.76

μνήμη, ης f
remembrance 29.7

μνημονεύω
a remember 29.7

b keep thinking about   *29.8*
c remember and re-
  spond *29.16*
d remember and
  mention *29.18*

μνημόσυνον, ου *n*
memorial *29.12*

μνησθήσομαι
see μιμνήσκομαι

μνήσθητι
see μιμνήσκομαι

μνηστεύομαι
promise in marriage . . *34.74*

μογιλάλος, ον
hardly able to speak . . . *33.107*

μόγις
see μόλις

μόδιος, ου *m*
container *6.151*

μοι
see ἐγώ

μοιχαλίς, ίδος *f*
adulteress *88.278*

μοιχαλίς, ί
unfaithful *31.101*

μοιχάομαι
commit adultery *88.276*

μοιχεία, ας *f*
adultery *88.276*

μοιχεύω
commit adultery *88.276*

μοιχός, οῦ *m*
adulterer *88.277*

μόλις
a scarcely *78.41*
b with difficulty *22.33*

Μολόχ or **Μόλοχ** *m*
Moloch *93.265*

μολύνω
a make dirty *79.56*
b defile *53.34*

μολυσμός, οῦ *m*
defiled *53.35*

μομφή, ῆς *f*
complaint *33.385*

μονή, ῆς *f*
dwelling place *85.76*

μονογενής, ές
unique *58.52*

μονόομαι
be without relatives . . . *10.13*

μόνος, η, ον
a only one *58.50*
b alone *58.51*
μόνος : unit
κατὰ μόνας
  alone *58.51*

μονόφθαλμος, ον
one-eyed *24.39*

μορφή, ῆς *f*
a nature *58.2*
b visual form *58.15*

μορφόω
form nature of *58.4*

μόρφωσις, εως *f*
embodiment *58.3*

μοσχοποιέω
make calf-idol *6.101*

μόσχος, ου *m*
calf *4.17*

μοῦ
see ἐγώ

μουσικός, οῦ m
musician 14.84

μόχθος, ου m
hard labor 42.48

μυελός, οῦ m
marrow 8.62

μυέομαι
learn secret 27.14

μῦθος, ου m
legend 33.13

μυκάομαι
roar 14.77

μυκτηρίζω
ridicule 33.409

μυλικός, ή, όν
of a mill 7.70

μύλινος, η, ον
of a mill 7.70

μύλος, ου m
a mill.............. 7.68
b millstone 7.69

Μύρα, ων n
Myra 93.534

μυριάς, άδος f
a ten thousand 60.45
b countless 60.8
μυριάς : unit
δισμυριάδες μυριάδων
countless 60.9

μυρίζω
anoint with perfume .. 6.206

μύριοι, αι, α
ten thousand 60.45

μυρίος, α, ον
countless 60.7

μύρον, ου n
perfume 6.205

Μυσία, ας f
Mysia............. 93.535

μυστήριον, ου n
secret 28.77

Μυτιλήνη
see Μιτυλήνη

μυωπάζω
fail to understand 32.48

μώλωψ, ωπος m
wound 20.29

μωμάομαι
criticize 33.414

μῶμος, ου m
blemish 79.60

μωραίνομαι
a become foolish..... 32.56
b lose taste 79.44

μωραίνω
(aor ἐμώρανα, aor
pass subj μωρανθῶ)
cause to become
nonsense 32.59

μωρία, ας f
foolishness.......... 32.57

μωρολογία, ας f
foolish talk.......... 33.379

μωρός, ά, όν
a foolish 32.55
b nonsense 32.58

Μωϋσῆς, έως m
a Moses 93.266
b the Law (of Moses) 33.59

Μωϋσῆς : unit
ἐπὶ τῆς Μωϋσέως κα-
θέδρας καθίστημι
  be authority on
  Law of Moses...... 37.44

Ναασσών *m*
  Nahshon 93.267

Ναγγαί *m*
  Naggai 93.268

Ναζαρά
  see Ναζαρέθ 93.536

Ναζαρέθ *f*
  Nazareth 93.536

Ναζαρέτ
  see Ναζαρέθ 93.536

Ναζαρηνός, οῦ *m*
  Nazarene 93.537

Ναζορηνός
  see Ναζαρηνός 93.537

Ναζωραῖος, ου *m*
  Nazarene 93.538

Ναζωρηνός
  see Ναζαρηνός 93.537

Ναζωρινός
  see Ναζαρηνός 93.537

Ναθάμ *m*
  Nathan 93.269

Ναθαναήλ *m*
  Nathanael 93.270

ναί
  yes 69.1

Ναιμάν *m*
  Naaman 93.271

Ναΐν *f*
  Nain............. 93.539

ναός, οῦ *m*
  a temple 7.15
  b model of a shrine ... 6.100

Ναούμ *m*
  Nahum 93.272

Ναραῖος
  see Ναζωραῖος 93.540

νάρδος, ου *f*
  perfume of nard 6.210

Νάρκισσος, ου *m*
  Narcissus.......... 93.273

ναυαγέω
  be shipwrecked 54.26

ναύκληρος, ου *m*
  ship owner.......... 54.29

ναῦς, acc. ναῦν *f*
  ship 6.43

ναύτης, ου *m*
  sailor 54.30

Ναχώρ *m*
  Nahor 93.274

νεανίας, ου *m*
  young man......... 9.32

νεανίσκος, ου *m*
  young man......... 9.32

Νέα Πόλις *f*
  Neapolis 93.541

νεῖκος, ους *n*
  see νῖκος

νεκρός, ά, όν
  a dead 23.121
  b useless 65.39
  c ineffective 74.28
  νεκρός : unit
  ἄφες τοὺς νεκροὺς θάψαι
  τοὺς ἑαυτῶν νεκρούς
    that is not the issue   33.137

νεκρόω
stop completely 68.48

νέκρωσις, εως f
a death 23.99
b barrenness 23.57

νεομηνία, ας f
new moon festival 51.5

νέος, α, ον
a new (time) 67.115
b new (class) 58.71
c young 67.116
νέος : unit
οἶνος νέος
new wine 6.198

νεότης, ητος f
youth 67.154

νεόφυτος, ου m
recent convert 11.21

νεύω
gesture 33.485

νεφέλη, ης f
cloud 1.34

Νεφθαλίμ m
a Naphtali (person) . . 93.275
b Naphtali (place) 93.542

νέφος, ους n
large crowd 11.3

νεφρός, οῦ m
desires 26.11

νεωκόρος, ου m
temple-keeper 53.95

νεωτερικός, ή, όν
youthful 67.155

νή
on basis of 89.14

νήθω
spin 48.2

νηπιάζω
be a child 9.44

νήπιος, α, ον
small child 9.43

Νηρεύς, έως m
Nereus 93.276

Νηρί m
Neri 93.277

νησίον, ου n
small island 1.67

νῆσος, ου f
island 1.66

νηστεία, ας f
a fasting 53.65
b hunger 23.31
c festival of atonement 51.11

νηστεύω
fast 53.65

νῆστις, ιδος, acc pl νήστεις
m, f
hunger 23.31

Νήφα
see Νύμφα 93.278

νηφάλιος, α, ον
restrained 88.87

νήφω
a be sober-minded . . . 30.25
b be restrained 88.86

Νίγερ m
Niger 93.279

νίθω
see νήθω

Νικάνωρ, ορος m
Nicanor 93.280

νικάω
conquer 39.57

νίκη, ης f
victory 39.57

Νικόδημος, ου m
Nicodemus 93.281

Νικολαΐτης, ου m
Nicolaitan 93.282

Νικόλαος, ου m
Nicolaus 93.283

Νικόπολις, εως f
Nicopolis 93.543

νῖκος, ους n
victory 39.57

Νινευίτης, ου m
Ninevite 93.544

νιπτήρ, ῆρος m
washbasin 6.122

νίπτω
(aor midd impv νίψαι)
wash 47.9
νίπτω : unit
πόδας νίπτω
a be very hospitable 34.59
b act humbly 88.58

νοέω
a understand 32.2
b consider well 30.3
c imagine 31.6

νόημα, τος n
a mind 26.14
b thought 30.15

νόθος, η, ον
illegitimate (child) 10.39

νομή, ῆς f
a pasture 1.98
b extension 84.1

νομίζομαι
do customarily 41.28

νομίζω
suppose 31.29

νομικός, ή, όν
about the law 33.337

νομικός, οῦ m
a interpreter of the
Law 33.338
b lawyer 56.37

νομίμως
correctly 72.18

νόμισμα, τος n
coin 6.70

νομοδιδάσκαλος, ου m
teacher of the Law 33.248

νομοθεσία, ας f
giving law 33.339

νομοθετέω
give law 33.339

νομοθέτης, ου m
lawgiver 33.340

νόμος, ου m
a law 33.333
b the Law 33.55
c the Scriptures 33.56
νόμος : units
ὁ νόμος καὶ οἱ προφῆται
the sacred writings 33.58
νόμος τοῦ ἀνδρός
marriage law 33.341

νοσέω
have morbid desire . . . 25.10

νόσημα, τος n
sickness 23.155

νόσος, ου f
sickness 23.155

νοσσιά, ᾶς f
brood 4.40

νοσσίον, ου *n*
young bird *4.39*

νοσσός, οῦ *m*
young bird *4.39*

νοσφίζομαι
embezzle *57.246*

νότος, ου *m*
a south *82.4*
b south wind *14.8*

νουθεσία, ας *f*
a teaching *33.231*
b warning *33.424*

νουθετέω
a instruct *33.231*
b admonish *33.418*
c warn *33.424*

νουνεχῶς
wisely *32.29*

νοῦς, νοός, νοΐ, νοῦν *m*
a mind *26.14*
b way of thinking *30.5*
νοῦς : unit
διανοίγω τὸν νοῦν
cause to be open-
minded *27.49*

Νύμφα, ας *f*
Nympha *93.284*

Νυμφᾶς, ᾶ *m*
Nymphas *93.284*

νύμφη, ης *f*
a bride *10.57*
b daughter-in-law *10.60*

νυμφίος, ου *m*
bridegroom *10.56*

νυμφών, ῶνος *m*
wedding hall *7.34*
νυμφών : unit
υἱοὶ τοῦ νυμφῶνος
wedding guests *11.7*

νῦν
a now *67.38*
b just now *67.39*

νυνί
see νῦν

νυνὶ δέ
and so *91.4*

νύξ, νυκτός *f*
a night (time) *67.192*
b night (darkness) *14.59*
νύξ : unit
ἡμέρας τεσσεράκοντα καὶ
νύκτας τεσσεράκοντα
long time *67.93*

νύσσω
(aor ἔνυξα)
pierce *19.15*

νυστάζω
grow drowsy *23.67*

νυχθήμερον, ου *n*
a night and a day *67.179*

Νῶε *m*
Noah *93.285*

νωθρός, ά, όν
lazy *88.249*
νωθρός : unit
νωθρὸς ταῖς ἀκοαῖς
slow to understand *32.47*

νῶτος, ου *m*
back *8.40*
νῶτος : unit
συγκάμπτω τὸν νῶτον
be overwhelmed
with trouble *24.94*

ξαίνω
comb wool *48.1*

ξενία, ας *f*
a guest room *7.31*
b hospitality *34.57*

ξενίζομαι
be surprised 25.206

ξενίζω
show hospitality 34.57

ξενοδοχέω
show hospitality 34.57

ξένος, η, ον
unknown 28.34

ξένος, ου m
a stranger 11.73
b host 34.60

ξέστης, ου m
pitcher 6.126

ξηρά, ᾶς f
land 1.60

ξηραίνομαι
(aor ἐξηράνθην, pf
ἐξήραμμαι)
a become dry 79.81
b become ripe 23.198
c become stiff 23.172

ξηραίνω
(aor ἐξήρανα)
cause to wither 79.82

ξηρός, ά, όν
a dry 79.80
b paralyzed 23.173

ξύλινος, η, ον
wooden 3.62

ξύλον, ου n
a wood 3.60
b firewood 3.61
c tree 3.4
d club 6.31
e stocks 6.21
f cross 6.28
ξύλον : unit
κρεμάννυμι ἐπὶ ξύλου
crucify 20.76

ξυράω
shave 19.24

ὁ, ἡ, τό
the 92.24

ὅ τι
see ὅστις

ὀγδοήκοντα
eighty 60.31

ὄγδοος, η, ον
eighth 60.55

ὄγκος, ου m
hindrance 13.149

ὅδε, ἥδε, τόδε
a this 92.32
b such and such 92.33

ὁδεύω
travel 15.19

ὁδηγέω
a guide 15.182
b guide in learning . . . 27.17

ὁδηγός, οῦ m
a guide 15.183
b leader 36.4

ὁδοιπορέω
travel 15.20

ὁδοιπορία, ας f
journey 15.20

ὁδός, οῦ f
a road 1.99
b journey 15.19
c way of life 41.16
d Christian way of
life 41.35
ὁδός : units
σαββάτου ὁδός
sabbath journey 81.28
κατασκευάζω τὴν ὁδόν
make ready 77.7

εὐθεῖα ὁδός
just way of life 88.18

ὀδούς, ὀδόντος m
tooth 8.20
ὀδούς : units
βρύχω τοὺς ὀδόντας
a gnash the teeth ... 23.41
b be furious 88.184
βρυγμὸς τῶν ὀδόντων
gnashing of teeth ... 23.41
τρίζω τοὺς ὀδόντας
gnash the teeth 23.41

ὀδυνάομαι
a be in great pain 24.92
b be terribly worried . 25.236

ὀδύνη, ης f
intense anxiety 25.235

ὀδυρμός, οῦ m
lamenting 52.3

Ὀζίας, ου m
Uzziah 93.286

ὄζω
stink.............. 79.47

ὅθεν
a from where 84.11
b because of 89.25

ὀθόνη, ης f
linen sheet 6.153

ὀθόνιον, ου n
linen cloth 6.154

οἶδα
(pf with pres mng, ἴστε
may be 2 pl ind or
impv, ind 3 pl οἴδασι
and ἴσασι, subj εἰδῶ,
inf εἰδέναι, masc ptc
εἰδώς, ἰδώς, fem ptc
εἰδυῖα, plpf ᾔδειν, fut
εἰδήσω)
a know 28.1
b know how to 28.7

c understand........ 32.4
d remember 29.6
e honor 87.12

οἰέσθω
see οἶμαι

οἰκεῖος, ου m
relative............ 10.11

οἰκετεία, ας f
household servants ... 46.6

οἰκέτης, ου m
house servant 46.5

οἰκέω
a dwell 85.67
b reside in 85.73

οἴκημα, τος n
quarters 7.26

οἰκητήριον, ου n
dwelling place 85.68

οἰκία, ας f
a house 7.3
b family............ 10.8
c property.......... 57.21

οἰκιακός, οῦ m
relative............ 10.11

οἰκοδεσποτέω
direct a household 46.2

οἰκοδεσπότης, ου m
master of household .. 57.14

οἰκοδομέω
a build............. 45.1
b make more able 74.15

οἰκοδομή, ῆς f
a building 7.1
b construction....... 42.34
c making more able .. 74.15

οἰκοδόμος, ου m
builder............. 45.7

οἰκονομέω
  manage a household .. *46.1*

οἰκονομία, ας *f*
  a task............. *42.25*
  b plan *30.68*
  c manage a household *46.1*

οἰκονόμος, ου *m*
  a manager of a house-
    hold *46.4*
  b administrator *37.39*
  οἰκονόμος : unit
  οἰκονόμος τῆς πόλεως
    city treasurer *57.231*

οἶκος, ου *m*
  a house, temple *7.2*
  b family........... *10.8*
  c lineage *10.24*
  d property......... *57.21*
  οἶκος : unit
  οἶκος Ἰσραήλ
    people of Israel *11.58*

οἰκουμένη, ης *f*
  a earth............. *1.39*
  b empire *1.83*
  c people *9.22*

οἰκουργός, όν
  homemaker *46.3*

οἰκτιρμός, οῦ *m*
  mercy............. *88.80*

οἰκτίρμων, ον
  merciful........... *88.81*

οἰκτίρω
  (fut οἰκτιρήσω)
  have mercy *88.80*

οἶμαι
  (impv 3 sg οἰέσθω,
  ptc οἰόμενος)
  suppose *31.29*

οἰνοπότης, ου *m*
  drunkard *88.288*

οἶνος, ου *m*
  wine *6.197*
  οἶνος : units
  οἶνος νέος
    new wine *6.198*
  ἐσμυρνισμένος οἶνος
    myrrhed wine *6.204*

οἰνοφλυγία, ας *f*
  drunkenness *88.284*

οἰόμενος
  see οἶμαι

οἷος, α, ον
  a such as *64.1*
  b what sort *58.30*

οἴσω
  see φέρω

ὀκνέω
  delay *67.125*

ὀκνηρός, ά, όν
  a lazy............. *88.250*
  b bothersome *22.8*

ὀκταήμερος, ον
  the eighth day *67.182*

ὀκτώ
  eight.............. *60.17*

ὄλεθρος, ου *m*
  a ruin (state) *20.33*
  b destruction....... *20.34*

ὀλιγοπιστία, ας *f*
  have limited faith *31.95*

ὀλιγόπιστος, ον
  of little faith........ *31.96*

ὀλίγος, η, ον
  a few *59.3*
  b slight *78.8*
  c little *59.13*
  ὀλίγος : units
  δι᾽ ὀλίγων
    in a short time *67.106*

ἐν ὀλίγῳ
a in a short time ... 67.106
b easily 22.41
πρὸς ὀλίγον
for a short time..... 67.106

ὀλιγόψυχος, ον
discouraged 25.290

ὀλιγωρέω
despise 88.197

ὀλίγως
hardly 78.41

ὀλοθρευτής, οῦ m
destroyer 20.36

ὀλοθρεύω
ruin 20.34

ὀλοκαύτωμα, τος n
whole burnt offering 53.24

ὀλοκληρία, ας f
complete health 23.131

ὀλόκληρος, ον
entire 59.30

ὀλολύζω
cry aloud 25.140

ὅλος, η, ον
a whole 63.1
b complete (quantity) 59.29
c complete (degree) .. 78.44

ὀλοτελής, ές
completely 78.47

'Ολυμπᾶς, ᾶ m
Olympas 93.287

ὄλυνθος, ου m
late fig 3.37

ὅλως
a completely 78.44
b really 70.1

ὄμβρος, ου m
rainstorm 14.12

ὀμείρομαι
have great affection for 25.47

ὁμιλέω
talk (with) 33.156

ὁμιλία, ας f
association 34.1

ὄμιλος, ου m
crowd 11.1

ὀμίχλη, ης f
mist 1.35

ὄμμα, τος n
eye 8.23

ὄμνυμι
(inf ὀμνύναι)
see ὀμνύω

ὀμνύω
(inf ὀμνύειν, aor
ὤμοσα, inf ὀμόσαι)
make an oath 33.463

ὁμοθυμαδόν
with one mind 31.23

ὁμοιοπαθής, ές
same kinds of desires 25.32

ὅμοιος, α, ον
similar 64.1

ὁμοιότης, ητος f
similarity 64.3

ὁμοιόω
a be similar to 64.4
b compare 64.5

ὁμοίωμα, τος n
similarity 64.3

ὁμοίως
similarly 64.1

ὁμοίωσις, εως *f*
similarity 64.3

ὁμολογέω
a profess 33.274
b admit 33.275
c declare 33.221

ὁμολογία, ας *f*
profession 33.274

ὁμολογουμένως
must be admitted 33.276

ὁμόσαι
see ὀμνύω

ὁμότεχνος, ον
of the same trade 42.52

ὁμοῦ
together 89.116

ὁμόφρων, ον
like-minded 30.21

ὅμως
a although 89.74
b similarly 64.11
ὅμως : unit
ὅμως μέντοι
nevertheless 89.75

ὀναίμην
see ὀνίναμαι

ὄναρ *n*
dream 33.486

ὀνάριον, ου *n*
foal 4.33

ὀνειδίζω
a insult 33.389
b reprimand 33.422

ὀνειδισμός, οῦ *m*
insult 33.389

ὄνειδος, ους *n*
disgrace 87.73

Ὀνήσιμος, ου *m*
Onesimus 93.288

Ὀνησίφορος, ου *m*
Onesiphorus 93.289

ὀνικός, ή, όν
of a donkey 4.32

ὀνίναμαι
(aor opt ὀναίμην)
receive benefit 35.4

ὄνομα, τος *n*
a name 33.126
b person 9.19
c reputation 33.265
d category 58.22
ὄνομα : units
ὀνομάζω τὸ ὄνομα κυρίου
say that one belongs
to the Lord 53.62
βαστάζω ὄνομα
inform 33.210
ἐκβάλλω τὸ ὄνομα
slander 33.396
ἐπιτίθημι ὄνομα
give a name to 33.128
ἐπικαλέομαι τὸ ὄνομά
τινος ἐπί τινα
be people of 11.28

ὀνομάζομαι
be known 28.22

ὀνομάζω
a give a name to 33.127
b pronounce a name . . 33.133
c speak about 33.93
ὀνομάζω : unit
ὀνομάζω τὸ ὄνομα κυρίου
say that one belongs
to the Lord 53.62

ὄνος, ου *m, f*
donkey 4.31

ὄντως
really 70.2

ὄξος, ους *n*
sour wine *6.201*

ὀξύς, εῖα, ύ
a sharp *79.95*
b swift *67.112*

ὅπερ
see ὅσπερ

ὀπή, ῆς *f*
hole *1.53*

ὄπισθεν
a from behind *84.12*
b on the back of *83.41*
c on the outside *83.21*

ὀπίσω
a behind *83.40*
b after *36.35*
ὀπίσω : units
ἀπέρχομαι εἰς τὰ ὀπίσω
no longer follow *36.36*
ἐπιβάλλω τὴν χεῖρα
ἐπ᾽ ἄροτρον καὶ
βλέπω εἰς τὰ ὀπίσω
start to do and then
hesitate *68.6*
ἀπέρχομαι ὀπίσω
σαρκὸς ἑτέρας
have homosexual
intercourse *88.279*

ὁπλίζομαι
prepare oneself *77.10*

ὅπλον, ου *n*
a tool *6.3*
b weapon *6.29*

ὁποῖος, α, ον
what sort of *58.30*

ὁπότε
when *67.30*

ὅπου
a where (place) *83.5*

b where (circum-
stances) *92.28*
c since *89.35*
d in the case of *89.5*

ὀπτάνομαι
be visible to *24.17*

ὀπτασία, ας *f*
vision *33.488*

ὀπτός, ή, όν
broiled, baked *46.15*

ὀπώρα, ας *f*
ripe fruit *3.34*

ὅπως
a how *89.86*
b so that *89.59*
c somehow *92.17*

ὅραμα, τος *n*
a something seen *24.2*
b vision *33.488*

ὅρασις, εως *f*
a vision *33.488*
b appearance *24.31*

ὁρατός, ή, όν
visible *24.3*

ὁράω
(impf 3 pl ἑώρων, fut
ὄψομαι, aor εἶδα and
εἶδον, ptc ἰδών, impv
ἴδετε, pf ἑώρακα and
ἑόρακα, aor pass ὤφ-
θην, ptc ὀφθείς, fut
pass ὀφθήσομαι)
a see *24.1*
b pay attention to *30.45*
c understand *32.11*
d visit *34.50*
e experience *90.79*
f learn about *27.5*
g cause to happen *13.134*

ὀργή, ῆς *f*
a anger *88.173*
b punishment *38.10*

ὀργίζομαι
be very angry *88.174*

ὀργίλος, η, ον
angry *88.175*

ὀργυιά, ᾶς f
fathom *81.26*

ὀρέγομαι
strive to attain *25.15*

ὀρεινός, ή, όν
mountainous region . . *1.47*

ὄρεξις, εως f
ὄρεξις : unit
ἐκκαίομαι ἐν τῇ ὀρέξει
  have strong desire . . *25.16*

ὀρθοποδέω
live right *41.36*

ὀρθός, ή, όν
straight *79.88*
ὀρθός : unit
τροχιὰς ὀρθὰς ποιέω
τοῖς ποσίν
  behave correctly *41.30*

ὀρθοτομέω
teach correctly *33.234*

ὀρθρίζω
get up early *67.190*

ὀρθρινός, ή, όν
early in the morning . . *67.189*

ὄρθρος, ου m
a early morning *67.187*
b daybreak *67.73*

ὀρθῶς
correct(ly) *72.13*

ὀρίζω
a decide *30.83*
b appoint *37.96*

ὅριον, ου n
region *1.79*

ὀρκίζω
put under oath *33.467*

ὅρκος, ου m
oath *33.463*

ὀρκωμοσία, ας f
oath *33.463*

ὀρμάω
rush *15.222*

ὀρμή, ῆς f
will *26.12*
ὀρμή : unit
ὀρμὴ γίνομαι
  make up mind *30.78*

ὅρμημα, τος n
sudden violence *68.82*

ὄρνεον, ου n
bird *4.38*

ὄρνις, ιθος f
bird *4.38*

ὁροθεσία, ας f
boundaries *80.5*

ὄρος, ους n
mountain *1.46*

ὅρος, ου m
totality *78.44*

ὀρύσσω
(aor ὤρυξα)
dig *19.55*

ὀρφανός, οῦ m, f
a orphan *10.40*
b friendless person . . . *34.21*

ὀρχέομαι
dance *15.244*

ὅς, ἥ, ὅ
who, which *92.27*
ὅς : units
ἐν ᾧ
   as long as *67.139*
ὅ ἐστιν
   that means *89.106*

ὁσάκις
ὁσάκις : unit
ὁσάκις ἐάν
   whenever *67.36*

ὅσιος, α, ον
a holy *88.24*
b dedicated *53.46*
ὅσιος : unit
τὰ ὅσια
   divine promises *33.290*

ὁσιότης, ητος f
a holiness *88.25*
b dedication *53.45*

ὁσίως
holy *88.24*

ὀσμή, ῆς f
odor *79.45*

ὅσος, η, ον
a as many as *59.7*
b as much as *59.19*
c to the degree that . . . *78.52*
d as long as *67.139*
ὅσος : unit
μικρὸν ὅσον ὅσον
   very soon *67.107*

ὀστέον, ου n
bone *8.61*

ὅστις, ἥτις, ὅ τι
whoever, whatever . . . *92.18*

ὀστοῦν, οῦ n
bone *8.61*

ὀστράκινος, η, ον
earthenware *2.20*

ὄσφρησις, εως f
sense of smell *24.71*

ὀσφῦς, ύος f
a waist *8.42*
b genitals *8.43*
ὀσφῦς : units
καρπὸς τῆς ὀσφύος
   offspring *10.34*
ἐξέρχομαι ἐκ τῆς ὀσφύος
   be born of *23.60*
περιζώννυμαι τὴν ὀσφύν
   get ready *77.5*
ἀναζώννυμαι τὰς ὀσφύας
τῆς διανοίας
   be ready to learn . . . *27.55*

ὅταν
a whenever *67.31*
b when *67.30*
c as often as *67.36*
d as long as *67.139*

ὅτε
a when *67.30*
b as long as *67.139*

ὅτι
a that *90.21*
b because *89.33*
c namely *91.15*

ὅτου
ὅτου : unit
ἕως ὅτου
   a until *67.119*
   b while *67.139*

οὖ
a where (place) *83.5*
b where (circum-
   stance) *92.28*
οὖ : units
ἄχρι οὖ
   a before *67.17*
   b until *67.119*
ἄχρις οὖ
   a until *67.119*
   b as long as *67.139*
μέχρις οὖ
   until *67.119*

πρὸς τὸ οὖς λαλέω
     whisper *33.91*

ἀκούω εἰς τὸ οὖς
     hear in secret *24.67*

ἔχω οὖς
     be able to hear *24.59*

συνέχω τὰ ὦτα
     refuse to listen *24.70*

τίθεμαι εἰς τὰ ὦτα
     a listen carefully to   *24.64*
     b remember well . . . *29.5*

τοῖς ὠσὶν βαρέως ἀκούω
     be mentally dull *32.46*

ἀπερίτμητος καρδίαις
καὶ τοῖς ὠσίν
     obstinate *88.224*

οὐσία, ας *f*
     property *57.19*

οὔτε
     nor *69.9*

οὗτος, αὕτη, τοῦτο
     this *92.29*
     οὗτος : unit
     τοῦτ᾽ ἔστιν
     that means *89.106*

οὔτω
     see οὕτως

οὕτως
     a thus *61.9*
     b as follows *61.10*
     c so (degree) *78.4*

οὐχ
     see οὐ

οὐχί
     a not *69.4*
     b marker of question   *69.12*

ὀφειλέτης, ου *m*
     a debtor *57.222*
     b one who must *71.27*
     c sinner *88.300*

ὀφειλή, ῆς *f*
     a debt *57.221*
     b what one should do   *71.24*

ὀφείλημα, τος *n*
     a debt *57.221*
     b obligation *71.26*
     c sin *88.299*

ὀφείλω
     a be in debt *57.219*
     b must *71.35*
     c ought *71.25*
     d sin against *88.298*

ὄφελον
     would that *71.28*

ὄφελος, ους *n*
     advantage *65.40*

ὀφθαλμοδουλία, ας *f*
     eyeservice *35.29*

ὀφθαλμός, οῦ *m*
     a eye *8.23*
     b sight *24.16*
     c understanding *32.24*
     ὀφθαλμός : units
     ὀφθαλμὸς πονηρός
         a jealousy *88.165*
         b stingy *57.108*
     καμμύω τοὺς ὀφθαλμούς
         refuse to learn *27.50*
     τυφλόω τοὺς ὀφθαλμούς
         cause to not under-
         stand *32.25*
     ἐν ῥιπῇ ὀφθαλμοῦ
         suddenly *67.114*
     ἀνοίγω τοὺς ὀφθαλμούς
         cause to be able to
         see *24.43*
     ἐπαίρω τοὺς ὀφθαλμούς
         look *24.34*
     κατ᾽ ὀφθαλμούς
         in presence of *83.34*
     ἦσαν οἱ ὀφθαλμοὶ
     βεβαρημένοι
         be very sleepy *23.69*

ὀφθαλμός
ἦσαν οἱ ὀφθαλμοὶ
καταβαρυνόμενοι
  be very sleepy *23.69*

ὀφθείς
see ὁράω

ὀφθήσομαι
see ὁράω

ὄφις, εως *m*
  a snake *4.52*
  b evil person *88.123*

ὀφρῦς, ύος *f*
  cliff *1.49*

ὀχλέω
  cause trouble *22.24*

ὀχλοποιέω
  gather a crowd *11.2*

ὄχλος, ου *m*
  a crowd *11.1*
  b common people *87.64*

ὀχύρωμα, τος *n*
  fortress *7.21*

ὀψάριον, ου *n*
  fish *5.16*

ὀψέ
  a late *67.76*
  b evening *67.197*
  c after *67.51*

ὀψία, ας *f*
  evening *67.197*

ὄψιμος, ου *m*
  late rain *14.13*

ὄψιος, α, ον
  late *67.76*

ὄψις, εως *f*
  a face *8.18*
  b appearance *30.14*

ὄψομαι
see ὁράω

ὀψώνιον, ου *n*
  a pay *57.166*
  b money for support   *57.118*
  c result *89.42*

παγιδεύω
  catch in mistake *27.30*

παγίς, ίδος *f*
  a snare *6.23*
  b danger *21.4*
  c control *37.15*

πάγος
see Ἄρειος Πάγος

παθεῖν
see πάσχω

πάθημα, τος *n*
  a suffering *24.78*
  b passion *25.30*

παθητός, ή, όν
  subject to suffering . . . *24.85*

πάθος, ους *n*
  passion *25.30*

παθών, παθοῦσα
see πάσχω

παιδαγωγός, οῦ *m*
  guardian *36.5*

παιδάριον, ου *n*
  child *9.42*

παιδεία, ας *f*
  a instruction *33.226*
  b discipline *36.10*
  c punishment *38.4*

παιδευτής, οῦ *m*
  a trainer *33.244*
  b punisher *38.5*

παιδεύω
a teach 33.226
b discipline 36.10
c punish 38.4

παιδιόθεν
since childhood 67.153

παιδίον, ου n
a child (generic) 9.42
b child (own) 10.37
c child (endearment) 9.46

παιδίσκη, ης f
slave girl 87.83

παίζω
play 50.8

παῖς, παιδός m, f
a child (generic) 9.41
b child (own) 10.36
c slave 87.77

παίω
a hit 19.1
b sting 19.16

πάλαι
a long ago 67.24
b all the time 67.141
c already 67.22

παλαιόομαι
become old 67.104

παλαιός, ά, όν
a old (time) 67.97
b old (class) 58.75
c long ago 67.24
παλαιός : unit
παλαιὸς ἄνθρωπος
    former behavior 41.43

παλαιότης, ητος f
a oldness (time) 67.100
b old way (class) 58.74

παλαιόω
make old 67.103

πάλη, ης f
fight 39.29

παλιγγενεσία, ας f
a rebirth 41.53
b new age 67.147

πάλιν
a again 67.55
b also 89.97
c on the other hand . . 89.129
πάλιν : unit
εἰς τὸ πάλιν
    again 67.55

παμπληθεί
all together 59.28

Παμφυλία, ας f
Pamphylia 93.545

πανδοχεῖον, ου n
inn 7.11

πανδοχεύς, έως m
innkeeper 7.12

πανήγυρις, εως f
celebration 51.4

πανοικεί
with entire household 10.10

πανοπλία, ας f
weapons and armor . . . 6.30

πανουργία, ας f
treachery 88.270

πανοῦργος, ον
scoundrel 88.269

πανταχῇ
everywhere 83.8

πανταχοῦ
everywhere 83.8

παντελής, ές
παντελής : unit
εἰς τὸ παντελές
  a forever 67.95
  b completely 78.47

πάντῃ
everywhere 83.8

πάντοθεν
  a from all directions . . 84.7
  b all over 83.8

παντοκράτωρ, ορος *m*
the Almighty 12.7

παντός
see πᾶς

πάντοτε
always 67.88

πάντως
  a certainly 71.16
  b indeed 91.10

παρά
  a at (location) 83.25
  b among (location) . . . 83.9
  c from (extension) . . . 84.5
  d from (source) 90.14
  e for (agent) 90.3
  f in opinion of (view-
    point participant). . . 90.20
  g contrary to (oppo-
    sition) 89.137
  h instead of (contrast) 89.132
  i with (association) . . . 89.111
  j because of (reason) 89.25
  k beyond (degree) 78.29
  l less (quantity) 59.76
παρά : units
οἱ παρ' αὐτοῦ
  his family 10.9
τίθημι παρὰ/πρὸς
τοὺς πόδας
  turn over to 57.82

παραβαίνω
(aor παρέβην)
  a disobey 36.28
  b cease 68.39

παραβάλλω
(aor παρέβαλον)
sail to 54.12

παράβασις, εως *f*
transgression 36.28

παραβάτης, ου *m*
transgressor 36.29

παραβιάζομαι
urge 33.299

παραβολεύομαι
risk 21.7

παραβολή, ῆς *f*
  a parable 33.15
  b archetype 58.63
παραβολή : units
παρατίθημι τὴν παρα-
βολήν
  tell a parable 33.16
ἐν παραβολῇ
  figuratively 33.17

παραγγελία, ας *f*
command 33.328

παραγγέλλω
(aor παρήγγειλα, ptc
παραγγείλας)
command 33.327

παραγίνομαι
(aor παρεγενόμην,
subj παραγένωμαι)
  a come 15.86
  b come to help 35.6
  c appear in a place . . . 85.7

παράγω
  a move along 15.15
  b pass by 15.28
  c pass away 13.93

παραδειγματίζω
disgrace publicly *25.200*

παράδεισος, ου *m*
paradise *1.14*

παραδέχομαι
a receive *31.52*
b welcome *34.53*

παραδίδωμι
(pres 2 sg παραδίδως,
subj 3 sg παραδιδῷ,
παραδιδοῖ, inf παραδι-
δόναι, ptc παραδιδούς,
impf 3 sg παρεδίδου,
3 pl παρεδίδουν, παρ-
εδίδοσαν, fut παρα-
δώσω, aor παρέδωκα,
3 pl παρέδωκαν, παρ-
έδοσαν, subj 3 sg πα-
ραδῷ, παραδοῖ, inf
παραδοῦναι, ptc πα-
ραδούς, pf ptc παρα-
δεδωκώς, plpf 3 pl
παραδεδώκεισαν, pf
midd παραδέδομαι,
aor pass παρεδόθην,
subj παραδοθῶ, inf
παραδοθῆναι, ptc πα-
ραδοθείς, fut pass πα-
ραδοθήσομαι)
a give over *57.77*
b betray, hand over . . . *37.111*
c instruct *33.237*
d grant *13.142*
παραδίδωμι : units
παραδίδωμι τὸ πνεῦμα
    die *23.110*
παραδίδωμι τὴν ψυχήν
    risk *21.7*
καρπὸς παραδίδωσι
    harvest is ripe *23.200*
παραδίδωμι εἰς χεῖρας
    deliver to control of *37.12*

παράδοξος, ον
a incredible *31.44*
b unusual *58.56*

παράδοσις, εως *f*
tradition *33.239*

παραδῶ
see παραδίδωμι

παραδώσω
see παραδίδωμι

παραζηλόω
make jealous *88.164*

παραθαλάσσιος, α, ον
by the seaside *1.71*

παραθεῖναι
see παρατίθημι

παραθεωρέω
disregard *30.48*

παραθήκη, ης *f*
what is entrusted *35.48*

παραθήσω
see παρατίθημι

παράθου
see παρατίθημι

παραινέω
(impf 3 sg παρῄνει)
advise strongly *33.295*

παραιτέομαι
(impf παρῃτούμην, pf
ptc παρῃτημένος)
a ask for *33.163*
b not pay attention . . . *27.60*
c reject *34.35*
d not associate with . . *34.41*
e refuse to obey *36.27*

παρακαθέζομαι
sit down by *17.14*

παρακαλέω
(pf pass παρακέκλημαι,
aor pass παρεκλήθην,
subj παρακληθῶ,
fut pass παρακληθήσο-
μαι)
a ask for earnestly *33.168*
b invite *33.315*
c call together to *33.310*
d encourage *25.150*

παρακαλύπτω
make secret *28.82*

παράκειμαι
be present *85.23*

παράκλησις, εως *f*
a encouragement *25.150*
b earnest request..... *33.168*

παράκλητος, ου *m*
a the Helper *12.19*
b helper.......... *35.16*

παρακοή, ῆς *f*
disobedience *36.27*

παρακολουθέω
a be follower of...... *36.32*
b investigate carefully *27.38*
c happen along *13.113*

παρακούω
a refuse to obey *36.27*
b overhear.......... *24.66*
c ignore........... *30.37*

παρακύπτω
a bend over *17.31*
b look into.......... *24.13*
c desire to learn *27.39*

παραλαμβάνω
(fut παραλήμφομαι,
aor παρέλαβον, impv
παράλαβε, fut pass
παραλημφθήσομαι)
a bring along with ... *15.168*
b lead aside *15.180*
c learn from someone *27.13*

d welcome *34.53*
e receive appointment *37.99*
f be taught by *33.238*

παραλέγομαι
sail along coast *54.8*

παράλιος, ου *f*
coastal region *1.61*

παραλλαγή, ῆς *f*
change *58.44*

παραλογίζομαι
deceive............ *88.153*

παραλύομαι
be paralyzed *23.170*
παραλύομαι : unit
τὰ παραλελυμένα
γόνατα ἀνορθόω
become encouraged *25.152*

παραλυτικός, η, ον
paralyzed *23.171*

παραμένω
(aor ptc παραμείνας)
a remain with *85.56*
b continue......... *68.11*

παραμυθέομαι
console............ *25.153*

παραμυθία, ας *f*
consolation *25.154*

παραμύθιον, ου *n*
consolation *25.154*

παρανομέω
disobey *36.28*

παρανομία, ας *f*
lawless act *88.142*

παραπικραίνω
(aor παρεπίκρανα)
rebel.............. *39.40*

παραπικρασμός, οῦ *m*
rebellion 39.40

παραπίπτω
(aor ptc παραπεσών)
forsake 34.26

παραπλέω
(aor inf παραπλεῦσαι)
sail past 54.9

παραπλήσιος, α, ον
very similar 64.9

παραπλησίως
very similarly 64.9

παραπορεύομαι
pass by 15.28

παράπτωμα, τος *n*
sin 88.297

παραρρέω
(aor pass subj παραρυῶ)
drift away from belief 31.69

παράσημον, ου *n*
emblem 6.51

παράσημος, ον
being marked 33.479

παρασκευάζομαι
get ready 77.8

παρασκευάζω
prepare a meal 46.12

παρασκευή, ῆς *f*
day of preparation 67.201

παραστήσομαι
see παρίστημι

παραστήσω
see παρίσταμαι

παρασχών
see παρέχω

παρατείνω
(aor παρέτεινα)
a prolong 67.120
b keep on 68.21

παρατηρέω
a watch closely 24.48
b observe custom 41.27

παρατήρησις, εως *f*
close watch 24.48

παρατίθεμαι
a entrust to 35.47
b show to be true 72.4

παρατίθημι
(fut παραθήσω, aor παρ-
έθηκα, inf παραθεῖναι,
aor midd παρεθέμην,
impv παράθου)
give food to 57.116
παρατίθημι : unit
παρατίθημι τὴν παρα-
βολήν
tell a parable 33.16

παρατυγχάνω
be in a place by chance 85.12

παραυτίκα
temporary 67.109

παραφέρω
(aor impv παρένεγκε)
a drive along 15.162
b mislead 31.75
παραφέρω : unit
παραφέρω τὸ ποτήριον
ἀπό
cause not to expe-
rience 90.97

παραφρονέω
be insane 30.24

παραφρονία, ας *f*
insanity 30.24

παραχειμάζω
spend the winter 67.166

παραχειμασία, ας *f*
spend the winter *67.166*

παραχρῆμα
suddenly *67.113*

πάρδαλις, εως *f*
leopard *4.13*

παρέβαλον
see παραβάλλω

παρέβην
see παραβαίνω

παρεγενόμην
see παραγίνομαι

παρεδίδοσαν
see παραδίδωμι

παρεδίδου
see παραδίδωμι

παρεδίδουν
see παραδίδωμι

παρεδόθην
see παραδίδωμι

παρέδοσαν
see παραδίδωμι

παρεδρεύω
serve *35.26*

παρέδωκα
see παραδίδωμι

παρεθέμην
see παρατίθημι

παρέθηκα
see παρατίθημι

παρειμένος
see παρίημι

πάρειμι
(inf παρεῖναι, ptc παρ-
ών, παροῦσα, παρόν,

impf 3 pl παρῆσαν)
a be present *85.23*
b arrive *15.86*
πάρειμι : units
τὸ παρόν
the present *67.37*
τὰ παρόντα
possessions *57.17*

παρεῖναι
see παρίημι and
πάρειμι

παρεισάγω
cause to happen *13.132*

παρείσακτος, ον
joined falsely *34.29*

παρεισδύω
slip into a group *34.30*

παρεισέρχομαι
(aor παρεισῆλθον)
slip into a group *34.30*

παρειστήκειν
see παρίσταμαι

παρεισφέρω
(aor ptc παρεισενέγκας)
παρεισφέρω : unit
σπουδὴν πᾶσαν παρ-
εισφέρω
do one's best *68.64*

παρεκλήθην
see παρακαλέω

παρεκτός
besides *58.38*

παρέλαβον
see παραλαμβάνω

παρελεύσομαι
see παρέρχομαι

παρεληλυθέναι
see παρέρχομαι

παρεληλυθώς
see παρέρχομαι

παρελθεῖν
see παρέρχομαι

παρεμβάλλω
(fut παρεμβαλῶ)
surround 85.39

παρεμβολή, ῆς f
a camp 1.94
b barracks 7.22

παρένεγκε
see παραφέρω

παρενοχλέω
cause extra difficulty . . 22.25

παρέξῃ
see παρέχω

παρεπίδημος, ου m
stranger 11.77

παρεπίκρανα
see παραπικραίνω

παρέρχομαι
(fut παρελεύσομαι, aor
παρῆλθον, inf παρελθεῖν,
pf inf παρεληλυθέναι,
ptc παρεληλυθώς)
a pass by 15.28
b arrive 15.86
c disobey 36.28
d pass away 13.93
e pass (of time) 67.85

πάρεσις, εως f
disregard 30.49

παρέστηκα
see παρίσταμαι

παρεστηκώς
see παρίσταμαι

παρέστην
see παρίσταμαι

παρέστησα
see παρίστημι

παρεστώς
see παρίσταμαι

παρέχω
(fut midd 2 sg παρέξῃ,
aor παρέσχον, ptc
παρασχών)
a continue to be 13.26
b cause to happen 13.127
c cause to experience 90.91

παρήγγειλα
see παραγγέλλω

παρηγορία, ας f
a comfort 25.155
b assistance 35.14

παρῆλθον
see παρέρχομαι

παρήνει
see παραινέω

παρῆσαν
see πάρειμι

παρῃτημένος
see παραιτέομαι

παρῃτούμην
see παραιτέομαι

παρθενία, ας f
virginity 23.64

παρθένος, ου f or m
a virgin (female) 9.39
b virgin (male) 9.33
c unmarried person . . 34.77

Πάρθος, ου m
Parthian 93.546

παρίεμαι
be weak 23.174

παρίημι
(aor inf παρεῖναι, pf
pass ptc παρειμένος)
avoid *13.145*

παρίσταμαι (+ 2 aor, pf,
plpf act)
(aor παρέστην, pf παρέσ-
τηκα, ptc παρεστώς, παρ-
εστηκώς, plpf παρειστή-
κειν, fut παραστήσομαι)
a stand near *17.3*
b be at *85.13*
c be in front of *85.18*
d be now *67.64*
e come *15.86*
f help *35.1*

παριστάνω
see παρίστημι[b]

παρίστημι
(fut παραστήσω, aor
παρέστησα)
a cause to be in a place *85.14*
b cause to be *13.11*
c cause to exist *13.83*
d provide *57.81*
e hand over *37.111*
f show to be true *72.4*

Παρμενᾶς, ᾶ *m*
Parmenas *93.292*

πάροδος, ου *f*
passing by *15.29*

παροικέω
a dwell temporarily . . *85.71*
b live as a foreigner . . . *85.78*

παροικία, ας *f*
time of residence *85.79*

πάροικος, ου *m*
stranger *11.77*

παροιμία, ας *f*
a proverb *33.14*
b parable *33.15*

πάροινος, ου *m*
drunkard *88.288*

παροίχομαι
(pf παρώχημαι)
pass (of time) *67.85*

παρομοιάζω
be very similar to *64.8*

παρόμοιος, ον
very similar *64.7*

παρόν
see πάρειμι

παρόντα
see πάρειμι

παροξύνομαι
be upset *88.189*

παροξυσμός, οῦ *m*
a encouragement *90.55*
b sharp argument *33.451*

παροργίζω
(fut παροργιῶ)
make angry *88.177*

παροργισμός, οῦ *m*
anger *88.176*

παροτρύνω
(aor παρώτρυνα)
incite *39.8*

παροῦσα
see πάρειμι

παρουσία, ας *f*
a presence *85.25*
b arrival *15.86*

παροψίς, ίδος *f*
plate *6.135*

παρρησία, ας *f*
courage 25.158
παρρησία : unit
ἐν παρρησίᾳ
in public 28.29

παρρησιάζομαι
a speak boldly 33.90
b have courage 25.159

παρών
see πάρειμι

παρώτρυνα
see παροτρύνω

παρώχημαι
see παροίχομαι

πᾶς, πᾶσα, πᾶν (gen *m, n*
παντός)
a all 59.23
b any 59.24
c total 78.44
d whole 63.2
e every kind of 58.28
πᾶς : units
διὰ παντός
a regularly 67.15
b always 67.86
πρὸ παντὸς τοῦ αἰῶνος
since all time 67.133
(εἰς) (παντὰς) τοὺς
αἰῶνας (τῶν αἰώνων)
forever 67.95
σπουδὴν πᾶσαν
παρεισφέρω
do one's best 68.64

πάσχα *n*
a Passover festival . . . 51.6
b Passover meal 51.7
c Passover lamb 4.27

πάσχω
(aor ἔπαθον, inf παθεῖν,
ptc παθών, fem ptc πα-
θοῦσα, pf πέπονθα)
a suffer 24.78
b experience 90.66

Πάταρα, ων *n*
Patara 93.547

πατάσσω
a strike a blow 19.3
b strike down 20.73

πατέω
a step on 15.226
b trample 19.51
c trample on 20.22
d conquer 39.54

πατήρ, πατρός *m*
a father 10.14
b parents 10.18
c ancestor 10.20
d Father (title for God) 12.12
e father (title for
person) 87.48
f elder 11.26
g archetype 58.64
h leader 36.8
πατήρ : units
προστίθημι πρὸς τοὺς
πατέρας αὐτοῦ
bury 52.7
θάπτω τὸν πατέρα μου
take care of one's
father until death . . . 35.46

Πάτμος, ου *m*
Patmos 93.548

πατριά, ᾶς *f*
a lineage 10.24
b nation 11.56

πατριάρχης, ου *m*
patriarch 10.22

πατρικός, ή, όν
of ancestors 10.21

πατρίς, ίδος *f*
homeland 1.81

Πατροβᾶς, ᾶ *m*
Patrobas 93.293

πατρολῴας, ου *m*
one who murders his
father *20.88*

πατροπαράδοτος, ον
teaching handed down *33.240*

πατρῷος, α, ον
of ancestors *10.21*

Παῦλος, ου *m*
Paul *93.294*

παύομαι
cease *68.34*

παύω
cause to cease *68.46*

Πάφος, ου *f*
Paphos *93.549*

παχύνομαι
be unable to under-
stand *32.45*

πέδη, ης *f*
fetter *6.17*

πεδινός, ή, όν
level *79.85*

πεζεύω
go by foot *15.224*

πεζῇ
on foot *8.50*

πειθαρχέω
obey *36.12*

πειθοῖς
see πειθός

πείθομαι
(impf ἐπειθόμην, pf
πέπεισμαι)
a obey *36.12*
b be a follower *36.34*
c be certain *31.46*

πειθός, ή, όν
persuasive *33.304*

πειθώ, οῦς *f*
persuasive power *33.306*

πείθω
(aor ἔπεισα, pf πέποιθα,
plpf ἐπεποίθειν, pf pass
πέπεισμαι, impf pass
ἐπειθόμην, fut pass
πεισθήσομαι)
a pcrsuade *33.301*
b trust (pf only) *31.82*
πείθω : unit
πείθω τὴν χαρδίαν
be assured *25.166*

πεῖν
see πίνω

πεινάω
a be hungry *23.29*
b desire strongly *25.17*

πεῖρα, ας *f*
πεῖρα : unit
πεῖραν λαμβάνω
attempt *68.58*

πειράζω
(aor pass ἐπειράσθην
and ἐπιράσθην)
a examine *27.46*
b try to trap *27.31*
c tempt *88.308*
d attempt *68.58*
πειράζω : unit
ὁ πειράζων
the Temptcr *12.36*

πειράομαι
attempt *68.58*

πειρασμός, οῦ *m*
a testing *27.46*
b temptation *88.308*

πεισθήσομαι
see πείθω

πεισμονή, ῆς f
　that which persuades　*33.303*

πέλαγος, ους n
　open sea *1.73*

πελεκίζω
　cut head off *20.80*

πέμπτος, η, ον
　fifth *60.52*

πέμπω
　a send (someone) *15.66*
　b send (by someone) . . *15.193*
　c send word *15.67*
　d cause to experience　*90.88*
　πέμπω : unit
　πέμπω τὸ δρέπανον
　　begin to harvest *43.17*

πένης, ητος m
　poor *57.50*

πενθερά, ᾶς f
　mother-in-law *10.59*

πενθερός, οῦ m
　father-in-law *10.58*

πενθέω
　be sad *25.142*

πένθος, ους n
　sorrow *25.142*

πενιχρός, ά, όν
　poor *57.49*

πεντάκις
　five times *60.72*

πεντακισχίλιοι, αι, α
　five thousand *60.43*

πεντακόσιοι, αι, α
　five hundred *60.37*

πέντε
　five *60.14*

πεντεκαιδέκατος, η, ον
　fifteenth *60.61*

πεντήκοντα
　fifty *60.28*

πεντηκοστή, ῆς f
　Pentecost *51.8*

πέπεισμαι
　see πείθω, πείθομαι

πεποιήκεισαν
　see ποιέω

πέποιθα
　see πείθω

πεποίθησις, εως f
　confidence *31.82*

πέπονθα
　see πάσχω

πέπραγμαι
　see πράσσω

πέπρακα
　see πιπράσκω

πέπραμαι
　see πιπράσκω

πέπραχα
　see πράσσω

πεπρησμένος
　see πίμπραμαι

πέπτωκα
　see πίπτω

πέπωκα
　see πίνω

περαιτέρω
　furthermore *89.99*

πέραν
　across *83.43*

πέρας, ατος *n*
a limit *80.6*
b conclusion *61.15*

Πέργαμος, ου *f*
Pergamum *93.550*

Πέργη, ης *f*
Perga *93.551*

περί
a around (location) . . . *83.18*
b about (content) *90.24*
c about (time) *67.35*
d because (reason) *89.36*
e on behalf of (bene-
  faction) *90.39*
f with (association) . . . *89.110*
g with regard to
  (specification) *89.6*

περιάγω
a travel about *15.23*
b bring/take along *15.170*

περιαιρέω
(aor inf περιελεῖν, ptc
περιελών, impf pass
3 sg περιῃρεῖτο)
a take from around . . . *15.204*
b lift anchor *54.24*
c do away with *13.38*
d stop *68.43*

περιάπτω
(aor ptc περιάψας)
  start a fire *14.65*

περιαστράπτω
shine brightly around *14.45*

περιβάλλω
(fut περιβαλῶ, aor
περιέβαλον, aor midd
impv περιβαλοῦ, pf
pass περιβέβλημαι)
a clothe *49.3*
b adorn *49.5*

περιβλέπομαι
look around *24.11*

περιβόλαιον, ου *n*
a clothing *6.163*
b cloak *6.172*

περιδέω
(plpf pass 3 sg
περιεδέδετο)
wrap up *18.14*

περιέδραμον
see περιτρέχω

περιεζωσμένος
see περιζώννυμι

περιέθηκα
see περιτίθημι

περιελεῖν
see περιαιρέω

περιελθών
see περιέρχομαι

περιελών
see περιαιρέω

περιέπεσον
see περιπίπτω

περιεργάζομαι
be a busybody *88.243*

περίεργος, ου *m*
a busybody *88.244*
b witchcraft *53.99*

περιέρχομαι
(aor περιῆλθον, ptc
περιελθών)
a travel about *15.23*
b go around *15.33*

περιέστησαν
see περιΐστημι

περιεστώς
see περιΐστημι

περιέτεμον
see περιτέμνω

περιετμήθην
see περιτέμνω

περιέχω
(aor περιέσχον)
a contain 90.27
b experience 90.69

περιζώννυμαι
(fut midd περιζώσο-
μαι, aor midd ptc πε-
ριζωσάμενος, pf midd
ptc περιεζωσμένος)
be girded 49.15
περιζώννυμαι : unit
περιζώννυμαι τὴν ὀσφύν
get ready 77.5

περιῆλθον
see περιέρχομαι

περιῃρεῖτο
see περιαιρέω

περιθείς
see περιτίθημι

περίθεσις, εως f
wearing 49.7

περιΐσταμαι
(pres impv 2 sg
περιΐστασο)
avoid 13.157

περιΐστημι
(aor 3 pl περιέστησαν,
pf ptc περιεστώς)
stand around 17.4

περικάθαρμα, τος n
garbage 79.53

περικαλύπτω
cover around 79.115

περίκειμαι
a be around 85.5
b be put around 85.54
c wear 49.4
d be in many ways . . . 13.6

περικεφαλαία, ας f
helmet 6.38

περικρατής, ές
have under control . . . 37.23

περικρύβω
conceal 28.79

περικυκλόω
surround 15.147

περιλάμπω
shine around 14.44

περιλείπομαι
be left behind 85.66

περίλυπος, ον
very sad 25.277

περιμένω
wait for 85.60

πέριξ
around 83.18

περιοικέω
live nearby 85.74

περίοικος, ου m
neighbor 11.89

περιούσιος, ον
a private possession . . 57.5
b peculiar 58.48

περιοχή, ῆς f
passage (in book) 33.10

περιπατέω
a walk 15.227
b behave 41.11
περιπατέω : unit
περιπατέω τοῖς ἴχνεσιν
imitate 41.47

περιπείρω
experience 90.73

περιπίπτω
(aor περιέπεσον, ptc
περιπεσών)
a run into 15.85
b fall into hands of . . . 37.11
c experience 90.71

περιποιέομαι
acquire 57.61
περιποιέομαι : unit
τὴν ψυχὴν αὐτοῦ περι-
ποιέομαι
save oneself 21.24

περιποίησις, εως f
a experience 90.74
b possessions 57.62

περιραίνω
(pf pass περιρέραμμαι)
sprinkle around 47.17

περιραντίζω
(pf pass περιρεράντισμαι)
sprinkle around 47.17

περιρήγνυμι
(aor ptc περιρήξας)
tear off 19.33

περισπάομαι
be distracted and
anxious 25.238

περισσεία, ας f
a abundance 59.53
b excessive 78.31

περίσσευμα, τος n
abundance 59.53

περισσεύω
a be in abundance 59.52
b provide in abun-
dance 59.54
c have more than
enough 57.24
d excessive 78.31
e cause to be intense 78.32
f have greater ad-
vantage 65.47

περισσός, ή, όν
a advantage 65.46
b exceptional 58.57
c superfluous 59.51
d unnecessary 71.40
περισσός : unit
ἐκ περισσοῦ
extremely 78.20

περισσότερος, α, ον
excessive 78.31

περισσοτέρως
excessive 78.31

περισσῶς
excessive 78.31

περιστερά, ᾶς f
dove, pigeon 4.44

περιτέμνω
(aor περιέτεμον, inf περι-
τεμεῖν, pf pass περιτέτμη-
μαι, aor pass περιετμή-
θην, inf περιτμηθῆναι)
circumcise 53.51

περιτίθημι
(pres 3 pl περιτιθέασιν,
aor περιέθηκα, ptc
περιθείς)
a put around 85.39
b assign 13.10

περιτομή, ῆς f
circumcision 53.51
περιτομή : unit
οἱ ἐκ περιτομῆς
those of the cir-
cumcision 11.51

περιτρέπω
change to 13.64

περιτρέχω
(aor περιέδραμον)
run about 15.231

περιφέρω
carry around 15.190

περιφρονέω
  disregard 76.25

περίχωρος, ου f
  surrounding region . . . 1.80

περίψημα, τος n
  garbage 79.53

περπερεύομαι
  brag 33.369

Περσίς, ίδος f
  Persis 93.295

πέρυσι
  last year 67.204

πεσεῖν
  see πίπτω

πεσοῦμαι
  see πίπτω

πεσών
  see πίπτω

πετεινόν, οῦ n
  bird 4.38
  πετεινόν: unit
  πετεινὰ τοῦ οὐρανοῦ
    wild birds 4.41

πέτομαι
  fly 15.245

πέτρα, ας f
  bedrock 2.21

Πέτρος, ου m
  Peter 93.296

πετρῶδες, ους n
  rocky ground 2.22

πεφίμωσο
  see φιμόω

πήγανον, ου n
  rue 3.22

πηγή, ῆς f
  a spring 1.78
  b well 7.57
  πηγή : unit
  πηγὴ αἵματος
    menstrual flow 23.182

πήγνυμι
  (aor ἔπηξα)
  erect 45.2

πηδάλιον, ου n
  rudder 6.50

πηλίκος, η, ον
  a how large 79.126
  b how important 87.32

πηλός, οῦ m
  clay 2.18

πήρα, ας f
  traveler's bag 6.145

πηρόω
  πηρόω : unit
  πηρόω τὴν καρδίαν
    make unable to learn 27.53

πῆχυς, εως m
  cubit 81.25

πιάζω
  a seize 18.3
  b arrest 37.110

πίε
  see πίνω

πιέζω
  press down 19.49

πιεῖν
  see πίνω

πίεσαι
  see πίνω

πιθανολογία, ας f
  convincing speech 33.31

πιθός
see πειθός

πικραίνομαι
be embittered *88.202*

πικραίνω
(fut πικρανῶ, aor
pass ἐπικράνθην)
make bitter *79.42*

πικρία, ας *f*
a bitterness *79.40*
b bitter resentment ... *88.201*
πικρία : unit
εἰς χολὴν πικρίας εἰμί
be terribly envious .. *88.166*

πικρός, ά, όν
a bitter *79.41*
b resentful......... *88.170*

πικρῶς
with agony......... *25.284*

Πιλᾶτος, ου *m*
Pilate *93.297*

πίμπλαμαι
a come to an end..... *67.70*
b completely *78.46*

πίμπλημι
(aor ἔπλησα, ptc πλήσας,
aor pass ἐπλήσθην, inf
πλησθῆναι, fut pass
πλησθήσομαι)
a fill completely *59.38*
b make happen *13.106*

πίμπραμαι
(inf πίμπρασθαι, aor
ptc πρησθείς, pf ptc
πεπρησμένος)
a sick with fever *23.159*
b swell up *23.163*

πινακίδιον, ου *n*
tablet *6.60*

πίναξ, ακος *f*
plate *6.134*

πίννω
see πίνω

πίνω
(fut πίομαι, 2 sg πίεσαι,
aor ἔπιον, subj πίω,
impv πίε, inf πιεῖν,
πεῖν, pf πέπωκα)
a drink *23.34*
b soak up.......... *14.35*
πίνω : unit
πίνω ποτήριον
suffer severely *24.81*

πιότης, ητος *f*
a rich sap.......... *3.59*
b value............ *65.7*

πιπράσκω
(pf πέπρακα, pf pass
πέπραμαι, aor pass
ἐπράθην, inf πραθῆ-
ναι, ptc neut πραθέν)
sell *57.186*

πίπτω
(fut πεσοῦμαι, aor ἔ-
πεσα, inf πεσεῖν, ptc
πεσών, pf πέπτωκα,
2 sg πέπτωκες)
a fall *15.118*
b fall down *15.119*
c prostrate oneself
before *17.22*
d be destroyed *20.60*
e die *23.105*
f cease............ *68.49*
g happen *13.122*
h worsen *13.59*
i come to an end..... *13.97*
j become inadequate *75.7*
k experience *90.71*
πίπτω : units
ἀχλὺς καὶ σκότος πίπτει
become blind *24.40*
πίπτω ἐπί τινα
cause to suffer...... *24.93*

ὁ κλῆρος πίπτει ἐπί τινα
   choose by lot 30.107
ὑπὸ κρίσιν πίπτω
   be condemned 56.32
τῷ ἰδίῳ κυρίῳ στήκει
ἢ πίπτει
   honor depends on
   master's judgment . . 87.56

Πισιδία, ας f
   Pisidia 93.552

Πισίδιος, α, ον
   Pisidian 93.553

πιστεύω
   a think to be true 31.35
   b trust 31.85
   c have Christian faith 31.102
   d entrust 35.50

πιστή, ῆς f
   a believer 31.103
   b Christian 11.17

πιστικός, ή, όν
   pure 79.97

πίστις, εως f
   a what can be believed 31.43
   b trust 31.85
   c trustworthiness 31.88
   d Christian faith 31.102
   e doctrine 31.104
   f promise 33.289

πιστόομαι
   come to believe 31.36

πιστός, ή, όν
   a trusting 31.86
   b trustworthy 31.87
   c sure 71.17

πίω
   see πίνω

πλανάομαι
   a wander about 15.24
   b stray from the truth 31.67

πλανάω
   deceive 31.8

πλάνη, ης f
   a deception 31.8
   b deceptive belief 31.10
   c perversion 88.262

πλανήτης, ου m
   wanderer 15.26

πλάνος, ον
   deceitful 31.9

πλάξ, πλακός f
   tablet 6.61

πλάσμα, τος n
   what is formed 58.12

πλάσσω
   (aor ptc πλάσας, aor
   pass ἐπλάσθην)
   a make 42.31
   b mold 58.11

πλαστός, ή, όν
   false 72.11

πλατεῖα, ας f
   wide street 1.103

πλάτος, ους n
   breadth 81.15

πλατύνω
   widen 81.17
   πλατύνω : unit
   πλατύνω τὴν καρδίαν
     show affection for . . 25.53

πλατύς, εῖα, ύ
   wide 81.16

πλέγμα, τος n
   what is woven 49.28

πλεῖστον
   see πλείων

πλείων, πλεῖον or πλέον,
ονος, pl πλείονες or πλείους
  (see also πολύς)
  a more (quantity) *59.1*
  b more (degree)...... *78.28*
  c more appropriate... *66.11*
  πλείων : unit
  τὸ πλεῖστον
    at most *59.8*

πλέκω
  braid *49.27*

πλέον
  see πλείων

πλεονάζω
  (aor opt 3 sg πλεονάσαι)
  a become more and
    more............ *59.67*
  b cause to increase ... *78.32*
  c be in abundance.... *59.48*
  d have more than
    enough.......... *57.23*

πλεονεκτέω
  exploit *88.144*

πλεονέκτης, ου m
  greedy person *25.23*

πλεονεξία, ας f
  a greed *25.22*
  b exploitation *88.144*

πλευρά, ᾶς f
  side of the body *8.41*

πλέω
  sail............... *54.1*
  πλέω : unit
  ὁ ἐπὶ τόπον πλέων
    sea traveller *54.27*

πληγή, ῆς f
  a hit.............. *19.1*
  b wound .... : *20.29*
  c plague .... : *23.158*
  d distress.......... *22.13*

πλῆθος, ους n
  a large number *59.9*
  b crowd *11.1*

πληθύνω
  a increase *59.68*
  b cause to increase ... *59.69*

πλήκτης, ου m
  bully *88.137*

πλήμμυρα, ης f
  flood *14.33*

πλήν
  but, except.......... *89.130*
  see also μέν ... πλήν

πλήρης, ες
  a full *59.35*
  b complete *59.31*
  c very many *59.10*

πληρόομαι
  a come to an end..... *67.70*
  b be completely *78.46*

πληροφορέομαι
  be completely certain *31.45*

πληροφορέω
  a make happen *13.106*
  b proclaim.......... *33.199*
  c accomplish........ *68.32*

πληροφορία, ας f
  complete certainty.... *31.45*

πληρόω
  a fill *59.37*
  b make complete..... *59.33*
  c finish *68.26*
  d provide fully *35.33*
  e proclaim completely *33.199*
  f give true meaning .. *33.144*
  g cause to happen *13.106*
  πληρόω : unit
  πληρόω τὴν καρδίαν
    cause to think...... *30.29*

πλήρωμα, τος *n*
a contents *59.36*
b completeness *59.32*
c end *67.69*

πλήσας
see πίμπλημι

πλησθῆναι
see πίμπλημι

πλησθήσομαι
see πίμπλημι

πλησίον
a nearby *83.27*
b neighbor *11.89*

πλησμονή, ῆς *f*
gratification *25.14*

πλήσσω
(aor pass ἐπλήγην)
strike *19.1*

πλοιάριον, ου *n*
small boat *6.42*

πλοῖον, ου *n*
boat *6.41*

πλοῦς, πλοός, acc πλοῦν *m*
sailing *54.1*

πλούσιος, α, ον
a rich *57.26*
b in abundance *59.57*

πλουσίως
a in abundance *59.57*
b extremely *78.15*

πλουτέω
a be rich *57.25*
b become rich *57.28*
c be generous *57.104*
d have great deal of *59.58*

πλουτίζω
a make rich *57.29*
b cause to have
abundance of *59.59*

πλοῦτος, ου *m*
a riches *57.30*
b extreme *78.15*

πλύνω
wash *47.8*

πνεῦμα, τος *n*
a Holy Spirit *12.18*
b spirit *12.33*
c evil spirit *12.37*
d ghost *12.42*
e inner being *26.9*
f way of thinking . . . *30.6*
g wind *14.4*
h breath *23.186*
πνεῦμα : units
πτωχὸς τῷ πνεύματι
be humble *88.57*
ἔχω πνεῦμα πύθωνα
be a fortuneteller . . . *33.285*
ζέω τῷ πνεύματι
show enthusiasm . . . *25.73*
τίθεμαι ἐν τῷ πνεύματι
make up mind *30.76*
ἀφίημι τὸ πνεῦμα
die *23.109*
παραδίδωμι τὸ πνεῦμα
die *23.110*
πνεῦμα ἀκάθαρτον
unclean spirit *12.39*
πνεῦμα πονηρόν
evil spirit *12.38*

πνευματικός, οῦ *m*
one who is spiritual . . . *12.20*

πνευματικός, ή, όν
a from the Spirit *12.21*
b spiritual *26.10*
c of spiritual conduct *41.40*
d not physical *79.3*
e supernatural *79.6*

πνευματικός : unit
τὰ πνευματικὰ τῆς πονη-
ρίας ἐν τοῖς ἐπουρανίοις
   supernatural powers *12.44*

πνευματικῶς
  a from the Spirit *12.21*
  b spiritual *26.10*
  c figuratively *33.17*

πνέω
  (aor ἔπνευσα)
  blow *14.4*

πνίγομαι
  drown *23.119*

πνίγω
  a choke *19.53*
  b cause plants to die . . *23.120*

πνικτός, ή, όν
  choked *19.54*

πνοή, ῆς f
  a wind *14.4*
  b breath *23.187*

ποδήρης, ους m
  long robe *6.175*

πόθεν
  a whence *84.6*
  b how *89.86*
  c why *89.38*

ποιέομαι
  ποιέομαι : unit
  λόγου ποιέομαι
   be of opinion *31.2*

ποιέω
  (unaugm plpf 3 pl
  πεποιήκεισαν)
  a do *90.45*
  b perform *42.7*
  c cause'to be *13.9*
  d work *42.41*
  e make *42.29*
  f behave toward *41.7*

g assign to a task *37.106*
h make profit *57.189*
ποιέω : units
ποιέω τὸ ἱκανόν
  act in a pleasing
  manner *25.96*
ποιέω καρπόν
  a produce fruit *23.199*
  b cause results *13.86*
τροχιὰς ὀρθὰς ποιέω
τοῖς ποσίν
  behave correctly *41.30*
μὴ γνώτω ἡ ἀριστερά
σου τι ποιει ἡ δεξιά σου
  do secretly *28.74*

ποίημα, τος n
  what is made *42.30*

ποίησις, εως f
  doing *42.7*

ποιητής, οῦ m
  a doer *42.20*
  b poet *33.25*

ποικίλος, η, ον
  of various kinds *58.45*

ποιμαίνω
  (fut ποιμανῶ, aor
  impv 2 pl ποιμάνατε)
  a shepherd *44.3*
  b guide and help *36.2*
  c rule *37.57*

ποιμήν, ένος m
  a shepherd *44.4*
  b minister *53.72*

ποίμνη, ης f
  a flock *4.28*
  b follower of Christ . . *11.31*

ποίμνιον, ου n
  follower of Christ *11.31*

ποῖος, α, ον
  a which *92.36*
  b what kind of *58.30*

πολεμέω
a wage war 55.5
b fight 39.26

πόλεμος, ου *m*
a war 55.5
b fight 39.26

πόλις, εως *f*
a town 1.88
b city 1.89
c inhabitants of city . . 11.61
πόλις : unit
οἰκονόμος τῆς πόλεως
     city treasurer 57.231

πολιτάρχης, ου *m*
city official 37.93

πολιτεία, ας *f*
a citizenship 11.70
b state 11.67

πολίτευμα, τος *n*
place of citizenship . . . 11.71

πολιτεύομαι
conduct one's life 41.34

πολίτης, ου *m*
citizen 11.68

πολλά (adv)
often 67.11

πολλάκις
often 67.11

πολλαπλασίων, ον
many times as much . . 59.20

πολυλογία, ας *f*
long speaking 33.87

πολυμερῶς
a fragmentary 63.19
b often 67.11
c many ways 89.81

πολυποίκιλος, ον
manifold 58.46

πολύς, πολλή, πολύ
(see also πλείων)
a many 59.1
b much 59.11
c great 78.3
πολύς : units
ἐπὶ πολύ
     for a long time 67.89
ὥρα πολλή
     (very) late 67.77

πολύσπλαγχνος, ον
very compassionate . . . 25.52

πολυτελής, ές
valuable 65.3

πολύτιμος, ον
valuable 65.3

πολυτρόπως
a in many ways
     (kind) 58.29
b in many ways
     (manner) 89.82

πόμα, τος *n*
drink 5.6

πονηρία, ας *f*
wickedness 88.108
πονηρία : unit
τὰ πνευματικὰ τῆς πονη-
ρίας ἐν τοῖς ἐπουρανίοις
     supernatural powers 12.44

πονηρίαι, ων *f*
wicked deeds 88.109

πονηρός, ά, όν
a wicked 88.110
b worthless 65.27
c guilty 88.314
d be sick 23.149
πονηρός : units
ὀφθαλμὸς πονηρός
     a jealous 88.165
     b stingy 57.108
ὁ πονηρός
     the Evil One 12.35

πνεῦμα πονηρόν
evil spirit *12.38*

πόνος, ου *m*
a pain *24.77*
b hard work *42.49*

Ποντικός, ή, όν
Pontian *93.554*

Πόντιος, ου *m*
Pontius *93.298*

Πόντος, ου *m*
Pontus *93.555*

πόντος, ου *m*
open sea *1.73*

Πόπλιος, ου *m*
Publius *93.299*

πορεία, ας *f*
a journey *15.18*
b business activity . . . *57.200*

πορεύομαι
a go *15.10*
b travel *15.18*
c go away *15.34*
d behave *41.11*
e die *23.101*

πορθέω
destroy *20.37*

πορισμός, οῦ *m*
gain wealth *57.194*

Πόρκιος, ου *m*
Porcius *93.300*

πορνεία, ας *f*
fornication *88.271*

πορνεύω
commit fornication . . . *88.271*

πόρνη, ης *f*
prostitute *88.275*

πόρνος, ου *m*
sexually immoral
person *88.274*

πόρρω
far away *83.31*

πόρρωθεν
a long before *67.46*
b far away *83.31*

πορρώτερον
farther *83.32*

πορφύρα, ας *f*
purple cloth *6.169*

πορφυρόπωλις, ιδος *f*
dealer in purple cloth *57.204*

πορφυροῦν, οῦ *n*
purple cloth *6.169*

πορφυροῦς, ᾶ, οῦν
purple *79.38*

ποσάκις
how often *67.14*

πόσις, εως *f*
a drink *5.6*
b drinking *23.34*

πόσος, η, ον
a how many *59.5*
b how much *59.17*
c how great *78.13*

ποταμός, οῦ *m*
river *1.76*

ποταμοφόρητος, ον
carried off by flood . . . *15.205*

ποταπός, ή, όν
what sort of *58.30*

ποτέ
a ever *67.9*
b when *67.30*

ποτέ : unit
ἤδη ποτέ
   now at last 67.40

πότε
   when 67.30

πότερον
   whether 89.70

ποτήριον, ου n
   cup 6.121
   ποτήριον : units
   πίνω ποτήριον
      suffer severely 24.81
   παραφέρω τὸ ποτήριον
   ἀπό
      cause not to expe-
      rience 90.97

ποτίζω
   a give to drink 23.35
   b irrigate 43.9

Ποτίολοι, ων m
   Puteoli 93.556

πότος, ου m
   orgy 88.287

ποῦ
   a where (place) 83.6
   b where (circum-
      stance) 92.28
   ποῦ : unit
   ποῦ φανεῖται
      what will happen to 13.118

πού
   a somewhere 83.7
   b almost 78.40

Πούδης, εντος m
   Pudens 93.301

πούς, ποδός m
   foot 8.49
   πούς : units
   πόδας νίπτω
      a be very hospitable 34.59
      b act humbly 88.58

κατευθύνω τοὺς πόδας
   guide behavior 41.17
τροχιὰς ὀρθὰς ποιέω
τοῖς ποσίν
   behave correctly 41.30
ἀνατρέφω παρὰ τοὺς
πόδας
   be taught by 33.232
ὑποπόδιον τῶν ποδῶν
   be under someone's
   control 37.8
ὑποκάτω τῶν ποδῶν
   be under complete
   control 37.8
τίθημι παρὰ/πρὸς
τοὺς πόδας
   turn over to 57.82
βῆμα ποδός
   square yard/meter .. 80.3
ὑπὸ τοὺς πόδας
   be in complete
   control of 37.8

πρᾶγμα, τος n
   a event 13.105
   b undertaking 42.9
   c lawsuit 56.2

πραγματεῖαι, ῶν f
   affairs 41.23

πραγματεύομαι
   do business 57.197

πραθέν
   see πιπράσκω

πραθῆναι
   see πιπράσκω

πραιτώριον, ου n
   a palace 7.7
   b palace guard 55.12

πράκτωρ, ορος m
   officer 37.92

πρᾶξις, εως f
   a deed 42.8
   b function 42.5

πραότης
see πραΰτης

πρασιά, ᾶς *f*
group (of people) *11.6*

πράσσω
(pf πέπραχα, pf pass
πέπραγμαι)
a do *42.8*
b receive *57.65*
c experience *90.76*

πραϋπαθία, ας *f*
gentleness *88.59*

πραΰς, πραεῖα, πραΰ
gentle *88.60*

πραΰτης, ητος *f*
gentleness *88.59*

πρέπει
be fitting *66.1*

πρεσβεία, ας *f*
representative *37.87*

πρεσβεύω
be a representative . . . *37.88*

πρεσβυτέριον, ου *n*
a high council of
the Jews *11.83*
b group of elders *11.84*

πρεσβύτερος, α, ον
a older *67.102*
b of ancient times *67.27*

πρεσβύτερος, ου *m*
a old man *9.31*
b elder *53.77*

πρεσβύτης, ου *m*
old man *9.31*

πρεσβῦτις, ιδος *f*
old woman *9.37*

πρηνής, ές
prostrate *17.20*

πρησθείς
see πίμπραμαι

πρίζω
(aor pass ἐπρίσθην)
saw in two *19.20*

πρίν (ἤ)
before *67.17*

Πρίσκα, ης *f*
Prisca *93.302*

Πρίσκιλλα, ης *f*
Priscilla *93.302*

πρό
a in front of (location) *83.33*
b before (time) *67.17*
c above (value) *65.54*
πρό : units
πρὸ θυρῶν
soon *67.58*
πρὸ προσώπου
previous *67.19*
πρὸ παντὸς τοῦ αἰῶνος
since all time *67.133*
πρὸ χρόνων αἰωνίων
since all time *67.133*

προάγω
(aor προήγαγον, inf
προαγαγεῖν)
a go prior to *15.142*
b go in front of *15.143*
c bring forward *15.171*
d happen previously . . *13.114*
e fail to obey *36.25*

προαιρέομαι
(pf προῄρημαι)
decide beforehand *30.84*

προαιτιάομαι
accuse previously *33.430*

προακούω
hear before *24.65*

προαμαρτάνω
(pf προημάρτηκα)
sin previously *88.293*

προαύλιον, ου *n*
forecourt *7.37*

προβαίνω
(aor ptc προβάς, pf
προβέβηκα)
move on *15.16*
προβαίνω : unit
προβαίνω ἐν ἡμέραις
be old *67.99*

προβάλλω
(aor subj προβάλω)
sprout leaves *23.195*

προβατικός, ή, όν
of sheep *4.23*

πρόβατον, ου *n*
a sheep *4.22*
b follower of Christ . . *11.30*
πρόβατον : unit
ἔρχομαι ἐν ἐνδύμασιν
προβάτων
    pretend to be good   *88.233*

προβέβηκα
see προβαίνω

προβιβάζω
urge *33.299*

προβλέπομαι
a provide for *35.35*
b select in advance . . . *30.100*

προγίνομαι
happen previously *13.114*

προγινώσκω
(aor προέγνων)
a know beforehand . . . *28.6*
b select in advance . . . *30.100*

πρόγνωσις, εως *f*
a have foreknowledge . *28.6*
b what is known be-
forehand *28.20*

πρόγονος, ου *m* or *f*
forefather *10.20*

προγράφω
a write beforehand . . . *33.66*
b describe vividly *33.191*

πρόδηλος, ον
very obvious *28.60*

προδίδωμι
(aor προέδωκα)
give beforehand *57.74*

προδότης, ου *m*
betrayer *37.113*

προδραμών
see προτρέχω

πρόδρομος, ου *m*
forerunner *36.9*

προέγνων
see προγινώσκω

προέδραμον
see προτρέχω

προέδωκα
see προδίδωμι

προεθέμην
see προτίθεμαι

προεῖπον·
see προλέγω

προείρηκα
see προλέγω

προέλαβον
see προλαμβάνω

προελεύσομαι
see προέρχομαι

προελθών
see προέρχομαι

προελπίζω
(pf προήλπικα)
hope beforehand *25.60*

προενάρχομαι
begin previously *68.4*

προεπαγγέλλομαι
(aor προεπηγγειλάμην,
pf προεπήγγελμαι)
promise beforehand . . *33.287*

προέρχομαι
(fut προελεύσομαι, aor
προῆλθον, ptc προελθών)
a go on *15.16*
b go along *15.27*
c go prior to *15.141*
d lead *15.181*

προεστώς
see προΐσταμαι

προετοιμάζω
make ready in advance *77.4*

προευαγγελίζομαι
bring good news
ahead of time *33.216*

προέχομαι
have advantage *65.47*

προήγαγον
see προάγω

προηγέομαι
a do with eagerness . . *68.70*
b do exceedingly *78.35*

προῆλθον
see προέρχομαι

προήλπικα
see προελπίζω

προημάρτηκα
see προαμαρτάνω

προῄρημαι
see προαιρέομαι

πρόθεσις, εως *f*
plan *30.63*
πρόθεσις : unit
ἄρτοι τῆς προθέσεως
consecrated bread . . *53.26*

προθεσμία, ας *f*
set time *67.2*

προθυμία, ας *f*
eagerness *25.68*

πρόθυμος, ον
eager *25.69*

προθύμως
eagerly *25.69*

προϊδών
see προοράω

πρόϊμος, ου *m*
early rain *14.14*

προΐσταμαι (+2 aor, pf act)
(aor inf προστῆναι,
pf ptc προεστώς)
a guide *36.1*
b be active in helping *35.12*
c strive to *68.67*

προκαλέομαι
provoke *88.188*

προκαταγγέλλω
(aor προκατήγγειλα)
foretell *33.283*

προκαταρτίζω
make ready in advance *77.4*

προκατέχομαι
have advantage *65.47*

πρόκειμαι
a exist openly *13.75*
b lie ahead *13.76*

προκηρύσσω
preach beforehand ... *33.257*

προκοπή, ῆς *f*
progress *13.57*

προκόπτω
a progress *13.57*
b accomplish *42.18*
c increase *59.64*
d draw to a close *67.118*

πρόκριμα, τος *n*
partiality *30.79*

προκυρόω
validate in advance ... *76.19*

προλαμβάνω
(aor προέλαβον, aor
pass subj προλημφθῶ)
a detect *27.33*
b do *90.49*

προλέγω
(aor προεῖπον, pf
προείρηκα)
a say already *33.86*
b predict *33.281*
c warn *33.423*

προμαρτύρομαι
predict *33.282*

προμελετάω
plan ahead *30.61*

προμεριμνάω
worry beforehand *25.227*

προνοέω
a have foresight *30.47*
b take care of *35.39*

πρόνοια, ας *f*
foresight *30.47*

προοράω
(aor ptc προϊδών)
a see beforehand *24.5*
b know beforehand ... *28.6*

προορίζω
decide beforehand *30.84*

προπάσχω
(aor ptc προπαθών)
suffer before *24.79*

προπάτωρ, ορος *m*
ancestor *10.20*

προπέμπω
a send on one's way .. *15.72*
b accompany *15.155*

προπετής, ές
reckless *88.98*

προπορεύομαι
a precede *15.143*
b lead *15.181*

πρός
a to (extension) *84.18*
b against (extension) *84.23*
c at (location) *83.24*
d among (location) ... *83.9*
e to (experiencer) *90.58*
f about (content)..... *90.25*
g with (association) ... *89.112*
h for (purpose) *89.60*
i end in (result)...... *89.44*
j according to (cor-
respondence) *89.9*
k toward (time) *67.162*
l at (time) *67.16*
m to the point of
(degree) *78.51*
n with regard to
(specification) *89.7*
o in opinion of (view-
point participant)... *90.20*
p against (opposi-
tion) *90.33*
q compared to (com-
parison) *64.17*
πρός : units
πρὸς ὀλίγον
for a short time..... *67.106*
πρὸς καιρὸν (ὥρας)
for a while *67.109*

πρὸς τὸ οὖς
   privately 28.73
στόμα πρὸς στόμα
   face to face 83.39
πρόσωπον πρὸς πρόσωπον
   face to face 83.37
τὸ στόμα ἀνοίγω πρός
   speak complete truth 33.252
πρὸς τὸ οὖς λαλέω
   whisper 33.91
προστίθημι πρὸς τοὺς
πατέρας αὐτοῦ
   bury 52.7
πρὸς κέντρα λακτίζω
   hurt by resistance . . 39.19
τίθημι παρὰ/πρὸς
τοὺς πόδας
   turn over to 57.82

προσάββατον, ου n
   Friday 67.202

προσαγορεύω
   give a name to 33.127

προσάγω
   (aor inf προσαγαγεῖν,
   aor pass προσήχθην)
   a bring into presence 15.172
   b approach 15.77

προσαγωγή, ῆς f
   right to speak 33.72

προσαιτέω
   beg 33.173

προσαίτης, ου m
   beggar 33.174

προσαναβαίνω
   (aor impv προσανάβηθι)
   move up to 15.106

προσαναλίσκω
   spend much 57.148

προσαναπληρόω
   provide fully 35.34

προσανατίθεμαι
   (aor προσανεθέμην)
   a add 59.72
   b ask advice 33.175

προσανέχω
   approach 15.77

προσαπειλέομαι
   threaten further 33.292

προσαχέω
   resound 14.81

προσβιβάζω
   urge 33.299

προσδαπανάω
   spend in addition 57.147

προσδέομαι
   need something more 57.45

προσδέχομαι
   a accept 31.53
   b welcome 34.53
   c wait for 85.60

προσδοκάω
   a wait with anxiety . . . 25.228
   b expect 30.55

προσδοκία, ας f
   expectation 30.55

προσδραμών
   see προστρέχω

προσεάω
   allow to go farther 13.139

προσεγγίζω
   approach 15.77

προσεθέμην
   see προστίθεμαι

προσέθηκα
   see προστίθημι

προσεκλίθην
see προσκλίνομαι

προσελαβόμην
see προσλαμβάνομαι

προσελεύσομαι
see προσέρχομαι

προσελήλυθα
see προσέρχομαι

πρόσελθε
see προσέρχομαι

προσενέγκαι
see προσφέρω

προσένεγκε
see προσφέρω

προσενεγκεῖν
see προσφέρω

προσένεγκον
see προσφέρω

προσενεχθείς
see προσφέρω

προσενήνοχα
see προσφέρω

προσέπεσον
see προσπίπτω

προσεργάζομαι
earn in addition 57.191

προσέρηξα
see προσρήγνυμι

προσέρχομαι
(fut προσελεύσομαι, aor
προσῆλθον, impv πρόσελθε,
pf προσελήλυθα)
a approach 15.77
b seek association with 34.23
c agree with 31.19

προσέταξα
see προστάσσω

προσετέθην
see προστίθημι

προσετίθει
see προστίθημι

προσευχή, ῆς f
a prayer 33.178
b place for prayer 33.179

προσεύχομαι
pray 33.178

προσέχω
(aor προσέσχον, pf
προσέσχηκα)
a be alert for 27.59
b consider carefully . . 30.35
c continue to believe 31.47
d continue to give
oneself to 68.19

προσῆλθον
see προσέρχομαι

προσηλόω
nail onto 18.20

προσήλυτος, ου m
proselyte 11.54

προσήνεγκα
see προσφέρω

προσηνέχθην
see προσφέρω

προσήχθην
see προσάγω

προσθεῖναι
see προστίθημι

προσθείς
see προστίθημι/εμαι

πρόσθες
see προστίθημι

προσθῶ
see προστίθημι

πρόσκαιρος, ον
temporary 67.109

προσκαλέομαι
(pf προσκέκλημαι)
a call to oneself 33.308
b call to a task 33.312

προσκαρτερέω
a persist 68.68
b associate closely 34.2
c serve personally 35.28

προσκαρτέρησις, εως f
persistence 68.68

προσκεφάλαιον, ου n
cushion 6.110

προσκληρόομαι
join 34.22

προσκλίνομαι
(aor προσεχλίθην)
join 34.22

πρόσκλισις, εως f
prejudice 88.241

προσκολλάομαι
join 34.22

πρόσκομμα, τος n
a stumbling 15.229
b offense 25.183
c occasion to sin 88.307

προσκοπή, ῆς f
a obstacle 22.14
b offense 25.183
c occasion to sin 88.307

προσκόπτω
a strike against 19.5
b stumble 15.228
c take offense 25.182

προσκυλίω
roll up to 15.249

προσκυνέω
a worship 53.56
b prostrate oneself
before 17.21

προσκυνητής, οῦ m
worshiper 53.57

προσλαλέω
speak to 33.71

προσλαμβάνομαι
(aor προσελαβόμην,
impv προσλαβοῦ)
a take hold of 18.2
b bring along 15.167
c lead aside 15.180
d gather together 15.127
e welcome 34.53

προσλέγω
reply 33.188

πρόσλημψις, εως f
acceptance 34.34

προσμένω
(aor inf προσμεῖναι)
a stay on 85.59
b keep on 68.11

προσορμίζομαι
moor 54.20

προσοφείλω
owe in return 57.220

προσοχθίζω
be angry 88.172

πρόσπεινος, ον
hungry 23.30

προσπήγνυμι
(aor ptc προσπήξας)
crucify 20.76

προσπίπτω
(aor προσέπεσον, f ptc
προσπεσοῦσα)
a prostrate oneself
before *17.22*
b strike against *19.11*

προσποιέομαι
act as though *41.49*

προσπορεύομαι
approach *15.77*

προσρήγνυμι
(aor προσέρηξα)
strike against *19.6*

προσρήσσω
see προσρήγνυμι

προστάσσω
(aor προσέταξα, pf
pass προστέταγμαι)
a command *33.325*
b arrange for *62.9*

προστάτις, ιδος *f*
helper *35.13*

προστεθῆναι
see προστίθημι

προστεθήσομαι
see προστίθεμαι/ημι

προστῆναι
see προΐσταμαι

προστίθεμαι
(aor προσεθέμην, 2nd
aor ptc προσθείς)
a continue *68.13*
b proceed to *89.89*

προστίθημι
(impf 3 sg προσετίθει,
aor προσέθηκα, impv
πρόσθες, inf προσθεῖ-
ναι, 2 aor ptc προσ-
θείς, subj προσθῶ,
aor pass προσετέθην,

inf προστεθῆναι, fut
pass προστεθήσομαι)
a add *59.72*
b give *57.78*
προστίθημι : unit
προστίθημι πρὸς τοὺς
πατέρας αὐτοῦ
bury *52.7*

προστρέχω
(aor ptc προσδραμών)
run up to *15.234*

προσφάγιον, ου *n*
fish *5.17*

πρόσφατος, ον
new *58.73*

προσφάτως
recently *67.23*

προσφέρομαι
behave toward *41.7*

προσφέρω
(aor προσήνεγκα,
impv προσένεγκον,
προσένεγκε, inf προσ-
ενέγκαι, προσενεγκεῖν,
pf προσενήνοχα, aor
pass προσηνέχθην, ptc
προσενεχθείς)
a bring to *15.192*
b bring into presence *15.172*
c present to *57.80*

προσφιλής, ές
pleasing *25.97*

προσφορά, ᾶς *f*
sacrifice *53.16*

προσφωνέω
a address *33.27*
b call out to *33.79*
c call to oneself *33.308*

πρόσχυσις, εως *f*
pouring *47.7*

προσψαύω
a touch 24.75
b touch to help 18.11

προσωπολημπτέω
be partial 88.238

προσωπολήμπτης, ου *m*
respecter of persons .. 88.239

προσωπολημψία, ας *f*
partiality 88.238

πρόσωπον, ου *n*
a face 8.18
b person 9.9
c surface 79.93
d appearance....... 24.24
e presence........ 85.26
f in front of........ 83.33
πρόσωπον : units
πρὸ προσώπου
  previous.......... 67.19
πρόσωπον πρὸς πρόσωπον
  face to face 83.37
κατὰ πρόσωπον
  a in front of 83.34
  b in person 83.38
τὰ κατὰ πρόσωπον
  outward appearance 31.31
θαυμάζω πρόσωπον
  flatter............ 33.365
λαμβάνω πρόσωπον
  show favoritism.... 88.238
στηρίζω τὸ πρόσωπον
  decide firmly 30.80
βλέπω εἰς πρόσωπον
  judge on external
  appearance 30.120
κλίνω τὸ πρόσωπον
εἰς τὴν γῆν
  prostrate oneself ... 17.21

προτείνω
stretch out 16.21

πρότερον
before 67.18

πρότερος, α, ον
a before 67.18
b the first time 60.47

προτίθεμαι
(aor προεθέμην)
a plan beforehand.... 30.62
b bring forth 13.15

προτρέπομαι
urge 33.300

προτρέχω
(aor προέδραμον, ptc
προδραμών)
run in front of 15.235

προϋπάρχω
exist formerly 13.78

πρόφασις, εως *f*
a pretense 88.230
b excuse .... : 33.437

προφέρω
produce 13.85

προφῆται, ων *m*
(the writings of) the
Prophets 33.60
προφῆται : unit
ὁ νόμος καὶ οἱ προφῆται
  the sacred writings 33.58

προφητεία, ας *f*
a inspired utterance .. 33.460
b ability to prophesy 33.461

προφητεύω
speak inspired
utterances 33.459

προφήτης, ου *m*
prophet (for the pl
προφῆται, see above).. 53.79

προφητικός, ή, όν
prophetic 33.462

προφῆτις, ιδος *f*
prophetess 53.80

προφθάνω
anticipate 67.29

προχειρίζομαι
choose in advance 30.89

προχειροτονέω
choose in advance 30.89

Πρόχορος, ου m
Prochorus 93.303

πρύμνα, ης f
stern (of a boat) 6.47

πρωΐ
early morning 67.187

πρωΐα, ας f
early morning 67.187

πρωϊνός, ή, όν
morning 67.188
πρωϊνός : unit
ἀστὴρ πρωϊνός
morning star 1.33

πρῷρα, ης f
bow (of a boat) 6.46

πρωτεύω
have first place 87.46

πρωτοκαθεδρία, ας f
seat of honor 87.18

πρωτοκλισία, ας f
seat of honor 87.18

πρῶτον
before 67.18

πρῶτος, η, ον
a first 60.46
b before 67.18
c prominent 87.45
d best 65.24
e most important 65.52

πρωτοστάτης, ου m
ringleader 87.52

πρωτοτόκια, ων n
birthright 10.44

πρωτότοκος, ον
a firstborn 10.43
b existing before 13.79
c superior 87.47

πρώτως
first(ly) 60.48

πταίω
sin 88.291

πτέρνα, ης f
heel 8.52
πτέρνα : unit
ἐπαίρω τὴν πτέρναν
oppose 39.3

πτερύγιον, ου n
pinnacle 7.53

πτέρυξ, υγος f
wing 8.29

πτηνόν, οῦ n
bird 4.38

πτοέομαι
be terrified 25.264

πτόησις, εως f
something alarming . . 25.265

Πτολεμαΐς, ΐδος f
Ptolemais 93.557

πτύον, ου n
winnowing shovel 6.6

πτύρομαι
be afraid 25.263

πτύσμα, τος n
saliva 8.71

πτύσσω
(aor ptc πτύξας)
roll up 79.120

214

πτύω
spit 23.43

πτῶμα, τος *n*
dead body 8.7

πτῶσις, εως *f*
a destruction 20.50
b falling (status) 87.75
c worsening 13.59

πτωχεία, ας *f*
poverty 57.52

πτωχεύω
become poor 57.54

πτωχός, ή, όν
a poor 57.53
b of little value 65.16
πτωχός : unit
πτωχὸς τῷ πνεύματι
   be humble 88.57

πυγμή, ῆς *f*
fist 8.35

Πύθιος, ου *m*
Pythius 93.304

πυθόμενος
see πυνθάνομαι

πύθων, ωνος *m*
spirit of divination . . . 12.48
πύθων : unit
ἔχω πνεῦμα πύθωνα
   be a fortuneteller . . . 33.285

πυκνά
often 67.12

πυκνός, ή, όν
often 67.12

πυκνότερον
as often as possible . . . 67.13

πυκτεύω
box 50.6

πύλη, ης *f*
gate, door 7.48
πύλη : unit
πύλαι ᾅδου
   death 12.50

πυλών, ῶνος *m*
a door, gate 7.48
b entrance 7.38

πυνθάνομαι
(aor ἐπυθόμην, ptc
πυθόμενος)
a inquire 33.181
b learn about 27.11

πῦρ, ός *n*
a fire 2.3
b bonfire 2.5
πῦρ : units
πῦρ βάλλω
   cause discord 39.15
λίμνη τοῦ πυρὸς (καὶ
θείου)
   place of punishment 1.22
σωρεύω ἄνθρακας πυρὸς
ἐπὶ τὴν κεφαλήν
   cause to be ashamed 25.199

πυρά, ᾶς *f*
bonfire 2.5

πύργος, ου *m*
(watch) tower 7.23

πυρέσσω
have fever 23.159

πυρετός, οῦ *m*
fever 23.159

πύρινος, η, ον
fiery red 79.33

πυρόομαι
a be on fire 14.63
b be greatly worried . . 25.229
c be sexually aroused 25.31

πυρόω
make fiery hot 79.72

πυρράζω
be fiery red 79.32

πυρρός, ά, όν
fiery red 79.31

Πύρρος, ου m
Pyrrhus 93.305

πύρωσις, εως f
a burning 14.63
b suffering 24.91
c intensity 78.37

πωλέω
sell 57.186

πῶλος, ου m
foal 4.33

πώποτε
ever 67.9

πωρόω
have closed mind 27.51

πώρωσις, εως f
stubbornness 27.52

πῶς
how? 92.16
see also μή πως

Ῥαάβ f
Rahab 93.306

ῥαββί
teacher 33.246

ραββουνι
my teacher 33.247

ῥαβδίζω
beat with a stick 19.8

ῥάβδος, ου f
a stick 6.218
b governing 37.53

ῥαβδοῦχος, ου m
policeman 37.89

Ῥαγαύ m
Reu 93.307

ῥᾳδιούργημα, τος n
wrongdoing 88.301

ῥᾳδιουργία, ας f
wrongdoing 88.301

ῥαίνω
(pf pass ἔρραμαι,
ῥέραμμαι)
sprinkle 47.16

Ῥαιφάν m
Rephan 93.308

ῥακά
fool 32.61

ῥάκος, ους n
patch 6.152

Ῥαμά f
Ramah 93.558

ῥαντίζω
(pf pass ptc ἐρραντισ-
μένος, ῥεραντισμένος)
a sprinkle 47.16
b purify 53.32
ῥαντίζω : unit
ῥαντίζομαι τὴν καρδίαν
be purified 88.31

ῥαντισμός, οῦ m
sprinkling 47.16

ῥαπίζω
whip 19.4

ῥάπισμα, τος n
whip 19.4

ῥαφίς, ίδος f
needle 6.215

Ῥαχάβ *f*
Rahab 93.309

Ῥαχήλ *f*
Rachel 93.310

Ῥεβέκκα, ας *f*
Rebecca 93.311

ῥέδη, ης *f*
carriage 6.53

ῥέραμμαι
see ῥαίνω

ῥεραντισμένος
see ῥαντίζω

ῥέω
(fut ῥεύσω)
flow 14.17

Ῥήγιον, ου *n*
Rhegium 93.559

ῥῆγμα, τος *n*
destruction 20.58

ῥήγνυμι
(fut ῥήξω, aor ἔρρηξα,
impv ῥῆξον
a rip 19.31
b begin to shout 33.85
c break forth with 68.81
d throw into fit 23.168

ῥηθείς
see λέγω

ῥῆμα, τος *n*
a word 33.9
b statement 33.98
c event 13.115

Ῥησά *m*
Rhesa 93.312

ῥήσσω
see ῥήγνυμι

ῥήτωρ, ορος *m*
lawyer 56.36

ῥητῶς
just as said 33.94

ῥίζα, ης *f*
a root 3.47
b descendant 10.33
c cause 89.17

ῥιζόομαι
(pf ἐρρίζωμαι)
be strengthened 74.18

ῥιπή, ῆς *f*
blinking 16.5
ῥιπή : unit
ἐν ῥιπῇ ὀφθαλμοῦ
suddenly 67.114

ῥιπίζομαι
be tossed about 16.11

ῥίπτομαι
be dejected 25.294

ῥίπτω
(aor ἔρριψα, ptc ῥίψας,
pf pass ἔρριμμαι)
a throw 15.217
b put down 85.37
c wave 16.10

Ῥοβοάμ *m*
Rehoboam 93.313

Ῥόδη, ης *f*
Rhoda 93.314

Ῥόδος, ου *f*
Rhodes 93.560

ῥοιζηδόν
with a shrill noise 14.85

ῥομφαία, ας *f*
a sword 6.32
b war 55.6

ῥομφαία : unit
τὴν ψυχὴν διέρχεται
ῥομφαία
  feel pain and
  sorrow 25.279

Ῥουβήν m
  Reuben 93.315

Ῥούθ f
  Ruth 93.316

Ῥοῦφος, ου m
  Rufus 93.317

ῥύμη, ης f
  narrow street 1.104

ῥύομαι
  (aor ἐρρυσάμην, impv
  ῥῦσαι, 3 sg ῥυσάσθω,
  aor pass ἐρρύσθην,
  subj ῥυσθῶ)
  rescue 21.23

ῥυπαίνομαι
  (aor impv 3 sg ῥυπαν-
  θήτω)
  be morally impure 88.258

ῥυπαρία, ας f
  moral impurity 88.256

ῥυπαρός, ά, όν
  a dirty 79.52
  b morally impure 88.257

ῥύπος, ου m
  dirt 79.55

ῥύσις, εως f
  flow 14.17
  ῥύσις : unit
  ῥύσις αἵματος
    menstrual flow 23.182

ῥυτίς, ίδος f
  wrinkle 8.54

Ῥωμαϊκός, ή, όν
  Roman 93.561

Ῥωμαῖος, ου m
  Roman 93.562

Ῥωμαϊστί
  Latin language 33.7

Ῥώμη, ης f
  Rome 93.563

ῥώννυμαι
  (pf impv ἔρρωσο, 2 pl
  ἔρρωσθε)
  a fare well 23.133
  b goodbye 33.24

σαβαχθανι
  forsake 35.56

Σαβαώθ
  Almighty 12.8

σαββατισμός, οῦ m
  Sabbath rest 67.185

σάββατον, ου n
  a Sabbath 67.184
  b week 67.177
  σάββατον : unit
  σαββάτου ὁδός
    Sabbath journey 81.28

σαγήνη, ης f
  seine net 6.13

Σαδδουκαῖος, ου m
  Sadducee 11.48

Σαδώκ m
  Zadok 93.318

σαίνομαι
  give up belief 31.66

σάκκος, ου m
  sackcloth 6.164

Σαλά m
  Shelah 93.319

Σαλαθιήλ *m*
Salathiel 93.320

Σαλαμίς, ῖνος *f*
Salamis 93.564

Σαλείμ
Salim 93.565

σαλεύομαι
be distressed 25.242

σαλεύω
a shake 16.7
b cause riot 39.44

Σαλήμ *f*
a Salem (name) 93.321
b Salem (place) 93.566

Σαλίμ *n*
Salim 93.565

Σαλμάν
Shelah 93.322

Σαλμών *m*
Salmon 93.323

Σαλμώνη, ης *f*
Salmone 93.567

σάλος, ου *m*
surging waves 14.26

σάλπιγξ, ιγγος *f*
a trumpet 6.89
b trumpet sound 6.93

σαλπίζω
a play the trumpet . . . 6.90
b a trumpet sounds . . . 6.92

σαλπιστής, οῦ *m*
trumpeter 6.91

Σαλώμη, ης *f*
Salome 93.324

Σαμάρεια, ας *f*
Samaria 93.568

Σαμαρίτης, ου *m*
Samaritan 93.569

Σαμαρῖτις, ιδος *f*
Samaritan woman 93.570

Σαμοθράκη, ης *f*
Samothrace 93.571

Σάμος, ου *f*
Samos 93.572

Σαμουήλ *m*
Samuel 93.325

Σαμψών *m*
Samson 93.326

σανδάλιον, ου *n*
sandal 6.183

σανίς, ίδος *f*
plank 7.79

Σαούλ *m*
Saul 93.327

σαπρός, ά, όν
a bad (value) 65.28
b harmful 20.14

Σάπφιρα, ης *f*
Sapphira 93.328

σάπφιρος, ου *f*
sapphire 2.31

σαργάνη, ης *f*
basket 6.148

Σάρδεις, εων *f*
Sardis 93.573

σάρδιον, ου *n*
carnelian 2.36

σαρδόνυξ, υχος *m*
(sard) onyx 2.35

Σάρεπτα, ων *n*
Zarephath 93.574

219

σαρχικός, ή, όν
a human 26.8
b material 79.1
c natural 79.4
d worldly 41.42

σάρχινος, η, ον
a of people 9.13
b human 26.8
c natural 79.4
d worldly 41.42

σάρξ, σαρκός f
a flesh 8.63
b body 8.4
c people 9.11
d human 9.12
e nation 10.1
f human nature 26.7
g physical nature 58.10
h life 23.90
σάρξ : units
σάρξ καὶ αἷμα
  human being 9.14
κοινωνέω αἵματος καὶ
σαρκός
  be a person 9.15
ἀπέρχομαι ὀπίσω
σαρκὸς ἑτέρας
  homosexual inter-
  course 88.279
σκόλοψ τῇ σαρκί
  trouble 22.20
σαρκὸς θέλημα
  sexual desire 25.29

σαρόω
sweep 46.19

Σάρρα, ας f
Sarah 93.329

Σαρών, ῶνος m
Sharon 93.575

Σατανᾶς, ᾶ m
a Satan (title) 12.34
b Satan (name) 93.330

σάτον, ου n
batch (measurement)   81.23

Σαῦλος, ου m
Saul 93.331

σβέννυμαι
stop burning 14.69

σβέννυμι
(fut σβέσω, aor
ἔσβεσα, inf σβέσαι)
a extinguish a fire 14.70
b stop 68.52

σέ
see σύ

σεαυτοῦ, ῆς
yourself 92.10

σεβάζομαι
worship 53.53

σέβασμα, τος n
a sanctuary 53.54
b object of worship . . . 53.55

σεβαστός, ή, όν
imperial 37.76

ὁ Σεβαστός
the Emperor 37.75

σέβομαι
worship 53.53

Σειλεᾶς
see Σιλᾶς 93.332

σείομαι
tremble 16.6

σειρά, ᾶς f
chain, rope 6.15

σειρός
see σιρός

σεισμός, οῦ m
a earthquake 14.87
b storm on the sea 14.22

σείω
  a shake 16.7
  b cause great anxiety   25.233

Σεκοῦνδος, ου m
  Secundus 93.333

Σελεύκεια, ας f
  Seleucia 93.576

σελήνη, ης f
  moon 1.29

σεληνιάζομαι
  be an epileptic 23.169

Σεμεῖν m
  Semein 93.334

σεμίδαλις, εως f
  fine flour 5.10

σεμνός, ή, όν
  honorable 88.47

σεμνότης, ητος f
  propriety 88.46

Σέργιος, ου m
  Sergius 93.335

Σερούχ m
  Serug 93.336

σέσηπα
  see σήπω

σέσωκα
  see σῴζω

Σήθ m
  Seth 93.337

Σήμ m
  Shem 93.338

σημαίνω
  (aor ἐσήμανα, inf
  σημᾶναι)
  make clear 33.153

σημεῖον, ου n
  sign 33.477

σημειόομαι
  take note of 29.3

σήμερον
  today 67.205
  σήμερον : unit
  ἐχθὲς καὶ σήμερον καὶ
  εἰς τοὺς αἰῶνας
    always 67.87

σήπω
  (pf σέσηπα)
  decay 23.205

σής, σητός m
  moth 4.49

σητόβρωτος, ον
  moth-eaten 20.20

σθενόω
  make more able 74.14

σιαγών, όνος f
  cheek 8.22

σιγάω
  keep quiet about 33.121

σιγή, ῆς f
  silence 33.120

σίδηρος, ου m
  iron 2.58

σιδηροῦς, ᾶ, οῦν
  made of iron 2.59

Σιδών, ῶνος f
  Sidon 93.577

Σιδώνιος, α, ον
  Sidonian 93.578

Σιδώνιος, ου m
  Sidonian 93.579

221

σικάριος, ου *m*
  terrorist *20.86*

σίκερα *n*
  beer *6.200*

Σιλᾶς, ᾶ *m*
  Silas *93.339*

Σιλουανός, οῦ *m*
  Silvanus *93.340*

Σιλωάμ *m*
  Siloam *93.580*

σιμικίνθιον, ου *n*
  apron *6.179*

Σίμων, ωνος *m*
  Simon *93.341*

Σινᾶ *n*
  Sinai *93.581*

σίναπι, εως *n*
  mustard plant *3.20*

σινδών, όνος *f*
  linen cloth *6.155*

σινιάζω
  sift *46.18*

σιρά, ᾶς *f*
  see σειρά

σιρικόν, οῦ *n*
  silk cloth *6.168*

σιρός, οῦ *m*
  deep hole *1.59*

σιτευτός, ή, όν
  a fattened *44.2*
  b prized *65.8*

σιτίον, ου *n*
  a grain *3.42*
  b food *5.2*

σιτιστός, ή, όν
  fattened *44.2*

σιτομέτριον, ου *n*
  food ration *5.3*

σῖτος, ου *m*
  a wheat (seed) *3.41*
  b wheat (plant) *3.31*

Σιών *f*
  (Mount) Zion *93.582*
  Σιών : unit
  θυγάτηρ Σιών
    people of Jerusalem *11.66*

σιωπάω
  a be silent *33.117*
  b not be able to speak *33.118*
  c become calm *14.24*

σκανδαλίζομαι
  a cease believing *31.77*
  b fall into sin *88.305*
  c take offense *25.180*

σκανδαλίζω
  a cause to no longer
    believe *31.78*
  b cause to sin *88.304*
  c give offense *25.179*

σκάνδαλον, ου *n*
  a trap *6.25*
  b sin *88.306*
  c offense *25.181*

σκάπτω
  a dig *19.55*
  b till ground *43.3*

Σκαριότα
  Iscariot *93.342*

Σκαριώθ
  Iscariot *93.342*

Σκαριώτης
  Iscariot *93.342*

σκάφη, ης *f*
small boat 6.45

σκέλος, ους *n*
leg 8.46

σκέπασμα, τος *n*
clothing 6.163

Σκευᾶς, ᾶ *m*
Sceva 93.343

σκευή, ῆς *f*
equipment 6.2

σκεῦος, ους *n*
a object 6.1
b vessel 6.118
c belongings 57.20
d person 9.21
e body 8.6
f wife 10.55
σκεῦος : unit
σκεῦος κτάομαι
    sexual life 23.63

σκηνή, ῆς *f*
a tent 7.9
b tabernacle tent 7.17

σκηνοπηγία, ας *f*
festival of the tents . . . 51.10

σκηνοποιός, οῦ *m*
tent-maker 7.10

σκῆνος, ους *n*
body 8.5

σκηνόω
take up residence 85.75

σκήνωμα, τος *n*
a dwelling 7.8
b dwelling place 85.77
c body 8.5
σκήνωμα : unit
ἀπόθεσις τοῦ σκηνώματος
    die 23.111

σκιά, ᾶς *f*
a shade 14.60
b shadow 14.61
c foreshadow 58.65

σκιρτάω
a jump for joy 15.243
b be extremely joyful   25.134

σκληροκαρδία, ας *f*
stubborn 88.224

σκληρός, ά, όν
a violent 20.3
b strong 76.15
c harsh 88.135
d demanding 88.136

σκληρότης, ητος *f*
stubbornness 88.223

σκληροτράχηλος, ον
stubborn 88.224

σκληρύνομαι
be stubborn 88.225

σκληρύνω
cause to be stubborn   88.226

σκολιός, ά, όν
a crooked 79.90
b unscrupulous 88.268

σκόλοψ, οπος *m*
σκόλοψ : unit
σκόλοψ τῇ σαρκί
    trouble 22.20

σκοπέω
a notice carefully 24.32
b watch out for 27.58
c be concerned about   27.36
d keep thinking about   30.20

σκοπός, οῦ *m*
goal 84.28
σκοπός : unit
κατὰ σκοπὸν διώκω
    strive for a purpose   89.56

σκορπίζω
a scatter 15.135
b give generously 57.95

σκορπίος, ου *m*
scorpion 4.56

σκοτεινός, ή, όν
dark 14.54

σκοτία, ας *f*
a darkness 14.53
b evil world 88.125
σκοτία : unit
ἐν τῇ σκοτίᾳ
secretly 28.71

σκοτίζομαι
a become dark 14.55
b unable to understand 32.44

σκοτόομαι
a become dark 14.55
b unable to understand 32.44

σκότος, ους *n*
a darkness 14.53
b evil world . . . . : . 88.125
σκότος : units
τὸ σκότος τὸ ἐξώτερον
abode of evil spirits 1.23
ὁ ζόφος τοῦ σκότους
gloomy hell 1.24
ἀχλὺς καὶ σκότος πίπτει
become blind 24.40

σκύβαλον, ου *n*
rubbish 6.225

Σκύθης, ου *m*
Scythian 93.583

σκυθρωπός, ή, όν
sad 25.287

σκῦλα, ων *n*
booty 57.243

σκύλλομαι
be troubled 22.16

σκύλλω
(midd impv σκύλλου,
pf pass ἔσκυλμαι)
trouble 22.23

σκῦλον
only in pl, see σκῦλα

σκωληκόβρωτος, ον
eaten by worms 23.166

σκώληξ, ηκος *m*
maggot 4.57

σμαράγδινος, η, ον
made of emerald 2.34

σμάραγδος, ου *m*
emerald 2.33

σμῆγμα, τος *n*
perfumed ointment . . . 6.207

σμίγμα
see σμῆγμα

σμύρνα, ης *f*
myrrh 6.208

Σμύρνα, ης *f*
Smyrna 93.584

σμυρνίζω
(pf ptc ἐσμυρνισμένος)
σμυρνίζω : unit
ἐσμυρνισμένος οἶνος
myrrhed wine 6.204

Σόδομα, ων *n*
Sodom 93.585

σοί
see σύ

Σολομών, ῶνος *m*
Solomon 93.344

Σολομῶν, ῶντος *m*
Solomon 93.344

σορός, οῦ *f*
bier 6.109

σός, σή, σόν
your 92.8

σοῦ
see σύ

σουδάριον, ου *n*
face cloth 6.159

Σουσάννα, ης *f*
Susanna 93.345

σοφία, ας *f*
a wisdom 32.32
b insight 32.37
c specialized knowl-
   edge 28.8
d Wisdom (title of a
   book) 32.41

σοφίζομαι
know how to contrive
cleverly 28.10

σοφίζω
make wise 32.36

σοφός, ή, όν
a skillful 28.9
b wise 32.33

σοφός, οῦ *m*
wise man 32.35

Σπανία, ας *f*
Spain 93.586

σπάομαι
pull 15.212

σπαράσσω
throw into a fit 23.167

σπαργανόω
clothe in swaddling
cloth 49.6

σπαταλάω
live indulgently 88.252

σπεῖρα, ης *f*
band of soldiers 55.9

σπείρω
(aor pass ptc σπαρείς,
pf pass ἔσπαρμαι)
sow 43.6

σπεχουλάτωρ, ορος *m*
a courier 33.196
b executioner 20.70

σπένδω
pour libation 53.27

σπέρμα, τος *n*
a seed 3.35
b descendants 10.29
c nature 58.13
σπέρμα : units
ἀνίστημι σπέρμα
   beget 23.59
ἐξανίστημι σπέρμα
   beget 23.59
καταβολὴ σπέρματος
   conceive 23.49

σπερμολόγος, ου *m*
a ignorant show-off . . 27.19
b foolish babbler 33.381

σπεύδω
a do quickly 68.79
b cause to happen soon 68.80
c be eager 25.74

σπήλαιον, ου *n*
cave 1.57

σπιλάς, άδος *f*
a hidden danger 21.5
b spot 79.57

σπίλος, ου *m*
spot 79.57

σπιλόω
spot 79.58

σπλάγχνα, ων n
a intestines 8.58
b desires 26.11
c compassion 25.49
d object of affection .. 25.50
σπλάγχνα : units
κλείω τὰ σπλάγχνα
  refuse to show
  compassion 25.55
στενοχωρέομαι ἐν τοῖς
σπλάγχνοις
  restrict one's affec-
  tion for 25.54

σπλαγχνίζομαι
feel compassion for ... 25.49

σπλάγχνον, ου n
only in pl, see
σπλάγχνα

σπόγγος, ου m
sponge 6.133

σποδός, οῦ f
ashes 14.73

σπορά, ᾶς f
parentage 10.23

σπόριμα, ων n
grain fields 43.7

σπόρος, ου m
seed 3.35

σπουδάζω
a do quickly 68.79
b do one's best 68.63
c be eager 25.74

σπουδαῖος, α, ον
eager 25.75

σπουδαίως
a doing one's best 68.65
b eagerly 25.75

σπουδή, ῆς f
a do quickly 68.79

b do one's best 68.63
c eagerness 25.74
σπουδή : unit
σπουδὴν πᾶσαν
παρεισφέρω
  do one's best 68.64

σπυρίς, ίδος f
large basket 6.149

στάδιον, ου n
arena 7.55

στάδιος, ου m
stade 81.27

σταθείς
see ἵσταμαι

σταθῆναι
see ἵσταμαι

σταθήσομαι
see ἵσταμαι

στάμνος, ου f
jar 6.125

στάς
see ἵσταμαι

στασιαστής, οῦ m
rebel............. 39.37

στάσις, εως f
a rebellion......... 39.34
b heated quarrel 33.448
c existence 13.72

στατήρ, ῆρος m
coin 6.80

σταυρός, οῦ m
cross............. 6.27
σταυρός : units
αἴρω τὸν σταυρόν
  suffer unto death ... 24.83
βαστάζω τὸν σταυρόν
  suffer unto death ... 24.83
λαμβάνω τὸν σταυρόν
  suffer unto death ... 24.83

σταυρόω
  crucify 20.76

σταφυλή, ῆς f
  (bunches of) grapes . . . 3.38

στάχυς, υος m
  head of wheat 3.40

Στάχυς, υος m
  Stachys 93.346

στέγη, ης f
  roof 7.50

στέγω
  endure 25.176

στεῖρα, ας f
  barren 23.56

στέλλομαι
  avoid 13.159
  στέλλομαι : unit
  στέλλομαι ἀπό
    avoid association . . . 34.41

στέμμα, τος n
  wreath 6.193

στεναγμός, οῦ m
  groan 25.143

στενάζω
  a groan 25.143
  b complain strongly . . 33.384

στενός, ή, όν
  narrow 81.19

στενοχωρέομαι
  a be restricted 37.18
  b cause to be in great
    trouble 22.19
  στενοχωρέομαι : unit
  στενοχωρέομαι ἐν τοῖς
  σπλάγχνοις
    restrict one's affec-
    tion for 25.54

στενοχωρία, ας f
  distress 22.10

στερεόομαι
  be strong 79.67

στερεός, ά, όν
  a solid 79.7
  b be firm 74.21

στερεόω
  a make strong 79.68
  b make firm 74.19

στερέωμα, τος n
  firmness 74.20

Στεφανᾶς, ᾶ m
  Stephanas 93.347

Στέφανος, ου m
  Stephen 93.348

στέφανος, ου m
  a crown 6.192
  b prize 57.121
  c accomplishment . . . 42.19

στεφανόω
  a give a prize 57.122
  b honor 87.13

στῆθι
  see ἵσταμαι

στῆθος, ους n
  chest 8.36
  στῆθος : unit
  ἀναπίπτω ἐπὶ τὸ στῆθος
    dine in place of
    honor 17.25

στήκω
  a stand 17.1
  b continue to be 13.30
  στήκω : unit
  τῷ ἰδίῳ κυρίῳ στήκει
  ἢ πίπτει
    honor depends on
    master's judgment . . 87.56

στῆναι
  see ἵσταμαι

στηριγμός, οῦ *m*
  a place of safety *21.13*
  b firm position *74.20*

στηρίζω
  a strengthen *74.19*
  b establish in a place   *85.38*
  στηρίζω : unit
  στηρίζω τὸ πρόσωπον
    decide firmly *30.80*

στήσομαι
  see ἵσταμαι

στήσω
  see ἵστημι

στιβάς, άδος *f*
  leafy branch *3.52*

στίγμα, τος *n*
  a scar *8.55*
  b mark *33.481*
  στίγμα : unit
  βαστάζω στίγματα
    experience being a
    slave *90.84*

στιγμή, ῆς *f*
  moment *67.149*

στίλβω
  glisten *14.47*

στοά, ᾶς *f*
  porch *7.40*

Στογύλιον
  Stogulium *93.587*

Στοϊκός, ή, όν
  Stoic *11.97*

στοιχεῖα, ων *n*
  a natural substances   *2.1*
  b supernatural powers   *12.43*
  c basic principles *58.19*

στοιχέω
  behave *41.12*
  στοιχέω : unit
  στοιχέω τοῖς ἴχνεσιν
    imitate *41.47*

στολή, ῆς *f*
  long robe *6.174*

στόμα, τος *n*
  a mouth *8.19*
  b speech (activity) *33.74*
  c speech (faculty) *33.75*
  d utterance *33.101*
  e sharp edge *79.109*
  στόμα : units
  στόμα φράσσω
    a put to silence *33.125*
    b keep from harming *20.30*
  δίδωμι στόμα
    help to say *33.105*
  ἀνοίγω τὸ στόμα
    start speaking *33.29*
  ἄνοιξις τοῦ στόματος
    starting to speak ... *33.29*
  τὸ στόμα ἀνοίγω πρός
    speak complete truth *33.252*
  στόμα πρὸς στόμα
    face to face *83.39*

στόμαχος, ου *m*
  stomach *8.66*

στρατεία, ας *f*
  warfare *55.4*

στράτευμα, τος *n*
  a army *55.7*
  b soldiers *55.10*

στρατεύομαι
  a engage in war *55.4*
  b be a soldier *55.18*

στρατηγός, οῦ *m*
  magistrate *37.90*
  στρατηγός : unit
  στρατηγὸς τοῦ ἱεροῦ
    commander of the
    Temple guard *37.91*

στρατιά, ᾶς *f*
στρατιά : units
στρατιὰ οὐράνιος
ranks of angels *12.30*
στρατιὰ τοῦ οὐρανοῦ
supernatural powers *12.45*

στρατιώτης, ου *m*
soldier *55.17*

στρατολογέω
a enlist soldiers *55.19*
b be an army officer . . *55.20*

στρατοπέδαρχος, ου *m*
camp commander *55.14*

στρατόπεδον, ου *n*
army *55.7*

στρεβλόω
misinterpret *33.155*

στρέφομαι
a turn around *16.13*
b come to believe *31.60*
c change one's ways *41.50*
d establish a relation
with *34.25*

στρέφω
(aor pass ἐστράφην,
ptc στραφείς)
a turn *16.14*
b change *13.63*
c carry back *15.195*
d pay back *57.157*
e reject *34.28*

στρηνιάω
live sensually *88.254*

στρῆνος, ους *n*
sensual living *88.254*

Στρογγύλιον
Strongulium *93.587*

στρουθίον, ου *n*
sparrow *4.46*

στρώννυμι
(aor ἔστρωσα, impv
στρῶσον, pf pass ptc
ἐστρωμένος)
a spread out *16.22*
b furnish a room *46.9*
c make one's bed *46.10*

στρωννύω
see στρώννυμι

στυγητός, ή, όν
hated *88.204*

στυγνάζω
a become dark and
gloomy *14.56*
b be downcast *25.286*
c be shocked *25.222*

στῦλος, ου *m*
a pillar *7.45*
b leader *36.7*

σύ, σοῦ, σοί, σέ
you *92.6*
σύ : unit
ἵλεώς σοι
God forbid *88.78*

συγγένεια, ας *f*
relatives *10.5*

συγγενής, οῦς *m*
a relative *10.6*
b fellow countryman *11.57*

συγγενίς, ίδος *f*
relative *10.7*

συγγνώμη, ης *f*
permission *13.141*

συγκάθημαι
sit down with *17.13*

συγκαθίζω
a sit down with *17.13*
b cause to sit down
with *17.18*

συγκακοπαθέω
join in suffering 24.84

συγκακουχέομαι
join in suffering 24.84

συγκαλέω
call together 33.309

συγκαλύπτω
conceal 28.81

συγκάμπτω
συγκάμπτω : unit
συγκάμπτω τὸν νῶτον
be overwhelmed
with trouble 24.94

συγκαταβαίνω
(aor ptc συγκαταβάς)
come/go down with . . . 15.154

συγκατάθεσις, εως f
joint agreement 31.18

συγκατατίθεμαι
(pf ptc συγκατατεθει-
μένος)
agree together 31.18

συγκαταψηφίζομαι
count 60.5

συγκεράννυμι
(aor συνεκέρασα, pf
pass συγκεκέρασμαι,
συγκέχραμαι)
fit together 62.2

συγκέχυμαι
see συγχέω

συγκινέω
stir up 39.8

συγκλείω
a catch fish 44.9
b cause to happen 13.125

συγκληρονόμος, ου m
fellow receiver 57.134

συγκοινωνέω
associate with 34.4

συγκοινωνός, οῦ m
a partner 34.6
b sharer 57.10

συγκομίζω
bury 52.5

συγκρίνω
a compare 64.6
b explain 33.154

συγκύπτω
be doubled up 17.32

συγκυρία, ας f
by coincidence 13.116

συγχαίρω
(aor impv 2 pl συγχά-
ρητε)
rejoice with 25.126

συγχέω
(impf συνέχεον, συνέχυν-
νον, aor pass συνεχύθην,
pf pass συγκέχυμαι)
cause consternation . . . 25.221

συγχράομαι
associate 34.1

συγχύννω
see συγχέω

σύγχυσις, εως f
uproar 39.43

συζάω
live with 23.96

συζεύγνυμι
(aor συνέζευξα)
join in marriage 34.73

συζητέω
a dispute 33.440
b talk with 33.157

συζήτησις, εως *f*
dispute *33.440*

συζητητής, οῦ *m*
debater *33.441*

σύζυγος, ου *m*
fellow-worker *42.45*

συζωοποιέω
raise to life with *23.95*

συκάμινος, ου *f*
mulberry tree *3.6*

συκῆ, ῆς *f*
fig tree *3.5*

συκομορέα, ας *f*
sycamore tree *3.7*

σῦκον, ου *n*
fig *3.36*

συκοφαντέω
make false charges *33.434*

συλαγωγέω
take control of *37.10*

συλάω
rob *57.234*

συλλαλέω
talk with *33.157*

συλλαμβάνομαι
join in helping *35.5*

συλλαμβάνω
(fut συλλήμφομαι, aor
συνέλαβον, inf συλλα-
βεῖν, pf συνείληφα, aor
pass inf συλλημφθῆναι)
a seize *37.109*
b become pregnant . . . *23.49*

συλλέγω
pick *18.10*

συλλογίζομαι
(aor συνελογισάμην)
talk with *33.157*

συλλυπέομαι
feel sorry for *25.276*

συμβαίνω
(aor συνέβην, ptc συμ-
βάς, pf συμβέβηκα)
happen *13.111*

συμβάλλομαι
(aor συνεβαλόμην)
help *35.1*

συμβάλλω
(aor inf συμβαλεῖν)
a think about seriously *30.7*
b confer *33.159*
c debate *33.439*
d meet *15.79*

συμβασιλεύω
reign with *37.66*

συμβιβάζω
a unite *63.5*
b conclude *30.82*
c prove *28.46*
d advise *33.298*

συμβουλεύομαι
plan against *30.74*

συμβουλεύω
advise *33.294*

συμβούλιον, ου *n*
a planning against . . . *30.74*
b council *11.86*

σύμβουλος, ου *m*
adviser *33.297*

Συμεών *m*
Simeon *93.349*

συμμαθητής, οῦ *m*
fellow disciple *36.42*

231

συμμαρτυρέω
testify in support *33.266*

συμμερίζομαι
share *57.7*

συμμέτοχος, ου *m*
sharer *57.8*

συμμιμητής, οῦ *m*
joint imitator *41.46*

συμμορφίζομαι
have same likeness . . . *58.6*

σύμμορφος, ον
similar in form *58.5*

συμπαθέω
a suffer with *24.80*
b have sympathy for   *25.57*

συμπαθής, ές
sympathetic *25.58*

συμπαραγίνομαι
(aor ptc συμπαραγε-
νόμενος)
come together *15.123*

συμπαρακαλέομαι
(aor inf συμπαρακλη-
θῆναι)
be encouraged
together *25.151*

συμπαραλαμβάνω
(aor inf συμπαραλαβεῖν)
take/bring along
with *15.169*

συμπάρειμι
be with *85.30*

συμπάσχω
join in suffering *24.84*

συμπέμπω
send with *15.69*

συμπεριλαμβάνω
(aor ptc συμπεριλαβών)
embrace *34.65*

συμπίνω
(aor συνέπιον)
drink together *23.36*

συμπίπτω
(aor συνέπεσον)
collapse *20.51*

συμπληρόομαι
a be swamped *54.14*
b come to an end *67.70*

συμπνίγω
a cause plants to die . . *23.120*
b crowd around *19.48*
c oppress *22.22*

συμπολίτης, ου *m*
fellow citizen *11.72*

συμπορεύομαι
a go with *15.148*
b come together *15.123*

συμπόσιον, ου *n*
eating group *11.5*

συμπρεσβύτερος, ου *m*
fellow elder *53.78*

συμφέρω
(aor ptc συνενέγκας)
a gather together *15.125*
b be advantageous . . . *65.44*

σύμφημι
agree *31.16*

σύμφορον, ου *n*
advantage *65.45*

συμφυλέτης, ου *m*
fellow countryman . . . *11.57*

συμφύομαι
(aor ptc fem nom pl
συμφυεῖσαι)
grow with 23.193

σύμφυτος, ον
be one with 89.117

συμφωνέω
a agree 31.15
b match 64.10

συμφώνησις, εως f
agreement 31.15

συμφωνία, ας f
music 14.83

σύμφωνον, ου n
agreement 31.15

συμψηφίζω
calculate 60.4

σύμψυχος, ον
harmonious 26.6

σύν
a with (association) . . . 89.107
b with (addition) 89.105
σύν : unit
σὺν χειρί
with the help of 90.2

συνάγομαι
come together 15.123

συνάγω
(aor συνήγαγον, inf
συναγαγεῖν, pf pass
ptc συνηγμένος, aor
pass συνήχθην, fut
pass συναχθήσομαι)
a gather together 15.125
b keep in a place 85.48
c turn into cash 57.144

συναγωγή, ῆς f
a assembly 11.44
b congregation of Jews 11.45
c synagogue 7.20

συναγωνίζομαι
join fervently in 34.20

συναθλέω
toil with 42.50

συναθροίζομαι
gather together 15.130

συναθροίζω
cause to gather to-
gether 15.131

συναίρω
(aor inf συνᾶραι)
check accounts 57.229

συναιχμάλωτος, ου m
fellow prisoner 37.118

συνακολουθέω
accompany 15.157

συναλίζομαι
a eat with 23.13
b live with 41.37

συναλλάσσω
reconcile 40.1

συναναβαίνω
(aor ptc συναναβάς)
come/go up with 15.153

συνανάκειμαι
associate in eating 34.10

συναναμίγνυμι
associate 34.1

συναναπαύομαι
rest with 23.86

συναντάω
happen 13.120

συναντιλαμβάνομαι
(aor subj συναντιλά-
βωμαι)
join in helping 35.5

συναπάγομαι
(aor pass συναπήχθην,
ptc συναπαχθείς)
a lead astray with *31.76*
b associate *34.1*
c share in doing *41.22*

συναποθνήσκω
(aor συναπέθανον, inf
συναποθανεῖν)
die with *23.118*

συναπόλλυμαι
(aor 3 sg συναπώλετο)
perish with *20.32*

συναποστέλλω
(aor συναπέστειλα)
send with *15.69*

συνᾶραι
see συναίρω

συναρμολογέομαι
fit together *62.1*

συναρπάζω
(aor συνήρπασα, plpf
συνηρπάκειν)
a seize *18.5*
b force off course *15.6*

συναυξάνομαι
grow with *23.192*

συναχθήσομαι
see συνάγω

συνβ-
see συμβ-

συνγ-
see συγγ-

συνδέομαι
be in prison with *37.116*

σύνδεσμος, ου *m*
a bond *18.17*
b unite *63.7*

συνδοξάζομαι
be honored with *87.10*

σύνδουλος, ου *m*
fellow slave *87.81*

συνδρομή, ῆς *f*
running together *15.133*

συνεβαλόμην
see συμβάλλω

συνέβην
see συμβαίνω

συνεγείρω
(aor pass συνηγέρθην)
raise to life with *23.95*

συνέδραμον
see συντρέχω

συνέδριον, ου *n*
a city council *11.79*
b Sanhedrin *11.80*

συνέζευξα
see συζεύγνυμι

συνέθεντο
see συντίθεμαι

συνείδησις, εως *f*
a be aware of *28.4*
b conscience *26.13*
συνείδησις : unit
καυστηριάζομαι τὴν
συνείδησιν
be insensitive to.... *27.54*

συνειδυῖα
see σύνοιδα

συνείληφα
see συλλαμβάνω

σύνειμι
(impf 3 pl συνῆσαν,
ptc συνιών, συνών)
a come together *15.123*
b be with *85.2*

συνείπετο
see συνέπομαι

συνεισέρχομαι
(aor συνεισῆλθον)
enter with *15.152*

συνέκδημος, ου *m*
travelling companion   *15.151*

συνεκέρασα
see συγκεράννυμι

συνεκλεκτός, ή, όν
one also chosen *30.94*

συνέλαβον
see συλλαμβάνω

συνελήλυθα
see συνέρχομαι

συνελθεῖν
see συνέρχομαι

συνελογισάμην
see συλλογίζομαι

συνενέγκας
see συμφέρω

συνέπεσον
see συμπίπτω

συνεπέστην
see συνεφίστημι

συνεπιμαρτυρέω
witness with *33.268*

συνέπιον
see συμπίνω

συνεπιτίθεμαι
(aor 3 pl συνεπέθεντο)
join in attack *39.50*

συνέπομαι
(impf 3 sg συνείπετο)
accompany *15.157*

συνεργέω
work together with . . . *42.15*

συνεργός, οῦ *m*
fellow worker *42.44*

συνέρχομαι
(aor συνῆλθον, inf συν-
ελθεῖν, pf συνελήλυθα)
a come together *15.123*
b go with *15.148*
c have sexual inter-
  course *23.61*

συνεσθίω
(aor συνέφαγον)
eat together *23.12*

σύνεσις, εως *f*
a what is understood *32.6*
b intelligence *32.26*

συνεσπάραξα
see συσπαράσσω

συνέσταλμαι
see συστέλλω

συνέστειλα
see συστέλλω

συνέστηκα
see συνίστημι

συνέστησα
see συνίστημι

συνεστώς
see συνίστημι

συνέσχον
see συνέχω

συνετάφην
see συνθάπτω

σύνετε
see συνίημι

συνετέθειντο
see συντίθεμαι

συνετός, ή, όν
intelligent 32.27

συνευδοκέω
agree 31.17

συνευωχέομαι
feast together 23.14

συνέφαγον
see συνεσθίω

συνεφίσταμαι (+ 2nd aor act)
(aor συνεπέστην)
join in attack 39.50

συνέχεον
see συγχέω

συνέχομαι
a experience 90.65
b be distressed 25.241
c continue 68.19
συνέχομαι : unit
συνέχομαι ἐκ
have conflicting
thoughts 30.18

συνεχύθην
see συγχέω

συνέχυννον
see συγχέω

συνέχω
(aor συνέσχον)
a restrain 37.17
b guard 37.122
c crowd around 19.45
συνέχω : unit
συνέχω τὰ ὦτα
refuse to listen 24.70

συνζ-
see συζ-

συνήγαγον
see συνάγω

συνηγέρθην
see συνεγείρω

συνηγμένος
see συνάγω

συνήδομαι
rejoice in 25.127

συνήθεια, ας f
custom 41.25

συνῆκα
see συνίημι

συνῆλθον
see συνέρχομαι

συνηλικιώτης, ου m
contemporary 67.159

συνηρπάκειν
see συναρπάζω

συνήρπασα
see συναρπάζω

συνῆσαν
see σύνειμι

συνήσω
see συνίημι

συνῆτε
see συνίημι

συνήχθην
see συνάγω

συνθάπτω
bury together with ... 52.8

συνθλάω
break into pieces 19.39

συνθλίβω
crowd around 19.45

συνθρύπτω
συνθρύπτω : unit
συνθρύπτω τὴν καρδίαν
cause great sorrow　25.282

συνιδών
see συνοράω

συνίημι
(pr 3 pl συνιᾶσιν and
συνίουσιν, inf συνιέ-
ναι, ptc συνιείς and
συνίων, subj 3 pl συν-
ιῶσιν, fut συνήσω,
aor συνῆκα, subj 2 pl
συνῆτε, 3 pl συνῶσιν,
impv 2 pl σύνετε)
a understand 32.5
b be intelligent 32.26

συνίσταμαι (+ pf act)
a stand with 17.2
b come into existence   13.82

συνιστάνω
see συνίστημι

συνίστημι
(aor συνέστησα, pf συν-
έστηκα, ptc συνεστώς)
a recommend 33.344
b demonstrate 28.49
c hold together 63.6

συνίω
see συνίημι

συνίων
see συνίημι

συνιών
see σύνειμι

συνιῶσιν
see συνίημι

συνκεχέραμμαι
alt. of συγκεχέρασμαι
see συγκεράννυμι

συνκεχέρασμαι
alt. of συγκεχέρασμαι
see συγκεράννυμι

συνκέχραμαι
alt. of συγχεχέρασμαι
see συγχεράννυμι

συνοδεύω
travel with 15.149

συνοδία, ας *f*
group of travelers 15.150

σύνοιδα
(ptc fem συνειδυῖα)
a be aware of 28.4
b know with 28.5

συνοικέω
live with 41.9

συνοικοδομοῦμαι
be built together 45.6

συνομιλέω
talk with 33.157

συνομορέω
be next to 85.15

συνοράω
(aor ptc συνιδών)
a learn about 27.5
b understand 32.13

συνοχή, ῆς *f*
distress 25.240

συνπ-
see συμπ-

συνσ-
see συσσ-

συνσπ-
see συσπ-

συνστ-
see συστ-

συντάσσω
command 33.325

συνταφείς
see συνθάπτομαι

συντέλεια, ας f
end 67.66

συντελέω
a complete 68.22
b cause to exist 13.88
c end 67.67

συντέμνω
(pf ptc συντετμημένος)
end 67.72

συντηρέω
a preserve 13.33
b keep in mind 29.1

συντίθεμαι
(aor 3 pl συνέθεντο,
plpf 3 pl συνετέθειντο)
agree together 31.18

συντόμως
briefly 67.108

συντρέχω
(aor συνέδραμον)
a run together 15.133
b join in living 41.15

συντρίβω
(pf pass inf συντετρῖφ-
θαι, ptc συντετριμμένος)
a break into pieces . . . 19.39
b crush 19.46
c overcome com-
pletely 39.53

σύντριμμα, τος n
destruction 20.59

σύντροφος, ου m
a foster brother/sister 10.51
b intimate friend 34.15

συντυγχάνω
(aor inf συντυχεῖν)
come near to 15.76

Συντύχη, ης f
Syntyche 93.350

συνυποκρίνομαι
pretend together 88.229

συνυπουργέω
join in helping 35.5

συνφ-
see συμφ-

συνχ-
see συγχ-

συνψ-
see συμψ-

συνωδίνω
suffer together 24.88

συνωμοσία, ας f
conspiracy 30.73

συνών
see σύνειμι

συνῶσιν
see συνίημι

Συράκουσαι, ῶν f
Syracuse 93.588

Συρία, ας f
Syria 93.589

Σύρος, ου m
Syrian 93.590

Συροφοινίκισσα, ης f
Syro-phoenician
woman 93.591

Σύρτις, εως f
the Syrtis 93.592

σύρω
a pull 15.212
b lead by force 15.178

συσπαράσσω
(aor συνεσπάραξα)
throw into a fit 23.167

σύσσημον, ου n
signal 33.476

σύσσωμος, ον
co-member 11.9

συστατικός, ή, όν
commendatory 33.345

συσταυρόω
crucify with 20.78

συστέλλω
(aor συνέστειλα, pf
pass συνέσταλμαι)
a draw to a close 67.118
b remove 15.200
c wrap up 79.119

συστενάζω
groan together 25.145

συστοιχέω
correspond to 58.68

συστρατιώτης, ου m
fellow struggler 34.19

συστρέφομαι
come together 15.123

συστρέφω
gather together 15.125

συστροφή, ῆς f
a revolt 39.43
b conspiracy 30.72

συσχηματίζομαι
shape one's behavior   41.29

Συχάρ f
Sychar 93.593

Συχέμ
a Shechem (person)   93.351
b Shechem (place).... 93.594

σφαγή, ῆς f
slaughter 20.72
σφαγή : unit
ἡμέρα σφαγῆς
day of condemnation 56.33

σφάγιον, ου n
sacrifice 53.20

σφάζω
slaughter 20.72

σφόδρα
exceedingly 78.19

σφοδρῶς
exceedingly 78.19

σφραγίζω
a put a seal on 6.55
b mark............ 33.484
c give in secure
manner........... 57.87
d deliver safely 15.180
e make known 28.53

σφραγίς, ῖδος f
a signet 6.54
b seal 6.62
c mark............ 33.483
d inscription 33.47
e proof 73.9

σφυδρόν, οῦ n
ankle 8.51

σχεδόν
almost 78.40

σχῆμα, τος n
a form 58.7
b appearance....... 58.17

σχίζω
a split 19.27
b divide 63.26

σχίσμα, τος n
a tear 19.28
b division 39.13

σχοινίον, ου n
rope 6.18

σχολάζω
a give time to 67.81
b be empty 59.43

σχολή, ῆς f
lecture hall 7.14

σχῶ
see ἔχω

σῴζω
(pf σέσωκα)
a rescue 21.18
b save 21.27
c heal 23.136

σῶμα, τος n
a body 8.1
b physical being 9.8
c church 11.34
d slave 87.78
e reality 58.66
σῶμα : units
σῶμα ἐπουράνιον
heavenly body 1.26
ἐνδημέω ἐν τῷ σώματι
be alive 23.91
ἐκδημέω ἐκ τοῦ σώματος
die 23.111

σωματικός, ή, όν
bodily 8.2

σωματικῶς
a bodily 8.2
b in reality 70.7

Σώπατρος, ου m
Sopater 93.352

σωρεύομαι
be engaged in 68.76

σωρεύω
σωρεύω : unit
σωρεύω ἄνθρακας
πυρὸς ἐπὶ τὴν κεφαλήν
cause to be ashamed 25.199

Σωσθένης, ους m
Sosthenes 93.353

Σωσίπατρος, ου m
Sosipater 93.354

σωτήρ, ῆρος m
a rescuer 21.22
b Savior 21.31

σωτηρία, ας f
a deliverance 21.18
b salvation (state) 21.25
c salvation (event) 21.26

σωτήριον, ου n
a salvation (means) . . . 21.29
b salvation (message) 21.30

σωτήριος, ον
saving 21.28

σωφρονέω
a be sane 30.22
b be sensible 32.34

σωφρονίζω
teach 33.229

σωφρονισμός, οῦ m
a sound judgment 32.34
b moderation 88.93

σωφρόνως
moderately 88.94

σωφροσύνη, ης f
a sound judgment 32.34
b moderation 88.93

σώφρων, ον
moderate 88.94

τά
see ὁ

ταβέρνη, ης f
inn 7.11

Ταβιθά *f*
Tabitha *93.355*

τάγμα, τος *n*
order *62.7*

Ταδδαῖον
Thaddaeus *93.356*

τακτός, ή, όν
determined *30.85*

ταλαιπωρέω
be sorrowful *25.136*

ταλαιπωρία, ας *f*
hardship *22.11*

ταλαίπωρος, ον
wretched *22.12*

ταλαντιαῖος, α, ον
weighing a talent *86.5*

τάλαντον, ου *n*
coin *6.82*

ταλιθα
little girl *9.48*

ταμεῖον, ου *n*
a inner room *7.28*
b storeroom *7.32*

τάξις, εως *f*
a sequence *61.3*
b good order *62.7*
c kind *58.21*

ταπεινόομαι
live in humble cir-
cumstances *87.63*

ταπεινός, ή, όν
a downhearted *25.295*
b humble *88.52*
c lowly *87.61*
d gentle *88.64*

ταπεινοφροσύνη, ης *f*
humility *88.53*

ταπεινόφρων, ον
humility *88.54*

ταπεινόω
a make low (spacial) . . *81.7*
b level off *79.87*
c make low (status) . . . *87.62*
d make humble *88.56*
e embarrass *25.198*

ταπείνωσις, εως *f*
a humility *88.51*
b low status *87.00*

ταράσσω
(pf pass τετάραγμαι,
3 sg τετάρακται, aor
pass ἐταράχθην, subj
ταραχθῶ)
a stir up *16.3*
b cause great distress   *25.244*
c cause a riot *39.44*

ταραχή, ῆς *f*
a movement *16.4*
b riot *39.42*

τάραχος, ου *m*
a commotion *39.5*
b great distress *25.243*

Ταρσεύς, έως *m*
person from Tarsus . . . *93.595*

Ταρσός, οῦ *f*
Tarsus *93.596*

ταρταρόω
cast into hell *1.25*

τάσσω
(pf inf τεταχέναι, pf
pass τέταγμαι, 3 sg
τέτακται)
a assign *37.96*
b cause to be *13.13*
c command *33.325*
d suggest *33.346*
e give oneself to *68.69*

ταῦρος, ου *m*
  bull *4.16*

ταφή, ῆς *f*
  burial place *52.9*

τάφος, ου *m*
  grave *7.75*

τάχα
  perhaps *71.12*

ταχέως
  a swift *67.110*
  b (very) soon *67.56*

ταχινός, ή, όν
  a swift *67.110*
  b (very) soon *67.56*

τάχιον
  swift *67.110*

τάχιστα
  see ταχύς

τάχος, ους *n*
  swift *67.111*
  τάχος : unit
  ἐν τάχει
    (very) soon *67.56*

ταχύ
  a soon *67.56*
  b quickly *67.110*

ταχύς, εῖα, ύ
  swift *67.110*
  ταχύς : unit
  ὡς τάχιστα
    as soon as possible *67.57*

τέ
  a and *89.95*
  b and then *89.88*

τε καί
  both . . . and *89.102*

τέ . . . καί
  both . . . and *89.102*

τε . . . τε
  not only . . . but also . . *89.103*

τέθεικα
  see τίθημι

τεθεικώς
  see τίθημι

τέθειται
  see τίθημι

τεθῆναι
  see τίθημι

τεθλιμμένος
  see θλίβω

τέθνηκα
  see θνήσκω

τέθραμμαι
  see τρέφω

τεθῶ
  see τίθημι

τεῖχος, ους *n*
  city wall *7.61*

τεκεῖν
  see τίκτω

τεκμήριον, ου *n*
  convincing proof *28.45*

τεκνίον, ου *n*
  child *9.46*

τεκνογονέω
  bear children *23.52*

τεκνογονία, ας *f*
  bearing children *23.52*

τέκνον, ου *n*
  a child (own) *10.36*
  b descendant *10.28*
  c inhabitants *11.63*
  d child (endearment) *9.46*

e disciple........... *36.40*
f kind of *58.26*
τέχνον : unit
τέχνα φωτός
   people of God *11.14*

τεχνοτροφέω
rear *35.51*

τέχτων, ονος *m*
builder *45.9*

τέλειος, α, ον
a perfect (moral) *88.36*
b genuine *73.6*
c perfect (physical) ... *79.129*
d complete *68.23*
e mature *88.100*
f adult............ *9.10*
g initiated *11.18*

τελειότης, ητος *f*
a maturity.......... *88.101*
b perfection *88.37*

τελειόω
a make perfect *88.38*
b make genuine...... *73.7*
c complete *68.22*
d succeed fully *68.31*
e initiate *53.50*
f make happen *13.126*
g become......... *13.18*

τελείως
completely.......... *78.47*

τελείωσις, εως *f*
a causing perfection .. *88.38*
b fulfillment *13.126*

τελειωτής, οῦ *m*
perfecter *68.24*

τελεσφορέω
bear ripe fruit *23.203*

τελευτάω
die *23.102*

τελευτή, ῆς *f*
death *23.102*

τελέω
a complete *68.22*
b end *67.67*
c make happen *13.126*
d obey *36.20*
e pay taxes *57.178*

τέλος, ους *n*
a end *67.66*
b result *89.40*
c purpose *89.55*
d completely *78.47*
e tax *57.179*
τέλος : units
τὸ τέλος
   finally *61.17*
εἰς τέλος
   completely....... *78.47*

τελώνης, ου *m*
tax collector *57.184*

τελώνιον, ου *n*
tax office *57.183*

τέξομαι
see τίχτω

τέρας, ατος *n*
portent............ *33.480*

Τέρτιος, ου *m*
Tertius *93.357*

Τέρτυλλος, ου *m*
Tertullus *93.358*

**τέσσαρες, n τέσσαρα, gen
τεσσάρων**
four *60.13*

τεσσαρεσχαιδέχατος, η, ον
fourteenth *60.60*

τεσσεράχοντα
forty.............. *60.27*
τεσσεράχοντα : units
ἡμέρας τεσσεράχοντα

(καὶ νύκτας τεσσερά-
κοντα)
  long time *67.93*

ἔτη τεσσεράκοντα
  very long time *67.94*

τεσσερακονταετής, ές
  period of forty years . . *67.172*

τέταγμαι
  (3 sg τέτακται)
  see τάσσω

τετάραγμαι
  (3 sg τετάρακται)
  see ταράσσω

τεταρταῖος, α, ον
  the fourth day *67.181*

τέταρτον, ου *n*
  fourth part *60.64*

τέταρτος, η, ον
  fourth *60.51*

τεταχέναι
  see τάσσω

τετρααρχέω
  be a tetrarch *37.79*

τετραάρχης, ου *m*
  tetrarch *37.78*

τετράγωνος, ον
  square *79.91*

τετράδιον, ου *n*
  group of four
  soldiers *55.11*

τετρακισχίλιοι, αι, α
  four thousand *60.42*

τετρακόσιοι, αι, α
  four hundred *60.36*

τετράμηνος, ου *f*
  four-month period *67.176*

τετραπλοῦς, ῆ, οῦν
  four times (as much) . . *60.76*

τετράπουν, ποδος *n*
  quadruped *4.4*

τέτυχα
  see τυγχάνω

τεφρόω
  reduce to ashes *14.72*

τεχθείς
  see τίκτω

τέχνη, ης *f*
  craft *42.51*

τεχνίτης, ου *m*
  craftsman *42.53*

τήκομαι
  become liquid *79.8*

τηλαυγῶς
  clearly *24.36*

τηλικοῦτος, αύτη, οῦτο
  a so great (size) *79.128*
  b so great (degree) *78.36*

τηρέω
  a keep *13.32*
  b guard *37.122*
  c obey *36.19*

τήρησις, εως *f*
  a custody *37.122*
  b prison *7.24*
  c obedience *36.19*

τί
  why? *92.15*
  see also τίς

τι
  see τις

Τιβεριάς, άδος *f*
  Tiberias *93.597*

Τιβέριος, ου *m*
Tiberius 93.359

τίθημι
(pres 3 pl τιθέασιν, ptc
τιθείς, impf 3 sg ἐτί-
θει, 3 pl ἐτίθουν, ἐτί-
θεσαν, fut θήσω, aor
ἔθηκα, subj θῶ, impv
2 pl θέτε, inf θεῖναι,
ptc θείς, pf τέθεικα,
ptc τεθεικώς, aor midd
2 sg ἔθου, 3 pl ἔθεντο,
impv 2 pl θέσθε, pf
pass 3 sg τέθειται,
aor pass ἐτέθην, subj
τεθῶ, inf τεθῆναι)
a put 85.32
b appoint 37.96
c take off 49.21
d explain 33.151
e deposit 57.217
f cause to be 13.9
g cause to experience 90.86
τίθημι : units
τίθημι βουλήν
　advise 33.296
τίθημι τὰ γόνατα
　kneel (down) 17.19
τὴν ψυχὴν τίθημι
　die willingly 23.113
τίθημι ἐν τῇ καρδίᾳ
　make up mind 30.76
τίθεμαι ἐν τῇ καρδίᾳ
　treasure up in mind 29.2
τίθεμαι ἐν τῷ πνεύματι
　make up mind 30.76
τίθεμαι εἰς τὰ ὦτα
　a listen carefully to . 24.64
　b remember well . . . 29.5
τίθημι παρὰ/πρὸς τοὺς
πόδας
　turn over to 57.82

τίκτω
(fut τέξομαι, aor ἔτεκον,
inf τεκεῖν, aor pass
ἐτέχθην, ptc τεχθείς)
a give birth 23.52
b grow 23.194

τίλλω
pick 18.9

Τιμαῖος, ου *m*
Timaeus 93.360

τιμάω
a honor 87.8
b set price on 57.165
c assist 57.117

τιμή, ῆς *f*
a honor 87.4
b value 65.1
c price 57.161
d pay 57.167

τίμιος, α, ον
a precious 65.2
b honored 87.6
τίμιος : unit
λίθος τίμιος
　gem 2.29

τιμιότης, ητος *f*
wealth 57.35

Τιμόθεος, ου *m*
Timothy 93.361

Τίμων, ωνος *m*
Timon 93.362

τιμωρέω
punish 38.6

τιμωρία, ας *f*
punishment 38.6

τίνω
(fut τίσω)
experience some-
thing bad 90.77

τίς, τί, gen τίνος
who?, what? 92.14
see also τί

τις, τι, gen τινός
a someone, something 92.12
b someone important 92.13

τράπεζα, ης *f*
a table *6.113*
b meal *23.26*
c bank *57.215*
τράπεζα : units
τραπέζης μετέχω
  belong to a reli-
  gious group *34.32*
διακονέω τραπέζαις
  handle finances *57.230*

τραπεζίτης, ου *m*
banker *57.216*

τραῦμα, τος *n*
wound *20.29*

τραυματίζω
hurt, wound *20.28*

τραχηλίζομαι
be easily known *28.61*

τράχηλος, ου *m*
neck *8.25*
τράχηλος : units
τράχηλον ὑποτίθημι
  risk one's life *21.8*
ἐπιπίπτω ἐπὶ τὸν
τράχηλον
  embrace *34.64*
ἐπιτίθημι ζυγὸν ἐπὶ
τὸν τράχηλον
  load down with
  obligations *22.27*

τραχύς, εῖα, ύ
rough *79.84*

Τραχωνῖτις, ιδος *f*
Trachonitis *93.598*

τρεῖς, τρία
three *60.12*

τρέμω
a tremble *16.6*
b fear *25.259*
c respect *87.14*

τρέφω
(aor ἔθρεψα, pf pass
τέθραμμαι)
a provide food for *23.6*
b take care of *35.45*
c rear *35.51*

τρέχω
(aor ἔδραμον, ptc
δραμών)
a run *15.230*
b try *68.61*
c behave *41.14*
τρέχω : unit
λόγος τρέχει
  message spread *28.25*

τρῆμα, τος *n*
eye of needle *6.216*

τριάκοντα
thirty *60.26*

τριακόσιοι, αι, α
three hundred *60.35*

τρίβολος, ου *m*
thorn plant *3.17*

τρίβος, ου *f*
path *1.100*

τριετία, ας *f*
three-year period *67.171*

τρίζω
τρίζω : unit
τρίζω τοὺς ὀδόντας
  gnash the teeth *23.41*

τρίμηνον, ου *n*
three-month period . . . *67.175*

τρίς
three times *60.71*

τρίστεγον, ου *n*
second or third story
of a building *7.36*

τρισχίλιοι, αι, α
three thousand 60.41

τρίτον, ου *n*
third part 60.63

τρίτος, η, ον
third.............. 60.50
τρίτος : unit
τρίτος οὐρανός
heaven 1.11

τρίχινος, η, ον
hairy 8.13

τριχός
see θρίξ

τρόμος, ου *m*
trembling.......... 16.6

τροπή, ῆς *f*
turning 16.15

τρόπος, ου *m*
a manner.......... 89.83
b way of life 41.10

τροποφορέω
put up with 25.173

τροφή, ῆς *f*
food 5.1

Τρόφιμος, ου *m*
Trophimus 93.365

τροφός, οῦ *f*
nurse 35.52

τροφοφορέω
take care of 35.45

τροχιά, ᾶς *f*
τροχιά : unit
τροχιὰς ὀρθὰς ποιέω
τοῖς ποσίν
behave correctly.... 41.30

τροχός, οῦ *m*
a course (sequence)... 61.5
b course (time) 67.83

τρύβλιον, ου *n*
bowl.............. 6.136

τρυγάω
pick 43.18

τρυγών, όνος *f*
pigeon, dove 4.44

τρυμαλιά, ᾶς *f*
eye of a needle 6.216

τρύπημα, ατος *n*
eye of a needle 6.216

Τρύφαινα, ης *f*
Tryphaena......... 93.366

τρυφάω
revel............. 88.253

τρυφή, ῆς *f*
revelling 88.253

Τρυφῶσα, ης *f*
Tryphosa.......... 93.367

Τρῳάς, άδος *f*
Troas 93.599

Τρωγύλλιον, ου *n*
Trogyllium 93.600

τρώγω
eat 23.3

τυγχάνω
(aor opt 3 sg τύχοι,
inf τυχεῖν, pf τέτυχα)
experience 90.61
τυγχάνω : unit
εἰ τύχοι
probably.......... 71.13

τυμπανίζω
torture 38.13

τυπιχῶς
example 58.60

τύπος, ου m
a scar 8.56
b image 6.96
c model 58.58
d example 58.59
e archetype 58.63
f kind 58.25
g contents 90.28

τύπτω
a strike 19.1
b harm 20.15

Τύραννος, ου m
Tyrannus 93.368

τυρβάζομαι
be upset 25.234

Τύριος, ου m
Tyrian 93.601

Τύρος, ου f
Tyre 93.602

τυφλός, ή, όν
a blind 24.38
b not able to under-
stand 32.42

τυφλόω
make not understand . . 32.43
τυφλόω : unit
τυφλόω τοὺς ὀφθαλμούς
cause to not under-
stand 32.25

τύφομαι
smolder 14.64

τυφόομαι
be extremely proud . . . 88.218

τυφωνικός, ή, όν
of a strong wind 14.7

τυχεῖν
see τυγχάνω

Τύχιχος, ου m
Tychicus 93.369

τύχοι
see τυγχάνω

τυχόν
perhaps 71.10

ὑακίνθινος, η, ον
blue 79.37

ὑάκινθος, ου m
hyacinth 2.41

ὑάλινος, η, ον
of glass 6.223

ὕαλος, ου f
a glass 6.222
b crystal 2.46

ὑβρίζω
a maltreat 88.130
b insult 33.390

ὕβρις, εως f
a maltreatment 88.131
b damage 20.19
c insult 33.391

ὑβριστής, οῦ m
a insolent person 88.132
b insulter 33.392

ὑγιαίνω
a be healthy 23.129
b be accurate 72.15

ὑγιής, ές
a healthy 23.129
b accurate 72.14

ὑγρός, ά, όν
wet 79.78

ὑδρία, ας f
pitcher 6.127

ὑπάρχω : unit
τὰ ὑπάρχοντα
    possessions 57.16

ὑπέβαλον
    see ὑποβάλλω

ὑπέδειξα
    see ὑποδείκνυμι

ὑπέθηκα
    see ὑποτίθημι

ὑπείκω
    obey 36.18

ὑπέλαβον
    see ὑπολαμβάνω

ὑπελείφθην
    see ὑπολείπομαι

ὑπέμεινα
    see ὑπομένω

ὑπεμνήσθην
    see ὑπομιμνήσκομαι

ὑπεναντίος, α, ον
    hostile 39.6

ὑπενεγκεῖν
    see ὑποφέρω

ὑπέπλευσα
    see ὑποπλέω

ὑπέρ
    a on behalf of (bene-
        faction) 90.36
    b about (content) 90.24
    c beyond (degree) 78.29
    d above (status) 87.30
    e because of (reason)   89.28
    ὑπέρ : unit
    μὴ ὑπὲρ ἃ γέγραπται
        observe rules 88.95

ὑπεραίρομαι
    a be overly proud 88.211
    b rise in pride against   39.39

ὑπέρακμος, ον
    past one's prime 67.158

ὑπεράνω
    a above (location) 83.49
    b above (status) 87.31

ὑπερασπίζω
    protect 21.12

ὑπεραυξάνω
    increase greatly 78.6

ὑπερβαίνω
    sin against 88.296

ὑπερβαλλόντως
    extremely 78.34

ὑπερβάλλω
    far more 78.33

ὑπερβολή, ῆς f
    far more 78.33

ὑπερέκεινα
    beyond 83.55

ὑπερεκπερισσοῦ
    extreme 78.34

ὑπερεκτείνω
    overextend 68.78

ὑπερεκχύννομαι
    overflow 14.19

ὑπερεντυγχάνω
    intercede 33.348

ὑπερέχω
    a surpass in value 65.4
    b control 37.17

ὑπερηφανία, ας f
    arrogance 88.213

ὑπερήφανος, ον
    arrogant 88.214

ὑπεριδών
see ὑπεροράω

ὑπερλίαν
extremely.......... 78.34

ὑπερνικάω
have complete
victory............ 39.58

ὑπέρογκος, ον
boastful........... 33.373

ὑπεροράω
(aor ptc ὑπεριδών)
disregard........... 30.49

ὑπεροχή, ῆς f
pompous........... 87.26

ὑπερπερισσεύω
a be more abundant .. 59.49
b extreme 78.34

ὑπερπερισσῶς
extremely.......... 78.34

ὑπερπλεονάζω
be more than 59.49

ὑπερυψόω
give exceptional honor 87.16

ὑπερφρονέω
be arrogant 88.210

ὑπερῷον, ου n
upstairs room 7.27

ὑπεστειλάμην
see ὑποστέλλω

ὑπετάγην
see ὑποτάσσομαι and
ὑποτάσσω

ὑπέταξα
see ὑποτάσσω

ὑπέχω
experience.......... 90.68

ὑπήκοος, ον
obedient........... 36.16

ὑπήνεγκα
see ὑποφέρω

ὑπηρετέω
a serve............ 35.19
b provide for........ 35.32

ὑπηρέτης, ου m
servant............ 35.20

ὕπνος, ου m
sleep.............. 23.66
ὕπνος : units
καταφέρομαι ὕπνῳ
  get sleepier........ 23.68
καταφέρομαι ἀπὸ τοῦ
ὕπνου
  be sound asleep 23.71
βαρέομαι ὕπνῳ
  be sound asleep 23.71

ὑπό
a under (location) 83.51
b under (control)..... 37.7
c by (agent)......... 90.1
d because of (reason) 89.26
e at (time).......... 67.161
ὑπό : units
εἰμὶ ὑπὸ ζυγόν
  be a slave 87.80
ὑπὸ τοὺς πόδας
  be in complete
  control........... 37.8
ὑπὸ τὸν οὐρανόν
  on earth.......... 1.43
ὑπὸ κρίσιν πίπτω
  be condemned 56.32

ὑποβάλλω
(aor ὑπέβαλον)
bribe.............. 57.176

ὑπογραμμός, οῦ m
example............ 58.59

ὑπόδειγμα, τος n
example............ 58.59

ὑποδείκνυμι
(fut ὑποδείξω, aor
ὑπέδειξα)
a make known 28.47
b explain 33.150

ὑποδέομαι
(aor impv ὑπόδησαι)
put on shoes 49.17

ὑποδέχομαι
welcome 34.53

ὑπόδημα, τος n
shoe 6.182

ὑπόδικος, ον
liable to judgment 56.17

ὑποδραμών
see ὑποτρέχω

ὑποζύγιον, ου n
pack animal 4.7

ὑποζώννυμι
brace a ship 54.25

ὑποκάτω
a under 83.51
b under surface of 83.52
ὑποκάτω : unit
ὑποκάτω τῶν ποδῶν
be under complete
control 37.8

ὑποκρίνομαι
pretend 88.227

ὑπόκρισις, εως f
pretense 88.227

ὑποκριτής, οῦ m
pretender 88.228

ὑπολαμβάνω
(aor ὑπέλαβον, ptc
ὑπολαβών)
a take up 15.102
b reply 33.187

c help 35.1
d suppose 31.29

ὑπόλειμμα, τος n
remnant 63.22

ὑπολείπομαι
(aor pass ὑπελείφθην)
be left behind 85.66

ὑπολήνιον, ου n
wine trough 7.67

ὑπολιμπάνω
leave behind 13.91

ὑπομένω
(aor ὑπέμεινα, ptc
ὑπομείνας, pf ptc
ὑπομεμενηκώς)
a resist 39.20
b stay behind 85.57
c continue 68.17
d endure 25.175

ὑπομιμνήσκομαι
(aor ὑπεμνήσθην)
remember 29.9

ὑπομιμνήσκω
(fut ὑπομνήσω, aor
inf ὑπομνῆσαι)
remind 29.10

ὑπόμνησις, εως f
reminding 29.10

ὑπομονή, ῆς f
endurance 25.174

ὑπονοέω
suspect 31.32

ὑπόνοια, ας f
suspicion 31.32

ὑποπλέω
(aor ὑπέπλευσα)
sail under shelter of . . . 54.10

ὑποπνέω
(aor ptc ὑποπνεύσας)
blow gently *14.5*

ὑποπόδιον, ου *n*
footstool *6.117*
ὑποπόδιον : unit
ὑποπόδιον τῶν ποδῶν
   be under someone's
   control *37.8*

ὑπόστασις, εως *f*
a substance *58.1*
b trust *31.84*

ὑποστέλλω
(aor midd ὑπεστειλάμην,
subj 3 sg ὑποστείληται)
a avoid *13.160*
b cease *68.53*

ὑποστολή, ῆς *f*
cease *68.53*

ὑποστρέφω
a return *15.88*
b turn back to belief . . *31.64*
c be again *13.24*

ὑποστρωννύω
spread out underneath *16.23*

ὑποταγή, ῆς *f*
obedience *36.18*

ὑποταγήσομαι
see ὑποτάσσομαι and
ὑποτάσσω

ὑποτάσσομαι
(fut ὑποταγήσομαι,
aor ὑπετάγην)
obey *36.18*

ὑποτάσσω
(aor ὑπέταξα, pf pass
ὑποτέταγμαι, aor
pass ὑπετάγην, fut
pass ὑποταγήσομαι)
bring under control . . . *37.31*

ὑποτίθεμαι
instruct *33.230*

ὑποτίθημι
(aor ὑπέθηκα)
ὑποτίθημι : unit
τράχηλον ὑποτίθημι
   risk one's life *21.8*

ὑποτρέχω
(aor ptc ὑποδραμών)
sail under shelter of . . . *54.10*

ὑποτύπωσις, εως *f*
example *58.59*

ὑποφέρω
(aor ὑπήνεγκα, inf
ὑπενεγκεῖν)
endure *25.175*

ὑποχωρέω
withdraw *15.53*

ὑπωπιάζω
a annoy and wear out *25.245*
b exercise self-control *88.89*

ὗς, ὑός *f*
sow *4.37*

ὑσσός, οῦ *m*
javelin *6.35*

ὕσσωπον, ου *n*
hyssop *3.26*

ὕσσωπος, ου *m, f*
hyssop *3.26*

ὑστερέω
a be in need *57.37*
b lack benefit *65.51*
c be inferior *87.65*
d fail to attain *13.21*

ὑστέρημα, τος *n*
a need *57.38*
b absence *85.29*

ὑστέρησις, εως f
  need 57.37

ὕστερος, α, ον
  a last 61.16
  b later 67.50

ὑφαίνω
  weave 48.3

ὑφαντός, ή, όν
  woven 48.4

ὑψηλός, ή, όν
  a tall 81.6
  b world above 1.13
  c very valuable 65.9
  d arrogant 88.208
  ὑψηλός : units
  ὑψηλὰ φρονέω
    be haughty 88.209
  βραχίων ὑψηλός
    great power 76.5

ὑψηλότερος, α, ον
  above 83.50

ὑψηλοφρονέω
  be arrogant 88.209

ὕψιστος, η, ον
  a world above 1.13
  b the Most High 12.4

ὕψος, ους n
  a height 81.3
  b world above 1.13
  c high rank 87.19
  ὕψος : unit
  ἀνατολὴ ἐξ ὕψους
    the dawn from on
    high 14.42

ὑψόω
  a lift up 81.5
  b exalt 87.20

ὕψωμα, τος n
  a world above 1.13
  b supernatural power 12.46
  c arrogance 88.207

φαγεῖν
  see ἐσθίω

φάγομαι
  see ἐσθίω

φάγος, ου m
  glutton 23.19

φαιλόνης, ου m
  cloak 6.172

φαίνομαι
  (fut φανουμαι, φανήσομαι,
  aor ἐφάνην, subj φανῶ)
  a become visible 24.18
  b make known 28.36
  c appear to be 28.55
  φαίνομαι : unit
  ποῦ φανεῖται
    what will happen to 13.118

φαίνω
  (fut φανῶ)
  shine 14.37

Φάλεκ m
  Peleg 93.371

φαν-
  see φαίνομαι and φαίνω

φανερός, ά, όν
  a widely known 28.28
  b evident 28.58
  c clearly seen 24.20

φανερόω
  a cause to be seen . . . 24.19
  b make known 28.36

φανερῶς
  a publicly 28.63
  b clearly seen 24.20

φανέρωσις, εως f
  revelation 28.36

φανός, οῦ m
  lantern 6.103

Φανουήλ m
Phanuel 93.372

φαντάζομαι
appear 24.26

φαντασία, ας f
pomp 87.57

φάντασμα, τος n
ghost 12.42

φανῶ
see φαίνομαι

φάραγξ, αγγος f
ravine 1.51

Φαραώ m
Pharaoh 93.373

Φάρες m
Perez 93.374

Φαρισαῖος, ου m
Pharisee 11.49

φαρμακεία, ας f
sorcery 53.100

φαρμακία
see φαρμακεία

φάρμακον, ου n
sorcery 53.100

φάρμακος, ου m
sorcerer 53.101

φασίν
see φημί

φάσις, εως f
report 33.211

φάσκω
declare 33.218

φάτνη, ης f
a feed box 6.137
b stall 7.64

φαῦλος, η, ον
bad 88.116

φέγγος, ους n
light 14.36

φείδομαι
a spare 22.28
b avoid 13.152

φειδομένως
sparingly 59.61

φέρομαι
a move 15.11
b progress 13.58

φέρω
(fut οἴσω, aor ἤνεγκα,
inf ἐνεγκεῖν and ἐνέγ-
και, ptc ἐνέγκας, aor
pass ἠνέχθην, ptc ἐνεχ-
θείς)
a carry 15.187
b bring 15.166
c drive along 15.160
d guide 36.1
e lead into 82.12
f bring about 13.133
g put 85.42
h experience 90.64
i sustain 13.35
j demonstrate reality
of 70.5
k accept 31.55
l endure 25.176
m bear fruit 23.199
φέρω : unit
καρπὸν φέρω
bear fruit 23.199

φεύγω
(aor ἔφυγον, inf φυγεῖν)
a flee 15.61
b escape 21.14
c disappear quickly . . 13.95
d avoid 13.161
e become invisible . . . 24.6

Φῆλιξ, ιχος m
Felix 93.375

Φίλητος, ου *m*
Philetus 93.378

φιλία, ας *f*
love 25.33

Φιλιππήσιος, ου *m*
Philippian 93.604

Φίλιπποι, ων *m*
Philippi 93.605

Φίλιππος, ου *m*
Philip 93.379

φιλόθεος, ον
loving God 25.40

Φιλόλογος, ου *m*
Philologus 93.380

φιλονεικία, ας *f*
desire to quarrel 33.449

φιλόνεικος, ον
quarrelsome 33.450

φιλοξενία, ας *f*
hospitality 34.57

φιλόξενος, ον
be hospitable 34.58

φιλοπρωτεύω
desire to be first 25.110

φίλος, ου *m*
friend 34.11

φιλοσοφία, ας *f*
human wisdom 32.38

φιλόσοφος, ου *m*
philosopher 32.39

φιλόστοργος, ον
very affectionate 25.41

φιλότεκνος, ον
loving one's
children 25.38

φιλοτιμέομαι
aspire to 25.78

φιλοφρόνως
friendly 88.72

φιμοῦμαι
say nothing 33.122

φιμόω
(pf impv πεφίμωσο)
a muzzle 44.6
b put to silence 33.123
c cease to make sound 14.86

Φλέγων, οντος *m*
Phlegon 93.381

φλογίζω
ignite 14.65

φλόξ, φλογός *f*
flame 2.4

φλυαρέω
talk nonsense 33.374

φλύαρος, ον
gossipy 33.375

φοβέομαι
a be afraid 25.252
b respect 87.14
c worship 53.58

φοβερός, ά, όν
fearful 25.255

φόβητρον, ου *n*
fearful thing 25.258

φόβος, ου *m*
a fear 25.251
b source of fear 25.254
c reverence 53.59

Φοίβη, ης *f*
Phoebe 93.382

Φοινίκη, ης *f*
Phoenicia 93.606

φοῖνιξ or φοίνιξ, ιχος m
  a palm tree 3.8
  b palm branch 3.53

Φοῖνιξ, ιχος m
  Phoenix 93.607

φονεύς, έως m
  murderer 20.85

φονεύω
  murder 20.82

φόνος, ου m
  murder 20.82

φορέω
  a wear 49.11
  b be 13.2
  φορέω : unit
  φορέω τὴν μάχαιραν
    have power to punish 38.3

Φόρον, ου n
  see Ἀππίου Φόρον 93.608

φόρος, ου m
  tribute 57.182

φορτίζω
  cause to carry 15.207

φορτίον, ου n
  load 15.208

Φορτουνᾶτος, ου m
  Fortunatus 93.383

φραγέλλιον, ου n
  whip 6.26

φραγελλόω
  beat with a whip 19.9

φραγμός, οῦ m
  a fence 7.59
  b byway 1.105
  c that which separates 34.39

φράζω
  explain 33.141

φράσσω
  (aor pass subj φραγῶ,
  fut pass φραγήσομαι)
  cause to cease 68.45
  φράσσω : unit
  φράσσω στόμα
    a put to silence 33.125
    b keep from harming 20.30

φρέαρ, ατος n
  a well 7.57
  b deep pit 1.58

φρεναπατάω
  deceive 31.12

φρεναπάτης, ου m
  deceiver 31.13

φρήν, φρενός f
  thoughtful planning . . 26.15

φρίσσω
  be extremely afraid . . . 25.260

φρονέω
  a have attitude 26.16
  b ponder 30.20
  c hold a view 31.1
  d honor 87.12
  φρονέω : unit
  ὑψηλὰ φρονέω
    be haughty 88.209

φρόνημα, τος n
  thoughtful planning . . 26.15

φρόνησις, εως f
  a thoughtful planning 26.15
  b wisdom 32.30

φρόνιμος, ον
  wise 32.31

φρονίμως
  wisely 32.31

φροντίζω
  keep thinking about . . 30.20

φρουρέω
 guard against 37.119

φρυάσσω
 rave 88.185

φρύγανον, ου n
 firewood 3.65

Φρυγία, ας f
 Phrygia 93.609

φυγεῖν
 see φεύγω

Φύγελος, ου m
 Phygelus 93.384

φυγή, ῆς f
 flight 15.61

φυέν
 see φύω

φυλακή, ῆς f
 a prison 7.24
 b guard post 37.123
 c period of night 67.196
 d haunt 85.85
 φυλακή : unit
 φυλάσσω φυλακάς
  guard against 37.119

φυλακίζω
 imprison 37.114

φυλακτήριον, ου n
 phylactery 6.195

φύλαξ, ακος m
 guard 37.121

φυλάσσομαι
 keep from 13.154

φυλάσσω
 a guard closely 37.120
 b obey 36.19
 φυλάσσω : unit
 φυλάσσω φυλακάς
  guard against 37.119

φυλή, ῆς f
 a tribe 10.2
 b nation 11.56
 φυλή : unit
 αἱ δώδεκα φυλαί
  all God's people 11.15

φύλλον, ου n
 leaf 3.51

φύραμα, τος n
 a lump 79.92
 b mixture (of dough) . . 63.12

φυσικός, ή, όν
 natural 58.9

φυσικῶς
 by nature 58.9

φυσιόομαι
 be proud 88.216

φυσιόω
 make proud 88.217

φύσις, εως f
 a nature 58.8
 b kind 58.24

φυσίωσις, εως f
 pride 88.215

φυτεία, ας f
 plant 3.1

φυτεύω
 plant 43.5

φύω
 (aor pass ptc neut
 φυέν)
 grow 23.191

φωλεός, οῦ m
 den 1.56

φωνέω
 a call 33.307
 b cry out 33.77
 c name 33.131

d invite *33.315*
e make a sound *14.76*

φωνή, ῆς *f*
a sound *14.74*
b voice *33.103*
c cry *33.80*
d language *33.1*
φωνή : unit
ἐπαίρω φωνήν
  speak loudly *33.78*

φῶς, φωτός *n*
a light *14.36*
b bonfire *2.5*
c torch *6.102*
φῶς : units
ἐν τῷ φωτί
  in public *28.64*
τέκνα φωτός
  people of God *11.14*
υἱοὶ τοῦ φωτός
  people of God *11.14*

φωστήρ, ῆρος *m*
a star *1.27*
b radiance *14.49*

φωσφόρος, ου *m*
morning star *1.32*

φωτεινός, ή, όν
a full of light *14.51*
b bright *14.50*

φωτίζω
a shine upon *14.39*
b make known *28.36*

φωτισμός, οῦ *m*
a truth *72.3*
b revelation *28.36*

χαίρω
(fut χαρήσομαι, aor pass
ἐχάρην, inf χαρῆναι)
a rejoice *25.125*
b greetings *33.22*

χάλαζα, ης *f*
hail *2.13*

χαλάω
let down *15.111*

Χαλδαῖος, ου *m*
Chaldean *93.610*

χαλεπός, ή, όν
a troublous *22.29*
b fierce *20.2*

χαλιναγωγέω
exercise self-control . . . *88.85*

χαλινός, οῦ *m*
bridle *6.7*

χαλκεῖον
see χαλκίον

χαλκεύς, έως *m*
metalworker *2.55*

χαλκηδών, όνος *m*
agate *2.32*

χαλκίον, ου *n*
bronze vessel *6.130*

χαλκολίβανον, ου *n*
(also -ος, ου *m*)
fine bronze *2.57*

χαλκός, οῦ *m*
a bronze *2.54*
b copper money *6.72*
χαλκός : unit
χαλκὸς ἠχῶν
  brass gong *6.95*

χαλκοῦς, ῆ, οῦν
(from εος, εα, εον)
made of bronze *2.56*

χαμαί
on the ground *1.45*

Χανάαν *f*
Canaan *93.611*

Χαναναῖος, α, ον
Canaanite 93.612

χαρά, ᾶς f
a gladness 25.123
b reason for gladness . 25.124

χάραγμα, τος n
a mark 33.482
b image 6.96

χαρακτήρ, ῆρος m
exact representation . . 58.62

χάραξ, ακος m
barricade 7.60

χαρῆναι
see χαίρω

χαρήσομαι
see χαίρω

χαρίζομαι
a give generously 57.102
b forgive 40.10
c cancel a debt 57.223
d hand over to 37.30

χάριν
a because of 89.29
b for the purpose of . . 89.60

χάρις, ιτος f
a kindness 88.66
b gift 57.103
c thanks 33.350
d good will 25.89

χάρισμα, τος n
gift 57.103

χαριτόω
show kindness 88.66

Χαρράν f
Haran 93.613

χάρτης, ου m
sheet of paper 6.58

χάσμα, τος n
chasm 1.54

χεῖλος, ους n
a shore 1.62
b speech 33.74

χειμάζομαι
undergo bad weather 14.3

χείμαρρος, ου m
a winter stream 1.77
b ravine 1.52

χειμάρρους, ου m
see χείμαρρος

χειμών, ῶνος m
a winter 67.165
b bad weather 14.2

χείρ, χειρός f
a hand, finger 8.30
b person 9.17
c power 76.3
d be in control of 37.14
χείρ : units
χείρ ἀνθρωπίνη
person 9.5
σὺν χειρί
with the help of 90.2
ἐπιβάλλω τὰς χεῖρας /
τὴν χεῖρα (ἐπί)
arrest 37.110
ἐκτείνω τὰς χεῖρας ἐπί
arrest 37.110
ἐπιβάλλω τὴν χεῖρα
ἐπ᾽ ἄροτρον καὶ
βλέπω εἰς τὰ ὀπίσω
start to do and
then hesitate 68.6
παραδίδωμι εἰς χεῖρας
deliver to control of 37.12

χειραγωγέω
lead by hand 15.184

χειραγωγός, οῦ m
guide 15.185

χειρόγραφον, ου *n*
record of debts *33.40*

χειροποίητος, ον
man-made *42.32*

χειροτονέω
a choose *30.101*
b appoint *37.103*

χείρων, ον
a very bad *88.107*
b worse *65.29*
χείρων : unit
εἰς τὸ χεῖρον ἔρχομαι
become more sick . . *23.150*

χερούβ, pl χερουβίν *n*
winged creature *6.99*

χήρα, ας *f*
widow *10.61*

χιλίαρχος, ου *m*
commanding officer . . *55.15*

χιλιάς, άδος *f*
group of a thousand . . *60.80*

χίλιοι, αι, α
thousand *60.39*

Χίος, ου *f*
Chios *93.614*

χιτών, ῶνος *m*
a tunic *6.176*
b clothing *6.162*

χιών, όνος *f*
snow *2.12*

χλαμύς, ύδος *f*
cloak *6.173*

χλευάζω
joke at *33.408*

χλιαρός, ά, όν
lukewarm *79.74*

Χλόη, ης *f*
Chloe *93.385*

χλωρόν, οῦ *n*
plant *3.13*

χλωρός, ά, όν
a light green *79.34*
b pale greenish gray . . *79.35*

χοϊκός, ή, όν
a made of dust *2.16*
b earthly *1.42*

χοῖνιξ, ικος *f*
quart *81.24*

χοῖρος, ου *m*
pig *4.36*

χολάω
be very angry *88.171*

χολή, ῆς *f*
gall *8.75*
χολή : unit
εἰς χολὴν πικρίας εἰμί
be terribly envious . . *88.166*

Χοραζίν *f*
Chorazin *93.615*

χορηγέω
provide for *35.31*

χορός, οῦ *m*
dancing *15.244*

χορτάζομαι
a eat one's fill *23.15*
b be content *25.82*

χορτάζω
cause to eat one's fill . . *23.16*

χόρτασμα, τος *n*
food *5.1*

χόρτος, ου *m*
a grass *3.15*
b sprout *3.48*

Χουζᾶς, ᾶ *m*
Chuza *93.386*

χοῦς, χοός, acc χοῦν *m*
dust *2.15*

χράομαι
(impv χρῶ, aor impv
χρῆσαι)
a behave toward *41.4*
b deal with *41.5*
c use *42.23*
d with *90.13*

χρεία, ας *f*
a what is needed *57.40*
b what should be *71.23*
c needed task *42.22*

χρεοφειλέτης, ου *m*
debtor *57.222*

χρή
should *71.22*

χρῄζω
need *57.39*

χρῆμα, τος *n*
a riches *57.31*
b money *6.68*

χρηματίζω
a reveal divine mes-
sage *28.39*
b give a name to *33.127*

χρηματισμός, οῦ *m*
divine revelation *28.40*

χρῆσαι
see χράομαι

χρήσιμος, η, ον
useful *65.30*

χρῆσις, εως *f*
sexual function *23.65*

χρῆσον
see κίχρημι

χρηστεύομαι
act kindly *88.67*

χρηστολογία, ας *f*
attractive speech *33.30*

χρηστός, ή, όν
a good (value) *65.25*
b good (moral) *88.9*
c kind *88.68*
d easy *22.40*

χρηστότης, ητος *f*
a benevolence *88.10*
b kindness *88.67*

χρῖσμα, τος *n*
assignment *37.107*

Χριστιανός, οῦ *m*
Christian *11.35*

Χριστός, οῦ *m*
a Messiah *53.82*
b Christ *93.387*

χρίω
assign *37.107*

χρονίζω
a be late *67.122*
b spend long time in . . *67.82*

χρόνος, ου *m*
a time *67.78*
b occasion *67.1*
χρόνος : units
χρόνοις αἰωνίοις
since all time *67.133*
πρὸ χρόνων αἰωνίων
since all time *67.133*

χρονοτριβέω
spend time *67.79*

χρύσεος
see χρυσοῦς

χρυσίον, ου *n*
a gold *2.49*
b gold ornaments *6.189*

χρυσίον : unit
ἀργύριον καὶ χρυσίον
money *6.69*

χρυσοδακτύλιος, ον
wearing a gold ring . . . *6.191*

χρυσόλιθος, ου *m*
chrysolite *2.37*

χρυσόπρασος, ου *m*
chrysoprase *2.40*

χρυσός, οῦ *m*
a gold *2.49*
b gold money *6.74*

χρυσοῦς, ῆ, οῦν
(from εος, εα, εον)
golden *2.50*

χρυσόομαι
be adorned with gold   *49.29*

χρῶ
see χράομαι

χρώς, χρωτός *m*
skin *8.53*

χωλός, ή, όν
lame *23.175*

χώρα, ας *f*
a land *1.60*
b region *1.79*
c countryside *1.87*
d field *1.95*
e inhabitants *11.64*

χωρέω
a move on *15.13*
b contain *80.4*
c accept *31.57*
d be friendly to *34.13*

χωρίζω
a separate *63.29*
b divorce *34.78*
c depart *15.49*
d remove *85.41*

χωρίον, ου *n*
field *1.95*

χωρίς
a without *89.120*
b separately *63.31*

χῶρος, ου *m*
northwest *82.5*

ψάλλω
(fut ψαλῶ)
sing praises *33.111*

ψαλμός, οῦ *m*
song of praise *33.112*

ψευδάδελφος, ου *m*
false fellow believer . . . *11.36*

ψευδαπόστολος, ου *m*
false apostle *53.75*

ψευδής, ές
liar *33.255*

ψευδοδιδάσκαλος, ου *m*
false teacher *33.250*

ψευδολόγος, ου *m*
liar *33.255*

ψεύδομαι
lie *33.253*

ψευδομαρτυρέω
give false witness *33.271*

ψευδομαρτυρία, ας *f*
false testimony *33.272*

ψευδόμαρτυς, υρος *m*
false witness *33.273*

ψευδοπροφήτης, ου *m*
false prophet *53.81*

ψεῦδος, ους *n*
lie *33.254*

ψευδόχριστος, ου m
false Christ 53.84

ψευδώνυμος, ον
falsely called 33.130

ψεῦσμα, τος n
lie................. 33.254

ψεύστης, ου m
liar 33.255

ψηλαφάω
(aor opt 3 sg ψηλα-
φήσειεν, 3 pl -σειαν,
-σαιεν, -σαισαν)
a touch 24.76
b try to find........ 27.40

ψηφίζω
a calculate.......... 60.4
b figure out 32.15

ψῆφος, ου f
pebble 2.27
ψῆφος : unit
καταφέρω ψῆφον
vote against 30.103

ψιθυρισμός, οῦ m
gossip............. 33.404

ψιθυριστής, οῦ m
gossiper 33.405

ψίξ, ψιχός f
crumb 5.5

ψιχίον, ου n
crumb 5.5

ψυγήσομαι
see ψύχομαι

ψυχή, ῆς f
a inner self 26.4
b life 23.88
c person 9.20
ψυχή : units
ζητέω τὴν ψυχήν
want to kill 20.66

ἀπόλλυμι τὴν ψυχήν
die 23.114
δίδωμι ψυχήν
die for 23.100
τὴν ψυχὴν τίθημι
die willingly 23.113
ψυχὴ ζωῆς
living creature 4.1
τὴν ψυχὴν διέρχεται
ῥομφαία
feel pain and sorrow 25.279
ψυχὴν βασανίζω
experience anguish 25.280
κάμνω τῇ ψυχῇ
become discouraged 25.291
κτάομαι τὴν ψυχήν
protect oneself 21.20
τὴν ψυχὴν αὐτοῦ
περιποιέομαι
save oneself 21.24
κακόω τὴν ψυχὴν κατά
cause to dislike 88.200
παραδίδωμι τὴν ψυχήν
risk 21.7
αἴρω τὴν ψυχήν τινος
keep in suspense ... 30.36

ψυχικός, ή, όν
a physical 79.2
b natural 79.5
c worldly 41.41

ψύχομαι
(fut ψυγήσομαι)
diminish greatly 78.39

ψῦχος, ους n
cold 79.75

ψυχρός, ά, όν
cold 79.77

ψωμίζω
a give to eat........ 23.5
b give away 57.113

ψωμίον, ου n
piece of bread 5.4

ψώχω
rub 19.50

Ω
last *61.18*

ὦ
o! *91.14*

ὧδε
a here *83.1*
b in this case *92.35*

ᾠδή, ῆς *f*
song *33.110*

ὠδίν, ῖνος *f*
a birth pains *23.54*
b great suffering *24.87*

ὠδίνω
a have birth pains *23.54*
b suffer greatly *24.87*

ὦμος, ου *m*
shoulder *8.27*

ὤμοσα
see ὀμνύω

ὠνειδίζομαι
see ὀνειδίζω

ὠνέομαι
buy *57.188*

ᾠόν, οῦ *n*
egg *5.18*

ὥρα, ας *f*
a occasion *67.1*
b a while *67.148*
c hour *67.199*
ὥρα : units
ὥρα πολλή
(very) late *67.77*
ἡ ἄρτι ὥρα
at this very moment *67.42*
πρὸς καιρὸν (ὥρας)
for a while *67.109*

ὡραῖος, α, ον
a beautiful *79.10*
b timely *67.3*

ὤρυξα
see ὀρύσσω

ὠρύομαι
roar *14.78*

ὡς
a like *64.12*
b that *90.21*
c how *89.86*
d when *67.45*
e while *67.139*
f because *89.37*
g in order to *89.61*
h with result that *89.52*
i approximately *78.42*
j how great *78.13*
ὡς : unit
ὡς τάχιστα
as soon as possible . . *67.57*

ὡσαννά
hosanna *33.364*

ὡσαύτως
in the same way *64.16*

ὡσεί
a like *64.12*
b approximately *78.42*

Ὡσηέ *m*
Hosea *93.388*

ὠσί(ν)
see οὖς

ὥσπερ
just as *64.13*

ὡσπερεί
just as *64.13*

ὥστε
a as a result *89.52*
b in order to *89.61*

ὦτα
see οὖς

267

ὠτάριον, ου n
  ear 8.24

ὠτίον, ου n
  ear 8.24

ὠφέλεια, ας f
  benefit 65.41

ὠφελέω
  a help 35.2
  b accomplish 68.33

ὠφέλιμος, ον
  beneficial 65.40

ὤφθην
  see ὁράω

ENGLISH INDEX

a
92.22

abandon
15.59; **31**.68; **85**.47, 65

abhor/rent
25.186-188

abide
85.58

ablaze
14.65

able, ability
35.9; **42**.4; **74**.1-27; **79**.64

aboard
15.96, 99, 100

abolish
76.22-26

abominate, abominable,
abomination
25.186, 188; **53**.38

abound
59.52

about (content)
89.5; **90**.23-25

about (degree)
78.40-43

about (space)
83.18-22

about (time)
67.35, 62, 161

above (space)
83.48-50; **84**.13

above (status)
87.30, 31, 47

absent, absence
85.21, 27-29

absorb
14.35

absurd
89.19

abundance (quantity)
59.48-61

abundance (wealth)
57.30, 31

abundant/ly (degree)
78.15

abyss
1.20

accent
33.102

accept/ance
31.50-57, 60; **34**.34, 35,
53-56; **56**.10; **57**.125

acceptable
25.85-98; **66**.11

access
33.72

accompany
13.113; **15**.148-157

accomplish/ment
13.88, 108, 126; **42**.7, 17-19;
68.22, 29-33

according/ly, accordance
89.9, 50-52, 137

account (financial)
33.39, 40; **57**.226-229

account (reason)
89.26, 31, 36; **90**.44

account (report)
33.11, 51

accurate/ly/ness
72.12-22

accursed
33.474, 475

accuse/r, accusation
33.426-434; **56**.4-11

achieve
13.16; **57**.61

acknowledge
31.26-28

acquaint/ance
27.18; **28**.1, 30; **34**.17

acquire
57.55-61

acquit/tal
56.34

across from
83.42-45

act/ive, activity
41.7, 49; **42**.6, 7, 11, 13-15;
76.2, 8, 14; **88**.149-151

actually
70.1-6

add, addition/al
58.38; **59**.72-76; **60**.4;
89.87-89, 92-104, 114

address
33.26-29, 71

adequate, adequacy
59.44-47; **75**.1-7

adhere to
34.24

adjourn a hearing
56.18

administrative area
1.82-85

administrator
37.39

admit/tedly
33.275-277

admonish
33.418

adopt/ion
35.53

close (intimate)
34.14, 15, 18

close (near)
83.28

close (shut)
79.112, 113

cloth
6.152-156, 165-170; **49.**6;
57.204

clothe, clothing
6.162, 163; **49.**1-29; **88.**233

cloud
1.34

club
6.31

coast
1.61

coat
6.172

cobra
4.53

cock
4.45; **67.**198

coffer
6.139

cohort
55.9

coin
6.68-82

coincidence
13.116

cold
78.39; **79.**75-77

collapse
20.51

collect/ion/or
15.132; **57.**65, 66, 115, 184,
185

colony
1.90

color
79.26-38

colt
4.33

comb wool
48.1

combine
63.5

combined with
89.123

come (happen)
13.109, 110, 119-123

come (movement)
15.1-11, 75-87, 93-117,
123-134, 141-155

come (tell to come)
33.311

come (visitation)
34.51

come here (extension)
84.24

come in sheep's clothing
(pretend)
88.233

come near (time)
67.21

come now (prompter)
91.13

come to be (appear)
85.7

comfort
25.153-155

command/ment/er
33.323-332; **36.**19; **37.**91;
55.14, 15, 20

commence
68.1, 3, 7, 9

commission
42.25

commit (oneself to)
25.73; **35.**47

commit suicide
20.81

common (defiled)
53.40

common (in common)
57.9; **89.**118

common people
87.64

commotion
39.5

communication
33.1-489

companion
34.8, 16

company (in the company of)
34.1; **89.**108, 110

comparable
65.17

compare
64.1-19

compassion/ate
25.49-52, 55; **88.**75, 80, 81

compel
37.33, 34

compensation
57.166, 167

compete
50.1, 2

competent
74.4

compile
62.3

complain/er
33.382-386

complaint (legal)
56.5, 10

complete/ness/ly, completion
59.29-34; **68.**22-33; **71.**29,
30; **78.**44-50

compose
62.2

disrobe
49.20

dissipation
88.286

dissociation
89.120-122

distant, distance
81.14; **83**.30, 31

distinction
30.113, 116; **58**.42

distinctive
58.47-49

distinctly
24.36

distort
33.155; **72**.9

distract/ing/ion
30.32, 33

distress/ed
22.1-14; **24**.89; **25**.223-250,
273, 274, 279, 281

distribute, distribution
57.89-95

distributive relations
89.90, 91

district
1.85

ditch
1.55

diversified
58.45

divest oneself of
87.70

divide/r, division (separation)
57.91; **63**.23-27

divine
12.13, 14; **88**.24, 25

division, divisive (opposition)
39.13-17

divorce
33.41; **34**.78

do/er/ing
13.131, 136; **41**.7, 11, 22;
42.4, 7-28; **68**.29, 33, 47,
62-79; **90**.45-49

do away with
13.38, 45; **20**.43; **76**.22, 23

do good
88.3, 5-8

doctor
23.141

doctrine
31.104; **33**.235, 236, 241

document
6.64; **33**.10

dog
4.34, 35; **88**.122

dole out
57.113

domineer
37.21

donation
57.112

donkey
4.31, 32

doomed
23.116

door
7.48, 49

doorkeeper
46.8

double
59.70; **60**.75

double-edged
79.94

doubleminded
31.38

double-tongued
88.235

doubled up
17.32

doubt/er
31.37, 38; **32**.9

doubtless
31.41; **71**.16

dough
63.12

dove
4.44

down/ward
84.21, 26

downcast, downhearted
25.286, 295

downpayment
57.170

drachma
6.76

drag
15.178, 179, 212-214

dragon
4.54

draw
15.212-214

draw a line between
30.116

draw away
31.74

draw to a close
67.118

draw water
47.1

dreadful
25.258

dream
33.486, 487

dress
49.1, 8-12

drift away
31.69

drink/er
5.6; **23**.1, 2, 34-39; **24**.81

sail/ing/or
  15.33; **54**.1-13, 24, 30

sake (for sake of)
  89.58, 60; **90**.36, 38, 43

salt/y
  5.25-28

salvation
  21.25-30

salve
  6.203, 207

same
  25.32; **26**.5; **58**.31-35; **64**.16;
  67.34

sanctuary
  7.15, 18; **53**.54

sand/bank
  1.68; **2**.28

sandal
  6.182, 183

sane
  30.22

Sanhedrin
  11.80, 83, 85

sapphire
  2.31

sardonyx
  2.35

Satan
  12.34

satiated
  57.22

satisfy
  23.15-18; **25**.80-84

saton
  81.23

Saturday
  67.184

save
  21.19-31

Savior
  21.22, 31

saw
  19.20

say/ing
  30.52; **31**.5; **33**.9, 14, 28, 69,
  70, 86, 94-98, 119-122, 139

scale
  8.57

scar
  8.55, 56; **33**.481

scarcely
  78.41

scared
  25.263

scarlet
  79.29

scarlet cloth
  6.170

scatter
  15.135-140

scent
  79.45

scheme, scheming
  30.68-72; **88**.158

scholar/ship
  27.21, 22; **32**.39

school
  7.14

scoff/er
  33.408; **88**.193

scold
  33.421

scorch
  14.67, 68

scorn
  88.192-197

scorpion
  4.56

scoundrel
  88.269

scrap
  5.5

scream
  33.81-84

Scripture
  33.10, 53-56

scroll
  6.64-67

scum
  79.53

sea
  1.69-75; **54**.4

sea creature
  4.58

sea (traveller/merchant)
  54.27

seal
  6.54, 55, 62; **33**.483, 484

seamless
  48.6

search
  27.34, 35, 42, 43

season
  46.14

seat/ed
  6.111; **7**.63; **17**.12-18

seat of honor
  87.18, 34-36

second
  60.49; **61**.12; **67**.180

secret/ly
  27.47; **28**.68-83

secretary
  37.94

sect
  11.50

secure, security
  21.9-11

see (visit)
  34.50

see/ing (sensory)
  24.1-51; **28**.37; **32**.11

see to (take care of)
35.39

seed
3.35; **23**.199

seek
13.20; **27**.34, 35, 42, 43;
34.23; **57**.59; **68**.60

seem
30.13, 97; **31**.30, 31

seize
18.3-7; **20**.62; **27**.32; **37**.11,
28, 108-110; **39**.49; **57**.235;
90.69

select
30.86-107

self (inner being)
26.2-4; **41**.43

self (emphatic)
92.37

self (haughtiness)
88.206, 211, 215

self-control
88.83-92

selfish
25.39; **88**.167

self-willed
88.206

sell
57.186-188

send
15.44, 66-74, 193; **90**.88

sense (meaning)
33.139

senseless (foolish)
32.49, 52

senseless/ly (behavior)
88.96-99

senses (mind)
30.26, 27

sensible, sensibility (behavior)
88.93-95

sensible, sensibly (sound)
32.34

sensual living
88.254

sentence
23.116; **56**.24, 26

sentinel
37.121

separate (distinguish)
30.116

separate (spacial)
85.17, 41

separate, separation
(interpersonal)
34.36, 39, 78

separate/ly, separation
(part-whole)
63.23, 27-31

sequence
61.1-19

serious/ly
78.17

servant
35.20-23; **46**.5, 6; **87**.76

serve, service
35.19-30; **37**.34; **42**.21; **46**.13

set (of the sun)
15.113

set (put)
85.40

set apart (for a task)
37.97

set aside (a belief)
31.100

set free
21.17; **37**.127-138; **56**.34

set up (erect)
45.2

settle
30.81; **40**.3; **56**.3; **57**.229;
85.63

seven/th
60.16, 44, 54, 73

seventy
60.30, 74, 77

several
60.70

severe
22.31; **78**.13-17; **88**.136, 138

sew
48.5

sex/ual
23.61-65; **25**.29-31;
88.271-282

shackle
6.17

shade, shadow
14.60-62; **58**.65

shake/n
16.2-8

shame/ful(ly)/less(ness)
25.189-202; **53**.60; **66**.12;
88.127, 149-151

shape behavior
41.29

shapes
79.104-109

share/r
34.7; **41**.22; **57**.6-10, 96-101,
129; **63**.13, 18

sharp
79.95, 96, 109

shatter
19.39

shave
19.24

she
92.11, 24, 32

shear
19.23

sheath
6.119

weed
3.30

week
67.177

weep/ing
25.137-139, 142

weight
86.1-5

welcome
34.53-56

well (circumstance)
22.47

well (degree)
78.21

well (for water)
7.57

well (not sick)
23.129-141

well (value)
65.23

well-disposed (attitude)
25.95

well-ordered
88.48

west
82.2

wet
79.78, 79

what/ever
92.14, 18, 27

wheat
3.31, 40, 41; **5**.2, 9

when/ever
67.30-33, 36, 45

whence
84.6

where/ver
83.5, 6; **84**.6, 11; **92**.28

whereas
89.35

whether
71.18; **89**.69, 70; **90**.26

which/ever
84.11; **92**.18, 27, 28, 36

while
67.106-111, 138, 139, 148

whip (artifact)
6.26

whip/ping (hit)
19.2, 4, 9

whirlwind
14.6

whisper
33.91

white/n
79.27, 28

whitewash
45.12

who/ever
92.14, 18, 27

whole
59.23, 29-31; **63**.1, 2

wholeheartedness
25.72

wholly
78.47

why
89.38; **92**.15

wick
6.158

wicked/ness
12.44; **88**.105, 108-110, 119, 120

wide/n
81.15-18

widow
10.61

width
81.15

wife
10.54, 55

will (desire)
25.3, 4

will (faculty)
26.12

will (purpose)
30.59

will (self-willed)
88.206

will (testament)
57.123, 124

willing/ly
25.65-67, 69

win
57.61

wind
14.4-9; **15**.164

winding
79.90

window
7.47

wine
6.197-201

wineskin
6.132

wine press
7.66

wine trough
7.67

wing
8.29

winged creature
6.99

winnowing shovel
6.6

winter
67.165, 166

wipe (away/off)
16.9; **47**.18

wipe (dry)
79.83

PASSAGE INDEX

JOHN

26.24	**13**.64, **27**.21, **30**.24	27.34	**21**.18	28.30	**57**.175, **67**.169, **85**.55
26.25	**30**.24, **32**.34	27.35	**18**.1	28.31	**13**.151
26.26	**42**.8, **79**.107	27.36	**18**.2, **23**fn3, **25**.147		
26.28	**22**.41, **67**.106	27.38	**57**.22, **86**.3		
26.29	**13**.48, **67**.89	27.39	**1**.63, **1**.74, **24**.51,		
26.30	**17**.13		**30**.43, **54**.17		

ROMANS

26.32	**56**.15
27.1	**37**.76, **37**.117
27.3	**35**.44, **41**.4, **54**.15,
	88.72
27.4	**54**.10
27.5	**1**.73, **54**.11, **83**.44,
	83fn16
27.6	**15**.96
27.7	**13**.139, **15**.1, **54**.2,
	83.44
27.9	**21**.3, **51**.11, **54**.1
27.10	**15**.208, **20**.19, **57**.69
27.11	**54**.28, **54**.29
27.12	**1**.75, **33**.296, **65**.35,
	67.166, **82**.5, **82**.6,
	82.10, **83**.45
27.13	**14**.5, **54**.8, **68**.29,
	83.28
27.14	**14**.7, **14**.9, **15**.112
27.15	**15**.6, **18**.5, **39**.21, **82**.9
27.16	**1**.67, **6**.45, **37**.23,
	54.10
27.17	**6**.1, **15**.160, **35**.10,
	54.25, **90**.13
27.18	**14**.3, **15**.220, **78**.19
27.19	**6**.2, **8**.31, **15**.217
27.20	**14**.2, **24**.21, **68**.43
27.21	**13**.137, **23**.32, **36**.12,
	71.21
27.22	**13**.103, **25**.146,
	33.295
27.23	**15**.86
27.24	**85**.18
27.27	**1**.60, **14**.81, **15**.77,
	15.163, **60**.60
27.28	**15**.12, **15**.50, **54**.23,
	59.14, **81**.26
27.29	**6**.48, **54**.19, **79**.84,
	83.7
27.30	**6**.46, **54**.30, **88**.230
27.31	**85**.55
27.32	**6**.18, **19**.18
27.33	**13**.27, **23**.32, **25**.228,
	25fn16, **67**.17

27.40	**6**.19, **6**.49, **15**.204,
	54.22
27.41	**1**.68, **6**.43, **14**.32,
	15.4, **15**.5, **15**.85,
	20.1, **20**.53, **54**.18
27.42	**15**.64, **15**.247, **30**.57,
	89.62
27.43	**15**.242, **15**.246,
	15fn10, **30**.57
27.44	**7**.79, **84**.3
28.1	**1**.66, **27**.8
28.2	**2**.5, **11**.94, **14**.65,
	68.7, **79**.75, **88**.71
28.3	**3**.65, **4**.53, **15**.125,
	18.7, **79**.70
28.4	**4**.3, 4fn3, **12**.27,
	18.22, **21**.19, **71**.16
28.5	**16**.8, **20**.18
28.6	**12**.22, **15**.119, **23**.159,
	23.163, **31**.58, **58**.54,
	67.89
28.7	**13**.77, **34**.53, **34**.57,
	57.2, **88**.72
28.8	**17**.27, **23**.160, **90**.65
28.10	**57**.78
28.11	**6**.51, **33**.479
28.13	**13**.107, **14**.8, **15**.33,
	54.24, **67**.180, **84**.11
28.15	**7**.11, **25**.157
28.16	**55**.14
28.17	**33**.309
28.18	**92**.23
28.19	**89**.37
28.20	**33**.168, **33**.310, **49**.4,
	89.15, **90**.43
28.21	**6**.63, **57**.125
28.22	**25**.5, **28**.21, **33**.455
28.23	**7**.31, 7fn7, **33**.346,
	67.187
28.25	**15**.38, **31**.24
28.26	**24**.63
28.27	**27**.50, **32**.46
28.28	**15**.67, **21**.30, **31**.56
28.29	**33**.440

1.1	**33**.314, **53**.74, **87**.76
1.2	**33**.287
1.3	**26**.9, **89**.4
1.4	**26**.9, **88**.25
1.5	**53**.73
1.7	**89**.92
1.8	**31**.102, **33**.204, **63**.1,
	92.7
1.9	**29**.18
1.10	**29**.18, **67**.40, **68**.30
1.11	**12**.21, **57**.103
1.12	**25**.151, **92**.26
1.13	**30**.62, **67**.43, **67**fn8
1.14	**11**.90, **11**.95, **32**.50
1.15	**25**.69
1.16	**31**.102, **33**.217
1.17	**31**.85, **34**.46, **34**.47,
	78.48
1.18	**13**.150
1.19	**28**.57, **28**.58
1.20	**12**.13, **27**.7, **27**fn3,
	67.96, **89**.48
1.21	**28**.1, **30**.10, **32**.44,
	32.49, **65**.38
1.22	**32**.56
1.23	**4**.51, 4fn7, **6**.96,
	23.125, **57**.142,
	58.35, **64**.3
1.24	**88**.261
1.25	**42**.38, **53**.53, **57**.142,
	72.6, **89**.132
1.26	**23**.65, **25**.30, **58**.9,
	68.50, **79**.103, **89**.137
1.27	**23**.65, **25**.16, **38**.15,
	79.102, **88**.149,
	88.262, **90**.47, **90**.63
1.28	**28**.2, **30**.98, **30**.114,
	31.28, **88**.111, **89**.34
1.29	**33**.388, **33**.405,
	88.113
1.30	**30**.69, **33**.388,
	88.132, **88**.205
1.31	**34**.45, **88**.82
1.32	**33**.334
2.1	**33**.438

2 CORINTHIANS

GALATIANS

EPHESIANS

1 TIMOTHY

HEBREWS

1:1	**58**.29, **63**.19, **67**.11, **67**.24, **89**.81, **89**.82
1.2	**1**.2
1.3	**1**.13, **12**.5, **13**.35, **14**.48, **58**.1, **58**.62
1.4	**78**.52, **87**.28
1.7	**14**.4
1.8	**37**.53, **67**.95, **88**.19
1.9	**34**.8
1.11	**13**.89, **13**.96, **67**.104
1.12	**6**.172, **13**.39
1.14	**35**.24
2.1	**31**.47, **31**.69
2.2	**28**.43, **31**.90, **38**.17
2.3	**30**.50, **31**.91
2.4	**25**.1, **33**.268, **57**.89
2.5	**1**.39
2.7	**78**.43, **87**.68
2.8	**37**.8, **37**.32
2.9	**87**.13
2.10	**36**.6, **68**.2
2.14	**9**.15, **64**.9, **76**.6
2.15	**37**.5, **37**.127
2.16	**30**.42, **30**fn7, **35**.1, **91**.7
2.17	**40**.9
3.1	**12**.17, **30**.4
3.4	**45**.1
3.5	**35**.20
3.8	**39**.40, **67**.33, **88**.226
3.9	**27**.45
3.11	**89**.52
3.12	**34**.26
3.13	**67**.139
3.14	**31**.84, **89**.68
3.15	**88**.226
3.16	**39**.40
3.17	**8**.8, **88**.172
3.18	**23**.81
4.1	**13**.92
4.2	**24**.52
4.3	**89**.72
4.6	**13**.140
4.7	**33**.86, **59**.18
4.8	**23**.85
4.9	**67**.185
4.10	**23**.81

4.12	**8**.59, **8**.62, **13**.124, **15**.32, **26**.4, **30**.66, **56**.23, **63**.24, **79**.96
4.13	**28**.61, **28**.62, **28**.68
4.15	**25**.57, **64**.3
4.16	**25**.158, **35**.1, **37**.72
5.1	**30**.86, **89**.102
5.2	**13**.6, **88**.65
5.4	**64**.15
5.6	**58**.21
5.7	**23**.90, **33**.172, **53**.7, **89**.102
5.8	**27**.15, **89**.71
5.9	**89**.15
5.10	**33**.127
5.11	**32**.47, **33**.149, **71**.3
5.12	**33**.97, **58**.19, **58**.20, **71**.3, **71**.23
5.13	**23**.2, **23**fn3, **28**.15, **71**.3
5.14	**9**.10, **32**.28, **42**.10, **71**.3, **79**.7
6.1	**13**.58, **41**.52, **53**.41, **58**.20, **71**.3, **85**.49, **85**fn11, **88**.101, **89**.12
6.2	**53**.41, **71**.3
6.3	**71**.3, **89**.68
6.4	**13**.67, **71**.3, **90**.78
6.5	**71**.3
6.6	**13**.67, **20**.77, **25**.200, **34**.26, **71**.3
6.7	**2**.10, **3**.14, **14**.35, **23**.194, **43**.1, **71**.3, **90**.63
6.8	**14**.63, **23**.194, **65**.13, **71**.3
6.9	**71**.3
6.10	**71**.3
6.11	**25**.12, **71**.3, **88**.249
6.12	**25**.167, **57**.131, **71**.3, **88**.249
6.13	**90**.29
6.14	**59**.69, **91**.8
6.15	**25**.168, **57**.60
6.16	**28**.44, **33**.445, **61**.15
6.17	**13**.61, **31**.21
6.18	**21**.15, **71**.3, **71**fn1, **78**.16

6.19	**7**.35, **83**.15
6.20	**36**.9
7.1	**20**.74, **33**.145
7.2	**33**.145, **57**.90, **60**.66, **89**.104
7.3	**10**.15, **10**.17, **10**.27, **10**fn3, **23**.88, **64**.4, **67**.95
7.4	**32**.11, **57**.244, **87**.32
7.5	**23**.60, **53**.86, **57**.115
7.6	**10**.25, **57**.115
7.7	**33**.456, **87**.67
7.8	**60**.66, **92**.35
7.9	**33**.139, **57**.114
7.10	**8**.43
7.11	**13**.81, **53**.92, **88**.38
7.12	**13**.52, **53**.86
7.13	**34**.31, **68**.19
7.14	**10**.35
7.15	**32**.20, **64**.3
7.16	**9**.13, **13**.47, **26**.8, **33**.333
7.18	**65**.50, **76**.24
7.19	**65**.21, **68**.10
7.20	**33**.463
7.21	**31**.59
7.22	**70**.8
7.23	**68**.11
7.24	**13**.61
7.25	**67**.95, **78**.47
7.26	**63**.29, **83**.50, **88**.2
8.1	**33**.12
8.2	**45**.2
8.5	**45**.2, **58**.58, **83**.47
8.6	**33**.339, **35**.25, **78**.52
8.8	**13**.88, **33**.431
8.9	**68**.11
8.10	**34**.43
8.11	**11**.68
8.12	**88**.77
8.13	**13**.98, **67**.103
9.1	**1**.40, **7**.18, **53**.14
9.2	**7**.35, **60**.46
9.3	**7**.35, **83**.56
9.4	**2**.49, **5**.22, **6**.61, **6**.116, **6**.125, **6**.139, **23**.195, **83**.8
9.5	**6**.99, **14**.62, **40**.13, **63**.16, **71**.1, **83**.49

2 PETER

CORRIGENDA

Greek-English Lexicon

Volume 2

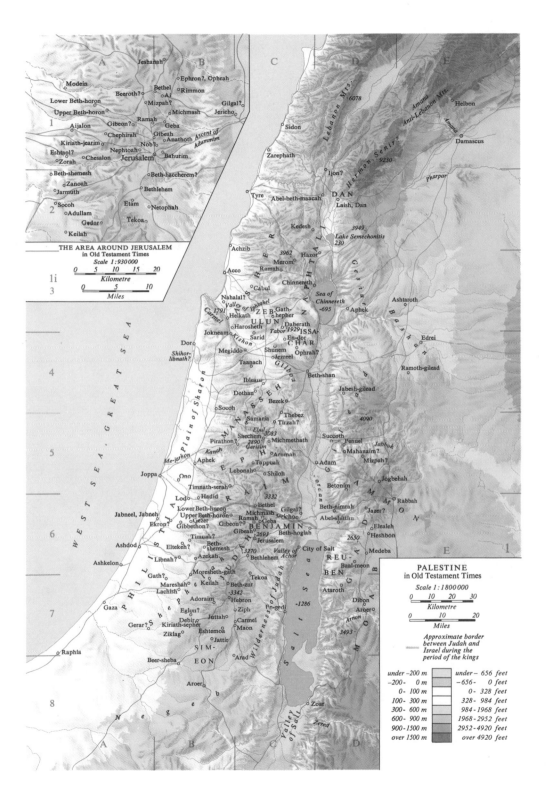

A B C D E

1

2

3

4

5

6

7

8

A B C D

MEDITERRANEAN SEA

Lebanon Mts.

6078

Hermon 9230 *Anti-Lebanon Mts.*

ABILENE

Sidon

Zarephath

Damascus

IV

Tyre

PHOENICIA

ITURAEA

Caesarea Philippi

Lake Semechonitis 230

GAULANITIS

BATANAEA

3949

III

TRACHONITIS

Gischala 3962

Chorazin

IIa

Capernaum

Julias Bethsaida

Ptolemais

Cana

Magdala

Sea of Galilee -695

Gergesa?

Raphana?

GALILEE

Tiberias

Sepphoris

Hippos

Dion

Ze-bulun

Tabor 1929

1791 *Carmel*

Nazareth

Abila

Nain

Gadara

VI

HAURAN

DECAPOLIS

Caesarea

Plain of Sharon

Scythopolis

Ginaea

Pella

SAMARIA

Salim?

Aenon?

Sebaste

4090

3083

Sychar? Shechem

Gerasa

2890

Acrabetta

Alexandrium ☆

Antipatris

Phaselis

IIb

Joppa

Arimathea?

Thamna

JORDAN

Lydda

Gophna 3332

Archelais

Philadelphia

Modein

Ephraim?

Jamnia

JUDEA

Jericho

Emmaus? 2693

Livias

Jerusalem

Bethany

2650

3270

Hyrcania ☆

Qumran

Medeba

Azotus

Bethlehem

Herodium ☆

PERAEA

Ascalon

Beth-zur

Machaerus ☆

3342

Hebron

En-gedi -1286

Gaza

Dead Sea

IDUMEA

Masada ☆

3493

Raphia

Zoar

Nabataea

PALESTINE
in New Testament Times

Scale 1 : 1 800 000

0 10 20 30
Kilometre

0 10 20
Miles

I   *Roman province of Judea*
    (4 B.C. - A.D. 6, Te-
    trarchy of Archelaus)
    Northern boundary
    of Judea proper
IIa *and IIb Tetrarchy of*
    Herod Antipas
    (4 B.C. - A.D. 39)
III *Tetrarchy of Philip*
    (4 B.C. - A.D. 34)
IV *Roman province of Syria*
V   *Tetrarch of Lysanias*
VI *Territory of Decapolis*

☆ *Fortresses*

For elevations, see
map of Palestine in
Old Testament Times

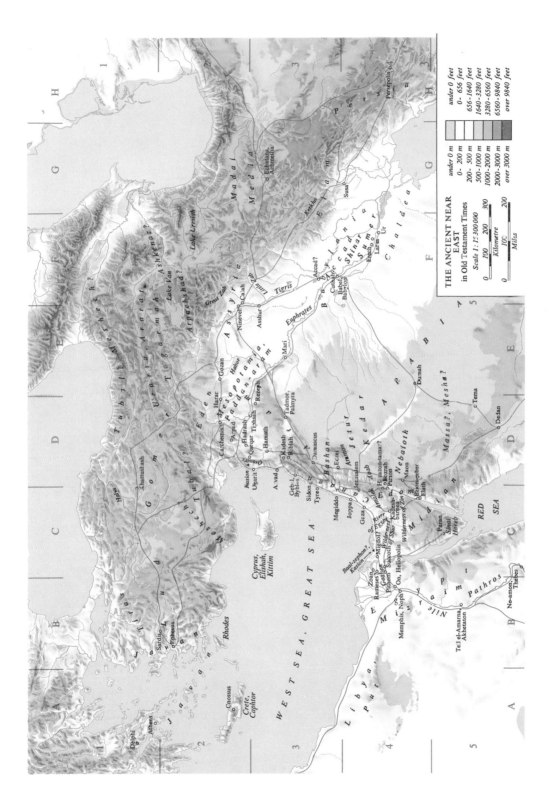

THE ANCIENT NEAR
EAST
in Old Testament Times

Scale 1: 1ʼ300000

| under 0 feet |
| 0 - 656 feet |
| 656 - 1640 feet |
| 1640 - 3280 feet |
| 3280 - 6560 feet |
| 6560 - 9840 feet |
| over 9840 feet |

| under 0 m |
| 0 - 200 m |
| 200 - 500 m |
| 500 - 1000 m |
| 1000 - 2000 m |
| 2000 - 3000 m |
| over 3000 m |

Kilometre
0   100   200   300

Miles
0   100   200

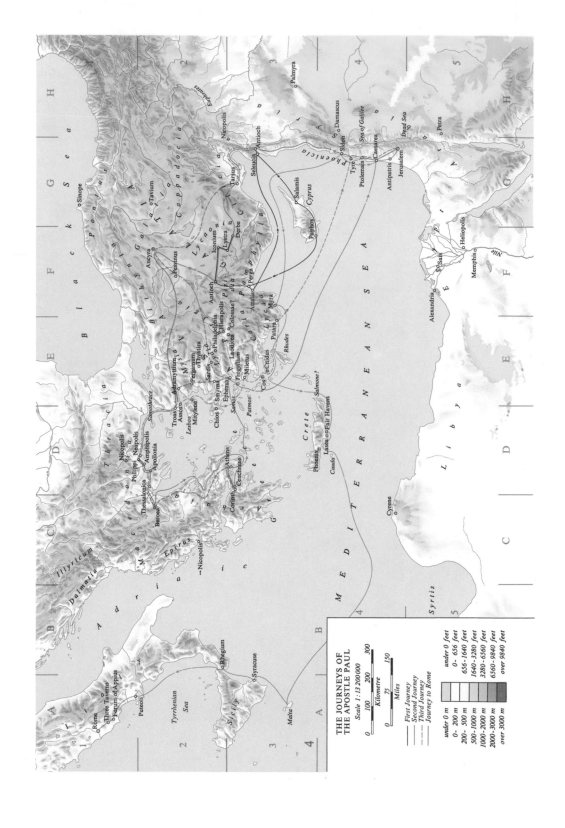

THE JOURNEYS OF
THE APOSTLE PAUL

Scale 1 : 13 200 000

Kilometre
0   100   200   300

Miles
0   75   150

————— First Journey
- - - - Second Journey
········· Third Journey
══════ Journey to Rome

	under 0 m	under 0 feet
	0 - 200 m	0 - 656 feet
	200 - 500 m	656 - 1640 feet
	500 - 1000 m	1640 - 3280 feet
	1000 - 2000 m	3280 - 6560 feet
	2000 - 3000 m	6560 - 9840 feet
	over 3000 m	over 9840 feet